SHADOWS
ON THE
SEA

SHADOWS
ON THE
SEA

The
MARITIME
MYSTERIES
of BRITAIN

NEIL ARNOLD

The
History
Press

This book is dedicated to my heroes – John Lennon,
Marc Bolan, Nikki Sixx and H.P. Lovecraft

Cover illustrations. Front & back: Boat in storm on the Ijsselmeer. (Courtesy of Patricia Dekker); Seagulls. (Courtesy of Lesli Lundgren).

First published 2013

The History Press
The Mill, Brimscombe Port
Stroud, Gloucestershire, GL5 2QG
www.thehistorypress.co.uk

British Library Cataloguing in Publication Data.
A catalogue record for this book is available from the British Library.

ISBN 978 0 7524 8772 4

Typesetting and origination by The History Press
Printed in Great Britain

CONTENTS

ACKNOWLEDGEMENTS

With many thanks and love to my mum Paulene, dad Ron, nan Win, granddad Ron, my sister Vicki and my wife Jemma. Thanks to The History Press; Jonathan Downes, Richard Freeman and The Centre For Fortean Zoology; Nick Redfern; Joe Chester; Karl Shuker; Medway Archives and Local Studies; WaterUFO; *Fortean Times*; *Dubuque Daily Herald*; *The Morning Herald*; *Auckland Star*; *Medway Messenger*; *Entiat Times*; *Ashburton Guardian*; *Daily Mirror*; *The Observer*; *Evening Post*; *Bygone Kent*; Wales Online; *Northern Echo*; *Chatham Standard*; *Falmouth Packet*; *Western Morning News*; *Kent Today*; *North Wales Chronicle*; KentOnline; UFOInfo; *Bristol Evening Post*; *Pembroke County Guardian*; *UFO Magazine*; *Daily Mail*; *Scottish Sunday Mail*; *Dorset Echo*; *Kentish Express*; *Grimsby Telegraph*; *The Metro*; *Folkestone Herald*; *Sunday Express*; and *Liverpool Echo*. Extra special thanks to Simon Wyatt, Joyce Goodchild, Stuart Paterson, Mark North, Terry Cameron, Dr Chris Clark, Matt Newton and Glen Vaudrey for contributing images.

FOREWORD

By Jonathan Downes
Director of the Centre for Fortean Zoology

They that go down to the sea in ships, that do business in great waters;
These see the works of the LORD, and his wonders in the deep.

Psalms, 107:23, KJV

My father was a sailor. During the Second World War he served in the Battle of the Atlantic, and after the war he was with the Blue Funnel Line in Australia and South East Asia. He came ashore in 1947 to marry my mother, but he never stopped being in love with the sea. Until he died in 2006 he would tell me stories of his time on the ocean, and from him I inherited a respect and fascination for life on the dark waters.

It seems from recent evidence that my use of the word 'inherited' might not be incorrect. The website genotopia.scienceblog.com about human genetics wrote in the summer of 2011:

> Researchers at Mystic University in Connecticut have identified a gene associated with seafaringness, according to an article to be published tomorrow in the journal *Genetic Determinism Today*. Patterns of inheritance of the long-sought gene offers hope for 'sailing widows,' and could help explain why the sailing life has tended to run in families and why certain towns and geographical regions tend historically to have disproportionate numbers of sea-going citizens. The gene is a form of the MAOA-L gene, previously associated with high-risk behavior and thrill-seeking.

So, did Odysseus, Sir Francis Drake, Thor Heyerdahl and my father have a genetic predisposition towards a life on the ocean waves? We probably will never know, and to be honest I don't really care. All I know is that, for as long as I can remember, I have been fascinated by stories of the strange things that happen on, over and under the sea, and they have been part of my personal iconography. Take mermaids, for example. When I was small my father used to sing a most unseemly song, which went:

My Father was the keeper of the Eddystone Light
And he slept with a mermaid one fine night.

Many years later I actually met a young lady called Phillipa, known to everyone as 'Flip'. Sadly, she has now left us, having succumbed to breast cancer about fifteen years ago. But both she and her mother told me (in a completely matter-of-fact manner) how she had seen a mermaid sitting on a rock off the Scilly Isles a few years before. When I came out with all the cryptozoological clichés about seals and manatees (not that I had any suspicion that a manatee should be off the coast of western Cornwall), she told me in no uncertain terms not to be so bloody stupid. She was a fisherman's granddaughter and knew perfectly well what a seal looked like.

I have been in search of Morgawr, the Cornish sea-giant. I know several people who have seen it, and I am friends with the notorious Tony 'Doc' Shiels, who has himself called up monsters from the 'vasty deep'. I have never seen this Irish wizard call up a sea monster, but I have seen him do something very similar on an Irish lake. But that is another story entirely.

I have known Neil Arnold for over fifteen years. He was a boy, only just out of school when I first knew him, and I have watched him mature into one of Britain's foremost writers on Fortean subjects, giving what help and guidance I have been able along the way. I can think of no one better to write about the mysteries of the realm of Poseidon, and I am very proud that he has asked me to write the foreword for this fascinating and excellent book.

INTRODUCTION

Sailors and other seafaring folk are extremely superstitious. Sea captains and trawler-men will happily chatter over a pint about the rough seas they've conquered, or the mighty fish they've caught in their nets, but the mention of ghosts and the like will send them running for their beds in terror. This book is a unique foray into sea-related superstition and folklore, and serves up several reasons as to why nautical-minded folk are wary of the waters around Britain's coastline. Those old, creaky stories of 'the one that got away' may be laughed at no more, because by delving into this compendium of the uncanny you'll see why sailors and their ilk are hesitant to dismiss maritime tales of monsters, mermaids, coastal spooks and spectres, and things that go bump on their boats.

Ever since man has had the ability to trawl and travel the rough seas around Britain, there have been weird stories told about unfathomable depths, remote bays and cliffs, and isolated beaches. Sea fishermen may seem like hardened souls; their faces battered by biting winds, their boats bombarded by grey waves, but in most cases, they would always respect those forces of nature and protect themselves accordingly. Sailors once believed it unlucky to take a woman on board a ship, and nowadays it is said to be of ill luck should a woman step over fishing nets. Others will tell you that, should they see a woman with a squint before setting sail, it would also be considered bad luck. In the book *Folklore Myths & Legends of Britain* it is written that '… prejudice against the Church is also found among merchant seamen', and that any heavy storms encoun-tered would be blamed on crews whose party consisted of priests and their ilk. Some words would not be mentioned on board ship by sailors, these include 'salt', 'eggs', 'salmon' and 'knives', as well as animal names such as 'cat', 'hare', 'fox' and more so the word 'pig'. In fact, the pig is one animal that fishermen are said to fear the most, maybe due to the fact that they bear the Devil's mark on their forefeet or because they can sense the wind. There is a legend that some fishermen dread the sight of a cormorant and often associate the bird with maritime misfortune. To spot such a bird at sea would mean imminent tragedy.

Some fishermen avoid setting sail on a certain day, whilst others carry out protective rituals before going to sea. Some boat owners refuse to purchase or have a boat built on a Friday, and in some cases to protect a boat against tragedy the shipwright will tie a red ribbon around the first nail he banged in. Other shipwrights may, for luck, embed pieces of silver or gold within the framework of the boats. When a large ship is christened you will often see someone smash a bottle of champagne against its bows, whilst Scottish fishermen were once said to sprinkle barley around a new vessel. Some fishermen would have their nets blessed before a trawl, which seems to contradict the belief that some seafaring folk opposed the Church. However, in some cases a blessing from a clergyman could actually be blamed if there was bad weather or a day of poor fishing. The weather, quite obviously, plays a great part in the traditions and superstitions of sailors, hence the fact that it is considered to be unlucky to whistle at sea. Those foolish enough to do so will trigger a storm.

Whatever their beliefs, those accustomed to the seas paid great attention to superstition. In the early nineteenth century it was known for sailors to purchase a caul to take on board their ship. A caul is the amniotic sac that some children are born in, hence the saying, 'born in the bag'. Sailors would pay large sums of money for a caul, often referred to as a 'sailor's charm', and having one on board gave the belief that no crew member would drown or suffer any other mishap.

I have no hesitation in admitting that I am afraid of the sea. It wasn't just the suspenseful 1975 film *Jaws* that put me off paddling along Britain's murky coastlines; I've always been terrified of those foaming waves as they lap away at rugged shores. Mind you, I'm even unsettled at the thought of a seemingly tranquil lake – maybe it is because, as a child, my imagination would run wild as I sat perched on river banks with my father and gazed, fishing rod at the ready, into the algae-ridden waters expecting some unseen monster to be lurking in the silted depths.

I've never learnt to swim, probably because I've felt no inclination to travel over or in the water. Family trips to seaside resorts would often leave me nervous, even as I waded into water just a few feet deep – I was petrified of possible encounters with jellyfish or stumbling and plummeting into some unseen hole. The oceans of the world are truly alien environments. I find it fascinating that science continues to investigate the depths of limitless space, and yet right in front of our noses our seas roll out as inhospitable abodes; places so dark and inaccessible that only trawlers and brave divers dare venture. There is indeed nothing more atmospheric than watching powerful waves smash into an eroded cliff face on a stormy night, or to drive or walk along a coastal road on a hot day to the soundtrack of gulls, as grey waters glisten for miles. There is something, too, about the roaring sea that suggests a lack of control: no human dare claim to have conquered such an abyss and as we sit, unsteadily on these plates we call land, we are surrounded by that blue void, which at any moment could wipe us all away.

It is estimated that around 70 per cent of the earth's surface is covered in water – that's a frightening statistic. Around 97 per cent of this coverage consists of salt water, the rest being fresh water from lakes and rivers. Great Britain – the largest island of the United Kingdom of Great Britain and Northern Ireland – is surrounded by a handful of large salt-water bodies: these being the Irish Sea, the Celtic Sea, the North Sea, the English Channel and the Atlantic Ocean, which is the second largest of the world's oceanic divisions, covering some 26 per cent of the earth's surface. The Irish Sea is approximately 576ft at its deepest point. It separates the islands of Ireland and Great Britain, and is connected to the Celtic Sea (which is approximately 650ft at its deepest point) in the south by the St George's Channel, and to the Atlantic Ocean in the north by the North Channel. The North Sea (which covers some 290,000 square miles and has a maximum depth of around 2,300ft) sits alongside the English Channel (which separates southern England and northern France, and is at its widest at the Strait of Dover), and is classed as a marginal sea of the Atlantic Ocean. The North Sea, according to *Wikipedia*, is 'located between Great Britain, Scandinavia, Germany, the Netherlands and Belgium'.

These great bodies of water have, for so many years, been navigated and fished. Their contents have been catalogued by science and almost every nook, cranny and crevice mapped. However, despite harbouring a bewildering variety of creatures, the waters around Great Britain exude further mystery. The ferocious waves continue to swallow ships – some having never been seen again – whilst other vessels line the shores like eerie, stranded skeletons as wrecks, half-consumed by the mud. Strange things have been reported by reputable seamen: from terrifying monsters to unexplained lights, which seem to slip in and out of the black deep. Not all of these stories are simply far-fetched tales spouted from the lips of drunken sailors in creaky old coastal inns, and the yarns pertaining to spectral ships and the like are not mere smugglers' creations, spun to ward off curious trespassers from places where illegal goods have been stashed. The seas around Britain take no prisoners; they rarely give up their dead and the esoteric secrets they hide only occasionally surface to leave us perplexed.

It is my fear of the sea that has driven me to write this book; a follow-on, to some extent, from my 2012 book *Shadows in the Sky: The Haunted Airways of Britain*. However much we fear the inky depths of space, or the steaming, inhospitable jungles of this planet, the crashing waves that batter ships on our coastlines are a bleak reminder of another mysterious place so close to home. Many books have been written concerning monster-inhabited lochs or eerie rivers, but this look at our haunted coasts is something different.

As children we visit the seaside to build sandcastles under warm summer skies and, as visitors, we cavort among the waves, yet someone, somewhere else in Britain may have had a more frightening or seemingly supernatural experience; maybe a monstrous head rearing above the foam, or an ancient vessel floating on the horizon only to suddenly vanish.

It was poet Matthew Arnold who wrote 'The sea is calm tonight' in his work *Dover Beach*, and yet was quick to speak of how '… now I only hear its melancholy, long, withdrawing roar'. Meanwhile, William Shakespeare spoke of 'sea nymphs' in his *Full Fathom Five*, and Samuel Taylor Coleridge, in his epic poem *Rime of the Ancient Mariner*, wrote of the 'Water, water, everywhere … nor any drop to drink.' For me, these haunting words sum up all of my fears of the seas I'll be speaking of in this tome, and I hope you enjoy the maritime mysteries I have to offer. Of course, I don't expect you to believe in any of these tales – especially if you are one to scoff at yarns pertaining to sea monsters, ghosts and the like – but I hope you'll agree that this volume of British sea riddles is impressive at least. So maybe, just maybe, you'll reconsider and, with open mind, venture forth next time onto that boat, pier or beach, and when casting an eye out across the glistening surface, you'll feel the same trepidation as me for the shadows on the sea.

Neil Arnold

The author. (Jemma Lee Arnold)

1

PHANTOM SHIPS

LEGENDS OF THE DEEP ...

As a child I often accompanied my dad on fishing trips to local freshwater lakes around Kent. My dad would set up the rod, tackle and bait, and I would happily gawp into the green waters beneath my feet for hours, waiting for that small, luminous float to bob as a hidden fish nibbled at it. The suspense made my spine tingle, and then, as the float disappeared beneath the lily pads, I'd stand up as quick as a shot and strike: lifting the rod (usually hitting an overhanging branch!) and reeling like mad, hoping that the hook would snag the lip of the maggot-hungry predator. More often than not, I would miss the bite, but on occasion the rod would bend and to me it felt like there was a monster on the end, even though by the time the silvery creature made its way to my dad's hands it rarely weighed more than a pound or two. Even so, angling was all about mystery, especially when the dusk used to draw in – bringing with it the darting bats and buzzing gnats – and my dad used to tell me ghost and monster stories. The great thing about these tales, which I listened to intently over a flask of tea and peanut butter sandwiches, was the fact that, according to my dad, they had taken place in and around the British Isles.

One of the first stories I heard – passed down from my granddad to my dad – concerned some deep-sea divers out at sea somewhere off the Scottish coast. One of the divers, whilst exploring the gloom of an old wreck, disturbed an angry eel of some kind, but the most terrifying aspect about the encounter was that the eel's head was said to have been the size of a chair! I was fascinated by this monster tale because, even as a youngster, I was obsessed with yarns pertaining to giant fish. I knew very well that an eel – especially a conger eel – could grow quite large, but certainly not to have a head the size of a chair. Was this story merely an exaggerated fisherman's tale? Probably. Yet conger eels weighing over 200lb have been caught off the British Isles from boats;

A phantom ship. (Illustration by Neil Arnold)

the record for the biggest conger caught offshore stands at 68lb, from Devil's Point in Cornwall. Even so, the tale of the giant eel got me hooked – excuse the pun. Another monster eel story I heard comes from good friend and cryptozoologist Richard Freeman, who told me recently:

When I was about seven years old, in 1977, I was on holiday in Torbay (an east-facing bay at the westernmost point of Lyme Bay). My granddad got talking to an old retired trawlerman in Goodrington harbour. He said that he and his crew used to fish off Brixham at a part of the coast called Berry Head. It is one of the deepest parts of the sea around the UK coast and is hence used to scuttle old ships so they wouldn't be a danger to shipping. The scuttle ships formed a man-made reef that was a magnet to fish. The trawlermen fished there for that very reason. One evening they were pulling up the nets and it felt like they had got a good, heavy catch. As the nets drew closer to the ship's lights however, they found that they had not caught thousands of fish but one huge one. The old man said it was a gigantic eel. He told my granddad that it was the only time in his many years at sea that he had felt frightened. He said it had a huge mouth, wide enough to swallow a man and teeth as long as his hand. He also recalled the large, glassy eyes.

So, I asked Richard, what happened to the monstrous eel?

'Once free of the support of the water,' he replied, 'the monster's great weight snapped the nets and it escaped back into the deep. The trawlerman was relieved to see it go.'

Although freshwater fishing at Kentish lakes involved occasional encounters with toothy pike, the tranquillity of the surroundings instilled warmth rather than dread – it was the salt water abode that intrigued but terrified me all the same. I couldn't deal with the possibility that beneath those cold British coastal waters there were such enormous creatures: beasts hiding in old wrecks, and leviathans concealed by silt, shingle and seaweed. It was these types of stories that instilled a fear of the sea in me and made my summer trips to the seaside with my family so unnerving.

On quite a few occasions I accompanied my dad to the Kent coast for a spot of sea fishing. These trips would usually take us to the beaches of Hythe, Dungeness or Deal. I was never one for braving the biting winds for too long, but I remember many a morning when I would wake for school at home and go into the bathroom and there, lying in the bath, would be a large dead cod or skate. These specimens – caught by my dad – would end up on the worktop in the kitchen where my dad would proceed to gut them and then later cook and eat them. I was constantly told that eating certain fish was very good for you, and I've always found cod, haddock et al, delicious.

Funnily enough, despite always having had a fascination with the creatures of the sea and spending much of my childhood sketching sharks and the like, my sister Vicki has an extreme phobia of water – especially those cold depths frequented by sharks. Anything shark-related absolutely petrifies her – I believe this is called geleophobia. So when the BBC ran the headline, 'Great white sharks could be in British waters' in the August of 2011, I made sure that I kept the newspaper cutting away from her! Of course, stories of such magnificent and man-eating beasts are unfounded, but the salty waters of Britain are known for porbeagle and shortfin mako sharks, as well as several other smaller species and a few less frequent visitors, such as the Blue shark. The porbeagle is, in fact, a member of the Great White family, and in 2012 a record 10ft long specimen was hooked off Cornwall by two men from Hampshire. The fish weighed more than 550lb, breaking the previous record by almost 50lb. Just like in the movie *Jaws*, the monster fish was said to have dragged the small boat of the fishermen for over a mile.

Sharks, alongside whales, are probably the closest thing we will get to seeing monsters in British waters. Elsewhere on the planet, however, there is one true monster that still eludes man and that is the giant squid of the genus *Architeuthis dux*.

This deep-ocean dweller is a formidable cephalopod that can grow to enormous size: in 2007 a colossal squid measuring 33ft in length was caught in Antarctica; in the same year a squid measuring almost 27ft was found on a beach in Australia. But despite a few, relatively large specimens being caught or washed up, the truly gigantic squid still eludes science. Yet we know such creatures are not just myth – large beaks have been found in the stomach of sperm whales, and such whales have been observed with enormous sucker marks on their bodies. Although the giant squid does not lurk in British waters – thankfully – it is the perfect example of how something huge can still evade man. No one knows just how big these monsters of the deep can get, but some researchers believe that a measurement of over 40ft would not be far-fetched. Despite the reluctance within the scientific community to accept the existence of monsters, the giant squid certainly fuelled my imagination as a child. Many people may dismiss such watery wonders as legends alongside the Cyclops, harpies, fairies and the like, but in the great waters of the world the impossible almost seems possible, rather than just fantasy or the stuff of old creaky Sinbad movies.

I do suggest, however, that before you begin to dismiss the salt waters of Britain as tame, you read Chapter 5, Denizens of the Deep, which may sway your judgement, especially when you consider the amount of accounts that exist to suggest that 'our' coastal environments do indeed harbour strange visitors. But first, I would like to share with you another weird story I was told of as a child that once and for all deterred me from those seaside visits …

Ungodly Goodwin Sands

The Goodwin Sands is a 10-mile stretch of sand situated 6 miles off Deal in the county of Kent. This sandbank has a reputation for being extremely challenging to ships, and over the centuries many vessels have perished in the waves that hide this stretch. The first ever recorded shipwreck from the Goodwin Sands comes from 1298, when a vessel returning from Flanders was consumed somewhere near Sandwich. Since then, many boats have broken their backs on the bank, forcing passengers – if they survived – onto the beach. Even then, survival was not assured because although crew would often light fires, if their pleas for help were missed, then shortly afterwards the foaming tide would roll back in, consuming them and sending them to a watery grave. Rumour has it that over the centuries more than 50,000 people have died along the Goodwin Sands.

When I first heard about the great number of shipwrecks on this stretch, I wondered if there had been any reports of ghosts haunting the coastline. Not surprisingly, I came across what is without doubt one of the most acknowledged cases regarding a spectral ship, and one of my favourite maritime mysteries. It is fair to say that the most famous ghost-ship legend concerns the *Flying Dutchman*, an ancient sailing vessel said

The treacherous Goodwin Sands sit several miles out at sea, off Deal. They can be seen from Deal Castle. (Neil Arnold)

to appear off the Cape of Good Hope in South Africa. Similarly, the Goodwin Sands are said to be haunted by a phantom ship called the *Lady Lovibond* (also spelt *Luvibund*). This three-masted schooner was bound for Oporto in Portugal in the February of 1748, but this journey was ill-fated from the start. At the time, sailors often considered a woman on board to be a bad omen, and yet the captain of the vessel, a chap named Simon Reed, was very keen to take his new bride Annetta on board. A further issue on the journey was the fact that another man aboard the boat, first mate John Rivers, was jealous of the captain's wife. Mr Rivers had once been a love rival, and it is believed that this caused a row and, in a fit of jealousy, the mate killed the captain. Some say that the crazed murderer then guided the ship onto the treacherous shore off Deal, where all crew died.

Ever since this terrible tragedy, which is said to have occurred on 13 February, a ghostly ship, reminiscent of the *Lady Lovibond*, has appeared in the waters off the Goodwin Sands, and every fifty years thereafter on 13 February. It is claimed that, on 13 February 1798, the master of a ship called *Edenbridge* made an entry into his log mentioning that his vessel had almost collided with a three-masted schooner. Captain James Westlake also recorded that he could hear female voices and much jollity below deck. Meanwhile, the crew of another boat out at sea at the time reported seeing the phantom ship beach itself upon the sandbank. In 1848 lifeboat men at Deal were called out to the sands when reports came in that a schooner had run aground, but their search proved fruitless. It is said that similar occurrences took place in 1898, though I can find no details to confirm this, but in 1948 it was claimed that a Captain Bull Prestwick had observed the phantom ship. The boat seemed very real except for the eerie glow about it as it came into view, and it was watched by the crew for some five minutes. Prestwick reported that, 'It came straight out of the fog like a mouldy shadow, its rotted old timbers creaking and groaning, its ripped and mangled sails flapping and cracking in the cold night wind like the laughter of Satan himself'.

Admittedly, this description of the encounter seems all too atmospheric; the words from Prestwick's mouth read like lines from a movie. It seems, however, that the legend is gradually fading, as in 1998 there were no reported encounters with the boat. Mind you, it is worth taking note of a snippet of information, which appeared in the *Evening Post* newspaper of 12 March 1969 in reference to a Goodwin Sands ghost boat. Under the heading 'Ghost ship hunt after collision', it was reported that a sea and air search had been conducted off Dover (a neighbouring town of Deal) after a tanker radioed to say they had avoided a collision with a small yet unknown vessel near the Goodwin Sands. The incident happened during a snowfall. Even more newsworthy is the incident that took place two years prior to this, in 1967, which involved the Hinckley family, consisting of Peter and Kim, and their two sons David and John. They had taken to the waters off Deal in their yacht *Grey Seal* on what began as a lovely day,

Looking out towards Goodwin Sands – Deal pier can be seen in the distance. (Neil Arnold)

but very soon a storm seemed to close in. Yet the most unnerving thing about the trip was the peculiar mist that seemed to sit on a specific area of the water. Large waves appeared to crash in this murky location but there was a still a surreal tranquillity around them. The Hinckleys waited, and waited, unsure what was going to happen but quite sure that *something* was going to happen, when they suddenly became aware of a terrific apparition that loomed out of the misty patch. A great ship, in combat with the sea, rode out of the aggressive waves in the distance and very quickly the Hinckleys passed around a set of binoculars, each of them confirming the startling sight before them as the crew members now began leaping out of the sailing craft in distress. At first the family felt that this was like some scene from a sea drama movie and, bravely, they approached the strange scene. But with that, the mist seemed to dissipate, the storm subsided and the ship and its despairing sailors were no more.

The Hinckleys were so confused that, like any normal family, they contacted the coastguard who stated that there had been no other reports of a ship having problems. Shortly after their unnatural encounter, the family did a bit of research. They all remembered that, as their yacht edged towards the ghostly ship, they saw the name *Snipe* written on its side, but when they looked into the archives they were astounded to find that such a boat had indeed sunk in the area – but in 1807! However, to confuse the matter they also found that a ship called *Snipe* had been in action until 1846 – so what type of surreal scenario had this family of four encountered? Some would argue, or prefer to state, that maybe the Hinckleys had seen the *Lady Lovibund* edging out of the mist, but this does not appear to be the case.

On 13 February 1998 several ghost-hunters visited the sands in the hope of catching a glimpse of the *Lovibund*. *Fortean Times* magazine, who have covered stories pertaining to the paranormal for several decades, sent their own investigative team of Paul Sieveking and Jonathan Bryant but, despite scanning the horizon for several hours, they saw nothing. *Fortean Times* did remark, however, that a map of wrecks displayed on the wall of a local cafe listed the *Lovibund* disaster as 1746; meanwhile, a very early, if not the earliest, reference concerning the wreck in the *Daily Chronicle* of 14 February 1924 writes of the ship sinking in 1724. To confuse matters further, *Fortean Times* added, 'At the time, correspondents for the magazine *Notes & Queries* were unable to find the origin of this yarn, either in history, local folklore or fiction.' To muddy the waters even more, G.M. Dixon, in his book *Folktales & Legends of Kent*, claims that the boat was run aground on 12 February, according to a 'reliable record', and that it was a man named Captain Whalley who manned the vessel. Dixon then goes on to name the murderous mate as a John Prior.

Did the incident involving the *Lady Lovibund* happen at all? Or is it merely a misty urban legend tied to 13 February simply because it is the eve of St Valentine, which in turn would make such a story a tale of lost love like so many other spook tales? Of course, as *Fortean Times* concluded, 'Even if the *Lady Luvibund* had no basis in fact, we cannot rule out ghost ships on the Goodwins.'

As a final note on this mysterious stretch of the Kent coast, I must share with you the case pertaining to the *Lucienne*, a wayward French ketch constructed in 1918, which a year later was found on the sands despite its home port being at St Malo in Brittany. The boat had all the ghost ship qualities about it: it was bereft of damage, and below deck there were several unfinished meals, suggesting the crew had simply disappeared into thin air or jumped overboard. The ship's wheel had also been roped, so that the *Lucienne* would make a straight course, but no one ever found or heard from the six crew members. The same could also be said for the barge named *Zebrina*, which, built at Faversham in 1873 was found, in 1917, without damage or crew at Rozel Point, south of Cherbourg. Eerie stuff, indeed.

LOST LANDS AND BELLS FROM HELL

Another strange characteristic about the sands is that the spot where these ships are said to have run aground, and then appear in ghostly fashion, is the same stretch said to harbour a lost island and another ghost story. Some people believe that an island known as Lomea once sat at the Goodwin Sands but, due to neglect sometime during the eleventh century, it was flooded and consumed by the waves. Legend has it that the sound of bells can be heard beneath the water, suggesting a ghostly church, but of course there is no evidence to prove that the mystical island ever existed. This tale may simply be the stuff of urban legend as it echoes an almost identical rumour from Dunwich in Suffolk. This area was once a major seaport of East Anglia but little now remains of the past after more than seven centuries of coastal erosion. Even so, locals often report that on certain nights the bells of the submerged church can be heard ringing out from beneath the waves. The sombre din is said to be a warning of a coming storm. It is also said that some of the people who used to reside in the village still haunt the cliff tops as shadowy figures. On 21 April 1974, the *Sunday Express* reported that a Suffolk diver named Stuart Bacon was attempting to solve the mystery of the watery bells. According to the article, Mr Bacon had a theory that 'the tidal flow causes the bell, supposed to be in one of the old churches, to ring,' but investigations would be difficult due to 'poor visibility'.

Another very similar legend of a sunken land emerges from Merionethshire, in Wales. The facts are that over 700 years ago the area of Cardigan Bay was dry land – but the folklore claims the land of Gwyddno was swallowed by water simply because the guardian of a fairy allowed it to overflow. And so, like the already mentioned legends, on certain nights when the wind refuses to howl, the bells of what became known as Cantref Gwaelod can still be heard to toll, only muffled by the lapping water. Pembrokeshire in the south-west of Wales also has a weird bell legend. The small village of St David's, once deemed the 'holiest ground in Britain', has a famous cathedral that sits in a hollow. Author John Harries writes, 'The first glimpse from the

Phantom bells are said to ring out from the sea near the Suffolk coastline. (Joyce Goodchild)

A487 of the famous cathedral is a memorable experience: just the tower is to be seen.' Legend has it that the dark forces stole the cathedral's largest bell and did so with ease, due to the fact that the high surrounding land enabled 'men possessed by imps' to gain easy access. The bell was then dropped out to the sea off Whitesands Bay and when a storm is near the buried bell rings. It is also worth noting that along the coast here are said to exist eerie lights, which are known as *canwll corfe*, or corpse candles.

From Land's End in Cornwall comes another similar legend, about the Isles of Scilly, as recorded by Jennifer Westwood in her book *Gothick Cornwall*. She states: 'The flash of the Seven Stones Light Vessel can be seen from here by night, marking the last visible remains of a lost country.' For it is said that during the sixteenth century, fishermen would often bring in their sturdy nets and find remains of sunken houses amongst their daily catch. Some 140 parishes are said to lie sunken between Land's End and Scilly; a neighbourhood wiped out by a flood, with only one man surviving. The legend, like those others before, claims that on moonlit nights one can see, if you look hard enough, the rooftops of those lost buildings. This could be the drowned land of Lyonesse, said to have existed a mile or so north of Land's End. Author Alasdair Alpin MacGregor wrote of the haunting bells and a report from the 1930s involving a chap named Stanley Baron, who, whilst staying with relatives at Sennen Cove, heard the sound of bells one night into the early hours. When Stanley mentioned the eerie sounds to a local fisherman he was told about the 'lost bells' and the land that was drowned in 1014 and 1094. MacGregor mentions another peculiar experience involving a lady named Edith Oliver who one Wednesday had driven to Land's End and, whilst staring across the sea, saw a town several miles out. She asked the local coastguard about the towers, spires and battlements she could see, to which he replied, 'There's no town there, only the sea …'.

Miss Oliver was bemused by what she'd seen, but was fortunate enough to get a second glimpse of the phantom land, this time when she was with a friend, a Miss MacPherson. One evening they had been driving towards Land's End when Miss Oliver spied the town in the distance and asked her friend if she too could see it, to which Miss MacPherson replied in the affirmative. Ghostly bells have also been heard from the waters at Carbis Bay, just up to coast from Land's End on the north coast of Cornwall.

Another fascinating tale of a Cornish lost village comes from Seaton Sands, where it was once said that between Downderry and Looe a town prospered, but when some local sailors insulted a mermaid, she placed a terrible curse on the town and eventually the foaming sea swallowed it, inhabitants and all. There is a slightly alternative version of this legend, which states that at Padstow a dreadful sandbank, known as the Doom Bar, was formed as a result of the mermaid's curse. It is said that a fisherman from the area once saw a woman sitting on a rock with her back to him, and she appeared to be combing her long hair. However, when the man attracted her attention, he was rather shocked to find she was in fact a mermaid and with that he pulled out a gun and shot her. As she slipped to her last breath the mermaid cursed the area and that night an appalling storm broke over Padstow and many ships and lives were lost.

Author Peter Underwood also wrote of the sound of bells from beneath the waves at the parish of Forrabury in Cornwall. According to Peter, 'They are supposed to have originated with the conveyance by sea of new bells for the local church …'. However, the tranquillity of the area was soon disturbed when a captain, whilst on board his boat, used blasphemous language, and a terrific storm began to swirl, sinking the boat and killing all on board. Where the ship sank there have been reports of a ghostly boat and spectral crewmen floundering in the waves.

At Bulverhythe – a suburb of Hastings – in East Sussex, there is legend of church bells being heard beneath the waves, which is also echoed at Bosham, in the west of the county. The noise could well be explained by the raking noise the sea makes as it combs the beach, but it has certainly spawned a degree of lore, for it is said that when the bells are heard then bad weather is imminent. Phantom sea bells have also been recorded a few miles seaward from Blackpool and also at Cromer, in Norfolk, although the main theme of the ghost story here is that on certain days the steeple of a sub-merged church – St Peter's – can be seen protruding from the water. This image appears about a quarter of a mile from the shore where there is, coincidentally, a rock named Church Rock. When the bells ring fishermen often flee to the safety of their homes because a storm is brewing, just like many years ago when unruly waves consumed the church. Another Norfolk-based legend of similar guise concerns St Mary's church.

On 4 January 1604 huge waves rushed through Eccles-on-Sea and swallowed literally everything, except the church tower, which somehow survived several more tempests over the next two centuries until, on 25 January 1895, the sea left only a stump. In December 1912 another flood swept through the area and some thirty-nine skeletons were exposed. The news of the skeletons spread like wildfire and visitors flocked from all over, including one man who had such a morbid curiosity that he – armed with a spade – dug into the earth and stole some of the bones.

The Cliffs of Moher can be found at the south-western edge of the Burren region on County Clare, Ireland. Between these 700ft cliffs and Ballard Cliffs further south, there used to be a few small towns, but these were sent to the depths of the sea by a terrific earthquake that struck many years ago. Everyone that resided within that farming community perished and it is said that on clear days when the sea is like a mirror, the spire of the monastery and the walls of some of the houses can still be observed. As Bob Curran writes, '… the monastery bell can yet be heard ringing out across the waves.' Again, it seems to be the stuff of legend, but Mr Curran does recall in his book, *Banshees, Beasts and Brides from the Sea*, that one summer's day, when he was about 14, he was on a boat in the shadow of the cliffs when he heard the sound, 'like the steady tolling of a bell'; a sound that instilled dread into those locals on board, who all at once pointed to the sea and maintained they could see the walls of the houses swept out to sea all those years ago. Mr Curran could not see anything as those waves rolled high, but suddenly the rush of excitement he'd experienced was turned to sadness when one of the men that had been shouting and pointing was hit by a wave, taken overboard and never seen again.

On Sunday 7 July 1878 a mysterious island was said to have appeared out at sea and been observed by the residents of Ballycotton, County Cork. The land looked rich in vegetation but when several boat loads of people put offshore to investigate, the island gradually faded into nothing. Many believed they had seen some type of enchanted island. Its magical properties are no doubt confirmed by the fact that it has also been seen off Carrigaholt at Clare, the mouth of Ballinaleame Bay in Galway, as well as in the vicinity of Ballysadare Bay, and numerous other locations around Ireland.

The Orkney Islands have rumour of a once-phantom island turned real. The land is known as the Isle of Enhallow and it is said to have only been visible during certain hours. Every time a boat was sent out to explore it, the island would vanish. However, one clever chap decided to head towards the isle one day, armed with a bar made of iron, which, according to writer Elliott O'Donnell, has an effect on some supernatural phenomena. As the man got to within a few metres of the mystical isle he cast his bar at it, and it landed on the beach. The man then leapt onto the island and from then on it remained stationary. A more thrilling story is told of by the natives of Rousay, who claim that near Enhallow there used to exist an extraordinary isle inhabited by fairy folk and that, of a night as fishermen passed in their boats, enchanting music could be heard soaring from the isle. It seems that the island was something akin to Heaven and Hell because those who got close enough to the shore often spoke of beautiful women but also hideous monsters. There is one rumour, which alleges that a young woman was abducted by a strange fellow and taken to this unusual place. Her parents went in search of her and accidentally landed upon the magic isle but their daughter refused to come home, saying she was happy with the man she had met. She did, however, give her father – a fisherman – a knife, and stated that all the time he kept it on him his fishing would never fail. Sadly, when the couple left the island the man dropped the knife overboard and his fishing days became numbered.

In contrast, on 8 August 1993 the *Scottish Sunday Mail* reported on an 'island' that had suddenly appeared over night; it makes a change from all those vanishing lands! The strange isle was found a quarter of a mile from the shores of Glenbuck Loch, near Douglas in south Ayrshire. A doctor from the British Geological Survey in Edinburgh was mystified as to its appearance but believed it may well have been a 'mass of peat', which had broken off from somewhere. Local fishermen blamed the phantom island for weeks of bad fishing.

Meanwhile, off Hayling Island (situated off the south coast of England not far from Portsmouth), there is more rumour of drowned churches. The buildings were said to have sat on South Hayling, which were consumed by the sea at some point in the fourteenth century. The bells can still be heard ringing out … or so it is said.

I'm amazed at the repetition in some of these tales, suggesting they are nothing more than folklore passed down through generations. This seems to happen through-out Britain, and you'll find that in this book, whether it is rumoured lost lands or phantom ships, there are many similarities in the stories from county to county.

WHEN THE BOAT COMES IN

Returning to the Kent coast, the *Lady Lovibond* is not the only ghostly vessel said to haunt the stretch of water around Deal. More than a century ago, the SS *Violet* – a paddle steamer – ran into trouble on the sands during a violent storm, which brought with it a heavy snowfall. The date was 6 January 1857. All crew, including a Captain Lyne and passengers, were said to have perished, but in 1947 a George Carter, who was a look-out on the East Goodwin lightship, claimed to have seen an old paddle steamer run aground. The lifeboat at Ramsgate was called into action but despite searching the area for more than an hour, there was no sign of the ghost boat. The *Shrewsbury* man-of-war and SS *Montrose*, a transatlantic ocean liner, are also said to occasionally be seen around the sandbank near Deal. SS *Montrose* was stationed at Dover to be used as a blockship but, on 20 December 1914, the ship broke free from its mooring during strong winds and was wrecked on the Goodwin Sands. One of the more recent sight-ings of the ghost boat, along with its phantom crew, took place in 1965. There have also been scant reports of a Spanish galleon around the coast. This boat sank during

The author at Deal. The Goodwin Sands are several miles in the distance. (Jemma Lee Arnold)

the Armada because of an attempted mutiny. The crew killed their own officers after Sir Francis Drake's attack, but those on board who were left were unable to navigate the galleon and so the boat perished. On 1 November 1919 a two-masted Estonian schooner named *Toogoo* fell foul of turbulent waters whilst journeying from Calais to South Shields. Distress signals sent out were heard by the North Deal lifeboat crew, however, as they arrived, a tremendous wave smashed into the boat sending several crew members into the water. The ghost story doesn't concern the boat, but those on board who lost their lives, for it is said that on certain nights of horrendous weather, one can, if one listens carefully enough, hear the screams of the suffering above the roaring waves and foul winds.

MORE SPECTRAL SHIPS

Whether or not we believe the stories pertaining to these lost ghost ships is not the question, but there is certainly something eerily romantic about forlorn vessels floating out at sea, stuck in some type of salty limbo bereft of crew. Such ghostly ships are dotted throughout world folklore and there are many treacherous coastlines said to harbour this type of ghost story. I've often thought to myself that if such phantasmal ships are true, then why hasn't anyone, on the anniversary of the wreck, visited the location and scanned the horizon with camera ready, and taken a photo? Well, maybe they have. In the May of 1998 Prince Edward presented a television series called *Crown and Country* and in one particular episode the focus was on HMS *Eurydice*, a twenty-six-gun frigate that had sunk in 1878 at Sandown Bay, Isle of Wight. The vessel had sailed from Portsmouth in 1877 to the West Indies and Bermuda, but upon its return had been caught in a ferocious blizzard, capsized and sank. More than 300 crew were killed; there were only two survivors. In a legend very much reminiscent of the *Lady Lovibond*, HMS *Eurydice* has apparently been seen around the coast since the tragedy.

In 1930 a captain of a submarine claimed that he ordered his crew to take drastic evasive action to avoid a three-masted vessel, but as some crew members watched, the boat vanished before their eyes. In 1978 a female magistrate named Julie Matthews observed the ghost ship whilst having a barbeque with friends on Compton beach. She commented at the time that, 'It came so close that if it had been real it would have run aground.' This mysterious event echoed another incident from 1959, when a Robin Ford – an ex-mayor and high-school teacher – also having a barbeque on the beach with friends, saw the boat just 100yds out. 'It moved slowly across the shore,' he commented, 'then just seemed to up-end and slipped silently out of view.' All witnesses present confirmed that as the night fell silent they could hear the distinct sound of the creaking timbers and clearly see the three masts of the vessel.

The mystery of the *Eurydice* deepened even further when Prince Edward and film crew stated they had seen the phantom boat whilst making their documentary. In fact, they even filmed the ethereal frigate. Some viewers of the documentary, which I was fortunate enough at the time to have recorded, claimed it had been an elaborate hoax. Prince Edward responded that, 'It just appeared … It was not arranged for us,' whilst director Robin Bextor added:

> We filmed it for a while, then decided to wait so we would catch it sailing off into the horizon. We assumed it was a training vessel. Like the rest of us, Edward was pleased at our stroke of luck at seeing it, because it saved time and money getting footage of something similar.

Luck indeed! But, was the three-masted vessel that appeared on the horizon on those glistening, silvery waves a phantom or a fraud? Suspicions were raised when Robin Bextor commented, 'We were packing up our cameras and took our eyes off it for a few minutes, but when we went to film it again, it had gone.'

I find it rather odd that a possible ghostly ship would only receive half-hearted attention from a film crew, who just happened to be making a documentary about the subject. Even stranger still, no one kept their eyes on it and saw it vanish, and yet were lacklustre enough to not only look away, but pack their filming equipment up! Hoax would seem to be the result, especially as there were no training vessels in the area at the time, and this was confirmed by Hilary Painter of the Sail Training Association, who commented that although they had two training ships of that design, neither were out at sea on that particular day. Had all this been an elaborate set-up by the film crew? As a strange coincidence, Prince Edward's great-grandfather, the Duke of York, had apparently had a similar experience off the Australian coast, which he recorded in his log book on 11 July 1881. He stated: 'At 4 a.m. the *Flying Dutchman* crossed our bows.' Thirteen witnesses were on hand to view the spectacle.

At Windsor on 22 March 1878, a Sir John MacNeill and the Bishop of Ripon were enjoying an afternoon meal when Mr MacNeill exclaimed, 'Good heavens! Why don't they close the portholes and reef the sails', as he claimed to have had a vision of a ship across the Channel some 70 miles away, which was being bombarded by a wind storm. It would seem that Sir MacNeill had in fact seen, in his mind, HMS *Eurydice*.

THERE IS A LIGHT THAT NEVER GOES OUT

Considering the amount of reports of ships that have gone missing over the centuries, coupled with the multitude of wrecks, it is no wonder the seas of the world occasionally re-enact such tragedies to those susceptible to seeing them. Amazingly, and rather eerily, even the coastal lights used to warn ships of danger have become part of the paranormal puzzle. Lighthouses – constructed to deter ships from harsh shores – have existed along the 7,000-mile coastline of the British Isles for several centuries, but when first constructed there were sinister rumours said to surround them. It has long been suggested that Sir John Killgrew, who built the first lighthouse in 1619 at the Lizard in Cornwall, didn't construct it to deter ships from the rocky outcrops, but instead to lure them closer to the beaches where they would succumb to ghastly pirates – with Mr Killgrew rumoured to be one of them!

Lighthouses have always appeared as eerie beacons shining out from the blackness of a storm-ravaged coast. There is a fascinating tale concerning a lighthouse from the eighteenth century. The Longships Lighthouse at Land's End was in terrible trouble one evening because the light-keeper had been kidnapped by local wreckers, and so it was up to his daughter to man the lighthouse. According to legend, the small child had to choose between Christian reverence and her duty to keep the light shining to warn ships of hazard. It is said that the girl could not reach up high enough to light the lamps but, showing great intuition, she placed a thick family Bible on the floor and stood on it, and thus continued her duty.

In 1772 the crew of the *Chantiloupe* had no such luck of a warning light when they hit rocks off Bantham in the south of Devon. Wreckers would often prey on those who had succumbed to devilish coastlines, and anyone who survived the waves would surely be robbed and possibly murdered. In the mammoth volume *Folklore Myths & Legends of Britain*, it is stated that: 'On stormy nights, people watched eagerly for the lights of a stricken vessel, and ghoulishly swooped on wreckage and survivors, whose chances of survival were considerably lessened by an ancient law.' It was once said to be illegal to claim salvage if anyone cast from a wrecked ship was still alive – in other words, if they were murdered, then their possessions could be taken. Mind you, some researchers dispute the possibility that wreckers purposefully lured ships onto rocks, but there are old tales of dastardly criminals attaching lights to the hind quarters of animals, such as horses and cows, in order to lure a ship in to the rocks. This legend is confirmed by author J.A. Brooks in his book *Cornish Ghosts & Legends*, when he writes of the mysterious number of ships wrecked on the coast. A stranger, possibly put ashore by a pirate vessel, would, of a night, fasten a lantern to the back of a horse that he would drive along the cliff, which in turn, according to Brooks, 'from its motion would be taken for a vessel's stern light'.

It seems that this devilish chap made quite a living for himself plying his terrible trade, but it is said that when on his deathbed, the local parsons reported seeing evil spirits in the house of the criminal. Sounds of splashing waves as if rising around his bed were also heard, suggesting the sea was getting its revenge on the man who had lured people to their deaths to rob them. Then, one night, the local farmhands heard a voice boom out over the sea, saying: 'The hour is come but the man is not come.' With that, they looked across the waves and saw a mighty black ship approaching the shore at pace. Huge, black clouds could be seen swirling above the boat, and the men fled in terror, warning others of some unknown yet impending doom. As locals scurried to safety, they all saw the ship of doom run fast to the abode of the sinful pirate, and with that the man died and the ship, seeming to reverse, floated back to the crashing waves and disappeared without trace.

Those brave enough to tend to the dead man's body suddenly noticed that the weather had become calm, but when his body was taken to the local churchyard, another tempest rose with lightning forks spearing the coffin, forcing the men to drop the casket and flee into the church. When the storm had abated the men resumed their task, only to find that all that remained of the coffin were its handles, for the lightning bolt that struck it had set it on fire, reducing it to dust. It seems that this incident may have forced many a criminal to think twice about luring ships onto the rocks.

At Seaford in East Sussex, legend claims that local people – once known as 'cormorants' or 'shags' – would lure ships onto the rocks by placing false lights on the cliffs. Another legend states that if one was a witch and wanted to wreck a ship, then all they had to do was stand on their head and chant, 'Sweery, sweery, linkum-loo! Do to them as I now do …'. This was certainly far easier, some would say, than waiting an age for a ship to be lured by a false light.

Witches were once thought to have the devil within them due to their ability to sink ships. So, imagine the horror of the man who, while walking one day with his daughter along the coast of Tobermory, Mull at the Inner Hebrides, got the shock of his life when she asked him what his reaction would be if she sunk every ship on the horizon. Of course, the man laughed, and with that, his daughter bent down and looked at the ships backwards between her legs, and at once, all except one, they began to rock and roll on the waves and then disappeared beneath the surface. The girl's father was shocked at his daughter's behaviour and asked where on earth she'd learnt of such a 'gift', to which she replied that her mother had taught her. Upon which, he took her home and the next day burnt her and her mother as witches. In another incident at Tobermory it is rumoured that some eighteen witches, disguised as seagulls, conjured a great storm in order to destroy a ship of the Spanish Armada. One of the weirdest witch stories in relation to a ship, however, dates back several centuries and concerns a seaman from Bristol, who claimed that on one occasion he saw the ghosts of four terrible witches in the cockpit of his ship. The hags were playing with dice! It was said that the witches sprinkled a magic dust throughout the ship to prevent it sailing, hence the fact it spent so long in Gibraltar. Eventually, a priest was summoned and blessed the vessel, and the hags appeared no more.

In Welsh folklore a master 'wrecker' was Thomas Vaughan, who would ruthlessly lure ships to their doom at Southerdown Beach, in the shadow of Dunraven's Castle, which held the seat of the Vaughans. Vaughan was often said to fasten lamps to an ivy-consumed tower or fix them to the back of sheep that grazed high on the cliff tops. As crewmen from the wrecked ships gasped for air on the beach, Vaughan's gang would creep from the shadows and strip the sailors of their valuables, and then cruelly roll them back towards the reaching tide.

It is also worth taking into consideration that Britain has several reputedly haunted lighthouses. This doesn't seem surprising either, when you consider some of the legends surrounding such beacons. The Eilean Mor lighthouse on the remote Flannan Isles, west of the Outer Hebrides, was bestowed an eerie legend in 1900 when passing ships reported that there was no light emanating from the structure. When the lighthouse was investigated it was found that the three keepers, Donald McArthur, James Ducat and head keeper Thomas Marshall, had simply vanished into thin air, never to be seen again. They had left orderly living quarters and a lamp that had been filled ready to be lit. The log retrieved from the lighthouse read:

12th December: Gale north by northwest. Sea lashed to fury. Never seen such a storm. Waves very high. Tearing at lighthouse. Everything shipshape. James Ducat irritable.

Later: Storm still raging, wind steady. Stormbound. Cannot go out. Ship passing sounding foghorn. Could see lights of cabins. Ducat quiet. Donald McArthur crying.

13th December: Storm continued through night. Wind shifted west by north. Ducat quiet. McArthur praying.

Later: Noon, grey daylight. Me, Ducat and McArthur prayed.

14th December: No entry in log.

15th December: Storm ended, sea calm. God is over all.

Southerdown beach in Wales. Legend has it that many ships were lured to their doom here. (Simon Wyatt)

And that was it. Where had the trio gone? Could three experienced lighthouse keepers be so afraid of a storm; storms that they had seen before? And what did 'God is over all' mean? Stranger still, on the night of 15 December two crew members of a passing ship claimed they had seen three men in a rowing boat who ignored their calls.

At Point of Ayr lighthouse, situated on the Flintshire coast, there have been eerie plans to construct a life-size replica figure of a ghost, after several reports of an apparition over the years. The lighthouse has been out of action for more than a century but reports persist of a ghostly old man wearing an old-fashioned keeper's coat. A woman reported to BBC Wales that, 'A few years ago my husband and I were on Talacre beach and saw a lighthouse keeper at the top of the lighthouse in front of the glass dome.' Even more peculiar was that the spectre had allegedly appeared in broad daylight, when there was not a hint of mist in the air. The figure remained for quite a while, despite the fact the lighthouse is locked up and chained to prevent trespassers. After a handful of recent sightings, the owners of the lighthouse, Talacre Beach Caravan Sales Limited, decided to apply for plans to Flintshire County Council for permission to erect a permanent ghost, albeit a 2m tall, stainless steel one. On 4 November 2011 the Wales Online website reported that the lighthouse is 'Yours for £100,000 …', after it was put on the market as a residence.

Another reputedly haunted lighthouse can be found at Anglesey and is known as South Stack. The lighthouse was opened in 1809 but on the night of 25 October 1853 a terrific storm hit the coastline and more than 200 ships were wrecked. Legend has it that the lighthouse keeper at the time, a man named Jack Jones, was on his way down the steep flight, which lead to the bridge that crosses to the lighthouse, when a strong gust of wind dislodged a piece of rock from a nearby cliff and it fell onto his head. Mr Jones dragged himself to the door of the lighthouse where he was eventually found the next day, bleeding heavily from his injury. Jack Jones died two weeks later and his ghost is still said to be heard thumping on the door of the building.

The reputation of the building attracted the *Most Haunted* team of investigators, who reported several peculiar incidents, including presenter Yvette Fielding being struck by a small horseshoe that had been thrown at her. It was also claimed that a figure was observed looking out of the window of the building, but when they approached, the person was said to have leapt over the cliff into the dark waters. South Stack lighthouse is reported to be so haunted that it has even earned itself a place in the AA ghost guide! The question is, though, is South Stack lighthouse more haunted than the lighthouse at Lizard Point, at Marsden? Souter lighthouse has also been investigated by *Most Haunted*. The lighthouse gets its name from Souter Point where it was originally going to be built, and the name was kept to avoid confusion with the lighthouse located in Cornwall called Lizard lighthouse. Souter Point lighthouse was opened in 1871 in order to warn ships of the treacherous reefs that surround the coast. It is claimed that the ghost of the building is one Isobella Darling, niece of one Grace Darling, who in 1838 rescued the crew of a sinking ship. Several people who work at Souter lighthouse have reported having items such as spoons thrown at them or about the place, and being grabbed by an unseen presence. It has also been rumoured that the spectre of an old-fashioned lighthouse keeper roams the building and was seen by a waitress before vanishing in front of her eyes.

On the coast of Whitby in North Yorkshire there are two lighthouses, and both are reported to be haunted. The lighthouse situated on the west pier is said to be haunted by a man who died when he fell over a section of cliff; meanwhile, the other building is rumoured to be the haunt of a young woman called Sylvia Swales. It seems that Sylvia was part of a tragic love triangle: two twin brothers were vying for her attention and so decided, in their macho nature, to have a boat race out at sea to see who could claim her hand. Sadly, both men died when they were battered by a huge wave and it is rumoured that Sylvia, so grief-stricken by the incident, never married. It is no wonder that her spirit is said to stand overlooking the sea, aching for the attention and love she never received.

In April 2003, journalist Paul Simon, writing for the *Observer*, spoke of his delight at staying in a haunted lighthouse 25 miles south of Dublin. Wicklow Head lighthouse stands almost 100ft in height and was erected in 1781. After being struck by lightning it, according to Paul, hadn't operated '… for more than 150 years', but has now been restored as a living quarters with six floors, each harbouring a room. As is the case of most lighthouses, staying at such a building would for some be an eerie experience, and Paul was quick to comment on the atmosphere of the place. He described the heavy drizzle and swirling winds that caused windows to rattle, but what concerned him most was some of the comments made in the visitor's book regarding an alleged headless ghost. One entry in the book stated that a party of six had all seen a wraith climbing the stairs, whilst another reported hearing the woman at the window. Legend states that the resident spectre is more than 150 years old and, according to Paul, 'lost her head to a suitor armed with a scythe who took exception to her betrothal to another man'.

But did Paul or his wife, or their young son, get to see the headless woman? Well, Paul did admit that one night he awoke and thought he'd seen a figure, but his wife comforted him, telling him it was a nightmare, and the rest of their stay passed without incident.

Kinnaird Head Lighthouse in Scotland also has a ghost story quite close to it. The lighthouse can be found at a headland projecting into the North Sea, and it occupies the stretch with Kinnaird Castle. The lighthouse was the first to ever be lit by the Commissioners of Northern Lights and within the vicinity of it sits a building known as the Winetower. In the cave below this it is said that a man, a member of a family named Fraser, imprisoned his daughter's boyfriend and there he drowned. Riddled with despair on losing her loved one, the daughter leapt from the top of the tower to the jagged rocks below. The woman is said to haunt the tower, and red paint has been daubed on the rocks to illustrate where she fell.

The area around Mumbles lighthouse in Swansea, Glamorgan, in south-west Wales is similarly haunted, by a man who drowned. In a 1967 edition of the *Herald of Wales* it was reported that the ghost sightings had increased, whereas in more recent years the ghost sightings seem to have transferred to the Beach House Club, which overlooked Swansea Bay.

These types of coast-related stories are intriguing, but I'll save such shoreline spectres for another chapter and return to those phantom ships.

More Ghoulish Galleons and the Like

In 2008 several witnesses came forward to report their sightings of a ghost ship off the coast of Abergele, situated on the north coast of Wales. Legend states that the vessel is the *Gwennon Gorn*, which belonged to one Prince Madoc who, according to folklore, sailed to America three centuries before Christopher Columbus. One such witness, Chris Steel, reported on the BBC Wales site that he'd seen such an apparition whilst walking along the shore with a friend one night. Other witnesses claimed to have seen an old-looking ship in the distance, shimmering on the horizon, but sceptics argued that such visions were a mere trick of the light or an illusion.

There have also been sightings of a ghostly galleon off Cefn Sidan – a long sandy beach in Wales. A man named Aaron reported that he had been walking with his dog along the beach at sunset when something caught his eye out at sea. An old-looking ship like 'something from *Treasure Island*' with tatty sails drifted on the horizon. The ship had a peculiar green hue about it and Aaron knew that something wasn't right as soon as his dog began to cower. Two other male witnesses came forward to say they had seen the ghostly ship whilst out jogging along the beach, while another witness claimed that one night whilst camping on the beach, he and his friends had heard a strange creaking noise. When they looked out of their tent, they saw a vessel that resembled a 'pirate ship'. This stretch of beach is several miles long and there is a history along the coast of shipwrecks. The ship *La Jeune Emma* lost thirteen of its nineteen-strong crew in 1828, while the last ship to be lost in the area was SS *Paul* in 1925, a four-masted windjammer.

A phantom shipwreck has similarly been observed on the shore close to Sker Rocks in south Wales. It is said that when the ship – a three-masted baroque – is seen, something bad will happen within a week. Those who know of the ghostly ship fear it greatly, for they say that they know it is near because it gives off an awful sulphuric smell. Others argue that the ship has come from the very depths of fiery hell and that its crew are sinners placed there by the Devil himself. A spectral light has also been seen floating along the shore and around the rocks, particularly when a storm is brewing. Is this weird light an unidentified flying object (UFO) in the truest sense, or, as some locals would say, a sign that something terrible is going to happen? It has often been connected to the appearance of the ghostly ship and in some cases, the light is said to be accompanied by a frightful soundtrack of moans. According to local fishermen, the waters around the spot where the light haunts are considered special, and three nets would always be cast out. Should the middle net, when retrieved, be full of lobster and crab then it is a sign of bad weather to come, but should it be filled with fish, then a good season of decent weather can be expected.

Anglesey has a bizarre phantom ship story attached to it, as well as the haunted lighthouse mentioned earlier. In 1734 a farmer named William John Lewis was ploughing a field with the help of a farmhand near Holyhead when into view came a monstrous ghostly ship – but from the sky! The farmer, so astounded by the manifestation, ran to fetch his wife and they came back just in time to see the craft head towards the mountains. It was recorded that the sails could be seen clearly and a flock of birds swarmed around the vessel. Stranger still, when the ship returned from whence it came, it moved backwards. And if this wasn't weird enough, Mr Lewis then claimed that he'd seen the sky ship before and expected a visit every decade or so! Another Anglesey ship-related ghost story is one I first read about in the *Tiswas Book of Ghastly Ghosts* when I was a child. In the book, it spoke of a man named John Jones who, one night in 1859 whilst resting his weary head in his cottage near Moelfre Bay, was disturbed by the lashings of a severe storm. At the time, John's son was away at sea and these types of nights always reminded him of his dear son. However, on this particular night, John felt compelled to leave the warmth of his quarters and take to the blustery cliff top. Once there, overlooking the violent waves, he heard the most despicable sound – the screams of men and then, as the wind seemed to blow the grim clouds free of the moon, he stood agog in horror as there, below him he could see a fully rigged steamship shattered by the sharp black rocks. As John strained his eyes, he noticed the face of his son, thrashing around in the waves, but this could not be, because his son was meant to be travelling the oceans on the other side of the world. The cries from the figure confirmed the horror but a second later the young man was eaten by the waves. As the remains of the crushed ship slipped into the depths, John could see the name the *Royal Charter* written on the side. John was so traumatised by the events that he staggered back home, stumbled through the door and collapsed. Finally, John managed to gather his senses, and told himself that it must have been a nightmare because he knew full well – and he kept on telling himself this – that his son was not in these local waters and eventually, tired from the experience, he fell asleep. When John awoke in the morning, he was told the shocking news that the *Royal Charter* and all of its crew had perished on the rocks at Moelfre. It seems, according to a letter received from the owners of the boat, that John's son had been transferred to the *Royal Charter*. Nevertheless, from where John had stood on the previous night, it should not have been possible to see the wreck or his son, because this tragedy had taken place on another part of the jagged coastline!

On the Sussex coast, the ghost of the *Good Ship Nicholas* is said to have been seen, although there has not been a reported sighting since the Second World War. During the twelfth century, the vessel was returning from a trip to Constantinople and was occupied by pilgrims who had been to visit the holy places of Jerusalem, when upon reaching the English Channel a strong wind began to blow and the boat was wrecked off Brighton. Witnesses to the phantom ship seem few and far between, as are witnesses of the ghostly tramp steamer (the name given to a steam ship that does not operate on a fixed schedule) also said to haunt the waters off Brighton. On 17 May 1916 a group of people strolling along the promenade were astonished to see a tramp steamer so close to shore, but the watchers were even more startled when it vanished into thin air before them.

It is worth noting that a phantom ship was seen to wreck in 1960 off East Sussex. A woman named Rita Newman had been working at a factory in Portslade and she was just finishing her tea break when she looked out of a large window in time to see a great ship, resembling a coal boat, leave the harbour and head off towards Brighton. Rita then returned to work but for some unknown reason felt an urge to look out the window again, and was astonished that in just a handful of seconds this boat seemed to have travelled a great distance. The oddest thing, however, was, despite its speed, the vessel suddenly stopped dead and then very slowly tipped forward so that the stern was pointing skywards as smoke began to billow from it. The ship was clearly in some distress but before Rita could even react, the boat disappeared beneath the waves.

The Sussex coast where ships, both real and ethereal, have run aground. (Terry Cameron)

Rita was unable to stay at the window as she had to get back to work, and no one else in the factory had seen the ship sink. However, that night Rita told her father about what she'd seen, and it transpired that he had seen the same thing. Rita's father worked at the nearby power station and where he was positioned there had been a clear, uninterrupted view of the sea stretching from Worthing to Brighton. He told Rita he had seen a ship come extremely close to shore and thought that surely it was about to run aground, and so he had moved to get an even better look – but there was no sign of the vessel.

Some suggestions put forward to explain the incident were that it was a mirage but, as Rita concluded, 'If it was a mirage, how could the size of the masts have taken up the whole view of the window where my father was working?'

Had this been the ghost ship reported off Brighton before the Second World War? Or does the Sussex coastline hide further secrets?

A spectral ship or two has also been sighted off the Scottish coast. One particular time the manifestation – a fishing boat – was said to have guided two other fishing boats through a heavy storm and enabled them to reach harbour at Aberdeen. According to a man named Walter McGregor, who had been told the tale many decades ago, it was believed that the ghostly boat had perished amongst the stormy waves long ago and the crew never seen again, and yet somehow the boat still manages to aid other vessels in distress.

Sandwood Bay, 5 miles south of Cape Wrath in north-west Sutherland, has an intriguing ghost story that reminds one of the Welsh wreck experienced by Mr Jones, who saw his son consumed by the waves at Moelfre. In this case, many people have reported seeing a ghostly sailor on the beach – particularly in the Oldshoremore area. One sighting involved two men who one winter were collecting driftwood from the beach when a sailor appeared and warned them off his property. Realising there was something unnatural about the man, the witnesses dropped their wood and ran in terror. A few years later, a farmer at Kinlochbervie had a similar experience and claimed that one evening, as dusk was drawing in, he was with several farmhands looking for a stray sheep when suddenly a man appeared on the rocks up ahead. Naturally, the men thought that it was a local chap and so approached him, but upon observing his sailor's uniform, the man disappeared into thin air. Now, the reason this ghost story is relevant to this chapter, is simply because a few weeks after the spooky encounter, a brutal squall hit the shore and an Irish boat was wrecked, and several dead bodies washed ashore. One of the men who had been looking for the sheep was at the scene and, to his horror, he recognised one of the men among the dead – it was the sailor he had seen weeks before. In 1969 ten hikers who knew nothing of the ghostly legends of the area, were walking along a remote path overlooking the bay when one of them – who had gone ahead – shouted that there was someone on the sands. However, by the time the other ramblers had caught up and looked, there was no one to be seen. When the hikers came on to flat ground they observed the wreck of a wooden boat sticking out of the sand, and to their amazement, there on the sand, emerging from the water, was a set of bare footprints that lead to the boat and then, oddly, returned to the sea.

A similar tale is told on the Shetland Islands, and concerns a trio of men who were killed when their boat was wrecked on the west coast of Scotland. Instead of being interred in the local churchyard, the bodies were laid to rest where they died – but rest was apparently the last thing on their minds. Soon after the burial, the crew were said to be seen wandering along the beach. So terrified were the locals that they decided to exhume the corpses, only to find that the graves and the bodies were full of water. With that, the villagers moved the bodies to dry land and the ghosts were never seen again.

One of the strangest reports in regards to spectral ships in Scotland originates from the island of Iona, situated in the Inner Hebrides. The area has several ghost stories, including ghostly monks said to loiter around the abbey, but one fascinating story that comes to mind involved a man who one day was walking along the shore when, to his amazement, he saw a fleet of phantom Viking longboats, which proceeded to take to the beach. Suddenly, from the boats several armed men rushed ashore and accosted a gathering of monks. After killing the monks, the Vikings made for the nearby abbey and then shortly afterwards returned with their booty. Once they had boarded their ship they set sail until out of sight, and with that, the stunned witness seemed to slip

Ghostly sailors have been seen on the Shetland Islands. (Glen Vaudrey)

back to his own time. Further investigations after the shocking encounter revealed that the man had possibly caught a glimpse of events of the tenth century. Interestingly, at Canvey Island in Essex, there is a legend that speaks of a ghostly Viking who, on moonlit nights, searches along the mudflats for his ship. The figure is said to take the form of a whitish mist.

In his excellent book *Ghost World*, from 1893, author T.F. Thiselton Dyer speaks of a spectral vessel said to materialise in the Solway, a stretch of water belonging to the Irish Sea that forms part of the border of Scotland and England. The ghost (boat) is always seen hovering near a ship that is doomed to be wrecked. According to Thiselton Dyer:

> The story goes that, for a time, two Danish pirates were permitted to perform wicked deeds on the deep, but were at last condemned to perish by wreck for the evil they had caused. On a certain night they were seen approaching the shore – the one crowded with people, and the other carrying on its deck a spectral shape.

Folklore claims that four young men had been sent from one ship to the other, but upon reaching it the vessel vanished. Of course, like in so many other spectral ship stories, on the anniversary of the wreck 'these two vessels are supposed to approach the shore, and to be distinctly visible', as in the case of the ghost ship known as the *Rotterdam*, which has become known in Highland folklore.

One such tale, which certainly brings to mind the Kentish story of the *Lady Lovibund*, is that concerning the ghost ship of the Orkneys. The Orkney Islands is a cluster of islands found 10 miles north of the coast of Caithness. The story here is that a couple of centuries ago the Laird of Graemsay, a chap named William Honyman, may have been a bit of a smuggler too, despite his wealth. Every time summer came round he would load up a boat with food and travel around the north-west tip of Scotland to the Hebrides. In 1758, however, one such voyage proved to be ill-fated. It is said that Honyman had a terrible row with his wife, Mary, as he wanted his son to come aboard but Mrs Honyman, thinking her son was too young to go on to a boat, opposed strongly. The laird was not going to back down and eventually got his way, but before voyage the laird and a friend of his decided to take to the hillside and bury a stash of treasure. When Honyman returned to the foot of the hill he visited his home and told his wife to remain vigilant and to keep an eye on his territory. That night, Honyman, his son and a servant took to the water and headed off for the Atlantic. Three months later there was no news of the boat and servants at Clestrain were becoming increasingly worried. Come August, all seemed well again when the boat was observed approaching Clestrain Sound. Mary Honyman ran to the shore-line accompanied by several servants, and there in the distance they could see the approaching boat and then the three figures on board. As the vessel came closer, how-ever, the shore party began to scream. Some later reported that, as they watched, the ship simply faded into nothing, whilst others claimed that the vessel was merely a pale shadow of its former self; a supernatural craft floating long after it had sunk.

Mary Honyman was said to have been so traumatised by the loss of her husband and son that she died soon afterwards. The tale of the spectral ship most certainly spawned another ghost story because many people claimed that they had seen Mary in her long white dress, still walking her husband's stomping ground, guarding his ter-ritory and treasure. Of course, the rumour of buried treasure lured many servants to the hillside where they searched, night after night, for the laird's stash, but to no avail. Unless, of course, you believe in the tale of the man who felt destined to find the treas-ure until, whilst digging at the earth, he became unsettled by the approaching figure of a woman dressed in all black. He continued digging regardless, but then, when the man looked again, the woman was wearing white, her face forlorn. Did he eventually find the treasure despite the ghostly sighting? Who knows?

Another ghost ship is said to appear off Lunan Bay, Arbroath. Around a century ago an elderly lady recalled how when she was a little girl she would stay near the bay with relations. During one such stay, she was talking to a local boatman and was told by him that one evening as he stood on the beach with several other men, a spectral ship had come into view. The vessel was about 1 mile offshore and despite the sea being relatively calm, the ship looked to be in some distress as it rolled and plunged as if in the throes of a severe storm. The witnesses decided to get into a small boat and row out to her aid, but as they left the bay the ship vanished. When the men arrived at the spot where the ship had been they could find no trace whatsoever – not a body nor piece of wreckage. From then on, the local boatman believed that every time the ghost vessel appeared it meant something bad was going to happen. This was confirmed when one evening the boatman and his brother were standing on the beach and they heard a mysterious voice, which called out the names of three men who they knew. Within days the three men had died: two of them drowned and the third killed in an accident. Then, on another night, the same boatman was aboard his craft alone and when, looking back toward shore, he saw a man in seaman attire standing on the beach. The figure appeared extremely pale and gaunt, and on the side of his face there was a hideous wound. The figure then shouted out, 'Tell my sister Mary Smith, who lives in Arbroath, that she must on no account marry Andrew, he is no good,' and with that, the seaman vanished.

When the stunned boatman finally managed to contact the Mary Smith in question, he discovered that she was in fact about to marry a man named Andrew, and although Andrew appeared to be a good man, Mary was rather concerned about the warning, because the ghostly seaman had in fact been her brother Keith. Mary never did marry Andrew, so unsettled was she by the caveat.

Another, similar incident is told of in Orkney folklore, particularly on the Island of Rousay, where it is said that a small spectral boat has been seen. The legend goes that a young fisherman was obsessed with a beautiful Orkney girl, but she told her admirer that she would only marry him if he proved his love by sailing through a treacherous strait alone in his diminutive boat. The naive fisherman agreed to the challenge but the girl's father, who was gifted with second sight, had told his daughter that this was not a challenge to be taken up, for he had seen a terrible image of the young man's boat being capsized and he being drowned. The woman refused to take the premonition seriously, threatening the fisherman with the fact that, if he did not carry out the journey, then she would marry another man. With that, the fisherman set sail, but the waves proved too dangerous, his boat was overturned and he drowned. Forevermore that small boat has been seen on the strait where the tides meet. And what of the young woman? Well, fate played a deadly part with her, too. Shortly after the death of the fisherman, she did indeed marry another man – a tradesman from Wick – but so bad did he treat her that she eventually killed herself – by jumping into the sea.

In another case a British ship named *Neptune*, manned by one Captain Grant, appeared off St Ives, Cornwall, even though it had already been wrecked at Gwithian. Around St Ives there are also tales of eerie lights, known as Jack Harry's Lights, named after the first local to be tempted by such phenomena. The ghostly lights seem to tie in with a phantom schooner that once appeared off the coast. The ship was sighted and approached by several men who rowed out to her. However, when one of the men tried to climb aboard he was shocked to find that his feet met nothing solid, and then the ship vanished into thin air. Many believe this apparition to be that of the *Neptune*. On another occasion a St Ives pilot gig was called out to assist a large vessel that had appeared in the bay, but as they drew alongside it the ship vanished, and then reappeared in a mysterious fashion some 3 miles away. At Porthcurno in Cornwall there are legends of a ghost ship dating back to the eighteenth century: a black square-rigger that bizarrely would be seen not to run aground, but actually travel over the dry sands with ease. Sadly, those who have witnessed such a phenomenon are hard to find. Mind you, to see such a sight is said to be bad luck, so perhaps that is not surprising. This tale may have simply been the sort to roll from the mouths of smugglers, who were said to dye their boats with luminous paint in order to spook people and scare them away from their illegal trades. Those who actually claim to have seen the vessel state that it is often mist-enshrouded and four figures appear on board: two men, a woman and a dog. And, even more remarkably, when the boat comes into shore it levitates oh so slightly, so that it skims the ground, and then the ship takes off above the town. The ship vanishes near a rock where many years ago a stash of coins were said to have been unearthed.

Paul Devereux and Craig Weatherhill wrote of a 'phantom lugger', too; said to be seen occasionally sailing in the shallow waters of the Goonhilly Downs at Croft Pascoe Pool. Tales of death ships around the Cornwall and Devon coasts are numerous, and though they appear to alter through time, they always maintain their stormy atmosphere. The *Ashburton Guardian* of 12 September 1919 reported that: 'A motor-boat which during the war had to patrol a certain stretch of water in the Bristol Channel reported, only a few months ago, that the apparition of the type used to convey fruit from the West Indies to Avonmouth had been encountered not far from Lundy.'

As the motor-boat travelled on a straight course, the spectral vessel seemed to rear up out of the waves and the smaller vessel careered straight through it. All that the witnesses on board could describe was how a white mist had enshrouded the motor-boat and how, when this cleared, there was no sign of the ship.

The county of Dorset has a few ghost ship legends. Of the weirdest pertains to a death ship steered by the Devil himself. The folklore claims that a Mayor Jones of Lyme Regis was despised by locals due to his persecution of anyone who didn't conform to his rules. And so it was no surprise to some when, as he lay on his death bed at what is now known as Chatham House, there was suddenly a terrible clatter and one end of his home caved in, causing great plumes of dust. When the dirt had settled, Satan appeared and accosted Jones, whose body was then taken on board a ship that was due to go to the Mediterranean. Legend states that a sailor, who was sailing back to Lyme Regis, had reached Scilly when he saw the amazing spectacle of the Devil at the helm of a ship. Oddly, the sailor asked the Devil where he was heading to (as you do!), to which the horned one replied, 'I'm transporting the body of Old Jones to Mount Etna.'

Soon afterwards, however, the ship exploded in to a great ball of fire, leaving the air thick with a sulphurous stench. It seems that this may have been the mayor's induction to Hell. This fiendish tale reminds us of the already mentioned ship of doom of Cornwall, which, accompanied by a sinister black cloud, wrenched a wrong-doer from his bed. It is also worth mentioning Dorset's other well-known phantom vessel, recorded in *Prodigies in Somerset and Dorset* from the seventeenth century. The report states that, on 23 April 1661 at around 3 p.m., a man riding his horse near Lyme Regis spotted an ominous dark cloud drifting above the region of the Isle of Portland. The 'cloud' then, bizarrely, turned into a great sailing ship complete with crew members. The man stood in amazement at the sight before him until thunder cracked and a storm ensued, and lightning bolts began to spear down through the pounding rain. The ship sailed off through the gloom until it was gone from view.

A ghostly ship called the *Mayfly* is said to occasionally visit Oulton Broad, which can be found in the shire county of Suffolk. Oulton Broad is formed of several man-made bodies of water and is linked to the east by a loch to Lake Lothing, which runs through Lowestoft and out into the North Sea. The boat is said to visit the area on 24 June every year – although it probably doesn't! To cut a long story short, the *Mayfly* was captained by a man named Stevenson at some point in the eighteenth century. He was on one occasion asked to transport a large amount of money to Yarmouth, and would be accompanied by the daughter of the boat's owner. However, being in the vicinity of the treasure was all too much for Stevenson, who decided to steer the wherry (a type of boat once used to carry passengers or cargo along canals and rivers) to a Dutch port. That night, as legend states, the captain heard screams and ran to see

At Oulton Broad a spectral 'wherry' has been observed. It travels on the manmade bodies of water and heads toward the North Sea. (Joyce Goodchild)

the boat owner's daughter bleeding from a neck wound, but as he approached she stabbed him in the heart with a knife, killing him. Shortly afterwards she died too. Three years later, the ghostly boat was said to have put in an appearance, and folklore has it that those who have observed the wherry hear of a death shortly afterwards.

A North Sea ghost ship has been seen travelling up the River Wear and around the coast. According to author Alan Robson, 'In 1923 a Hong Kong newspaper reported a sailor's tale of how he had witnessed a ghostly ship sailing into the River Wear.' The ship, said to have had tall masts and fronted by a figurehead of a busty woman bearing the name *Plato*, had in fact been built in the mouth of the Wear, but little did the seaman realise that the boat had already perished, along with its crew, in the South China Seas. Legend has it that a majority of the crew were eaten by sharks as the ship sank; whilst those who escaped fled to shore in lifeboats, but to their misfortune ended up on an island of cannibals. There was only one survivor of the horror: a chap named John Collins who was eventually rescued by a Royal Navy vessel. The seaman who observed the ghostly ship decided to assemble a team to visit the island that Mr Collins spoke of, but this is where the tale ends with a terrible twist of fate. The seaman's boat was never seen again; some say he fell foul to the bloodthirsty cannibals, whilst others suggest that he never found the island, but was instead murdered by his own crew of rogues and criminals.

The Irish city of Galway has a ghost ship story attached to it, too. It was written about by one of my favourite writers on the supernatural, Elliott O'Donnell, who claimed to have seen the phantom barge on three occasions, always at night. His third encounter took place in the spring of 1932 as they 'were just passing the Headland of Mallin More in County Donegal …'. The second time was under a full moon at Clew Bay, which is a natural ocean bay in County Mayo. O'Donnell described the apparition as a bridal barge, which dazzled with red and gold.

Researcher Michael G. Crawford wrote of a phantom fetch-ship, a spectre said to haunt the waters of County Kerry. Crawford comments that, 'Warrenpoint can claim its phantom ship also, which is the ghost of the *Lord Blaney* steam packet': an apparition said to float up the pier and then disintegrate into nothing. The ghost loiters in the area because, on a stormy night in 1833, the boat was due to travel to Liverpool but never made it. It had been packed with people, including a young man and his bride, but also animals, ranging from pigs to geese. As the ship reached the Irish Sea a dreadful storm hit, and under blackening skies the ship was tossed and rolled on monstrous waves. The vessel was eventually thrown to a sandbank, snapping the masts and jolting the passengers into a state of confusion as they were cast to the decks by the howling gales. Those on board who were still alive hoped and prayed that they could latch onto a piece of floating wreck, which would maybe, just maybe, take them safely to shore. So many lives were lost as exhaustion claimed the last passengers who were swept out into the grey depths, and yet amidst the despair there is one remarkable story. It is said that on board the *Lord Blaney* was a champion racehorse named Monteagle. The horse had beaten so many others in its trade, but now its race was for life, and Monteagle successfully braved the waves and bounded ashore.

It is worth quickly mentioning that in February 1984 the *Daily Express* reported that a £3,000 Irish mare called Russell's Touch had been training on the shore of Dungarvan, County Waterford, when it unseated its rider – trainer David Kiely – and bolted towards the sea. Kiely rushed to find a phone (which took him two hours on this remote stretch) and eventually a rescue boat was employed. The horse was spotted by a trawler and fortunately the mare was roped and brought ashore, and recovered a few days later. Weirder still, in 1989 crew of a Welsh yacht rescued a dog that was found swimming some 2 miles out at sea off St David's Head!

Some people will say that the ghostly ship *Lord Blaney* appears as a strange white cloud that seems to drift along the surface of the water; whereas others will tell you that, on certain nights, you can hear the sound of the waves crashing away at the body; and there are also those who will claim that they have seen the steamer clearly as a vessel that rides out of the cloud and then disappears into darkness. Many have rowed out to find the wreckage of the ship they have seen sink, but to no avail, and like so many others the encounters, as well as the ships, forever nestle in some watery grave. Mr Crawford, who claims to have seen the phantom ship, was told by many a fisherman that every time a ghost vessel appears around Warrenpoint it is a bad omen; a sign that another wreck is due to occur. When a 1,100-ton passenger ferry ran into a 500-ton coal boat on 3 November 1916, 6 sea miles from Warrenpoint, there was a rumour that there had been a sighting of the *Lord Blaney* a few days previous.

Despite this ghost ship drifting into the realms of folklore, the *Lord Blaney* is not the most well-known phantom boat of Ireland. A more well-known ghost vessel is a ship called the *Sea Horse* which was wrecked in Tramore Bay in 1816. Of the 393 people on board, only a mere thirty survived. This British transport vessel is still seen – allegedly – on the anniversary of the tragedy and nearly always before a drowning or a wreck. My advice would be to not go swimming or travelling across the south-east coast of Ireland on or around 31 January!

The Waterford coast near Helvick Head in the Republic of Ireland also has a ghost ship legend. A student named Arthur Frewen, who later became a playwright and schoolmaster, was taking a stroll along the coast of Waterford one day when suddenly the sky began to grow dark and mist seemed to filter in from nowhere. Rather perturbed, Mr Frewen decided it best to find somewhere to stay the night and came upon a small village, which seemed extremely desolate. When in the vicinity of the pier Arthur noticed a light coming from the water, and upon looking down from the pier saw a fishing boat and the figure of an elderly seaman. Arthur asked the seaman if there was anywhere on the boat he could stay for the night and, as it happened, there was a bunk going spare. Arthur, rather pleased, was shown around the boat and given some hot soup by the man. After supper Arthur decided it best to get some rest, and took his red scarf off and hung it on the door, but as he snuggled up he became suddenly unsettled; in fact, such a strong feeling of dread came over him that he leapt to his feet and made sure that the door was locked. Seconds later the door knob began to rattle, as if someone was trying to get in, and from the other side of the door he heard a voice shout, 'Open up!'. Arthur declined to do so, feeling so sure that something bad was going to happen. So scared was the young student that he then climbed onto his bunk and smashed the nearby window, hauled himself up on deck and then ran for his life toward the pier, never once looking back.

Arthur didn't even attempt to sleep again that night but when the morning drew in he decided to go back to the village, and found the people there very friendly. One person in the village asked Arthur if he was unwell due to his gaunt appearance and he just had to tell them about his weird experience aboard the boat. Upon closer investigation, however, Athur and the villagers found there was now no boat tied to the pier. All that sat there was the skeletal remains of a boat; a vessel in such a state that no one could even attempt to get on board. Yet Arthur knew this had been the same boat which he had climbed aboard the previous night.

'This boat has been mouldering here for nearly fifty years,' a local man told Arthur. 'And there is a bad story about it ...'

To Arthur's astonishment, the man told the tale of how, many years ago, a young student had been killed on the boat by a fisherman, who was eventually arrested and then hanged at Dungarvan. The most startling detail was yet to occur, however: for when as Arthur peered into the gloom of the boat, there on the hook near where the old bunk would have been located was his red scarf!

And, just to round off this segment, I leave you with mention of some very old reports of phantom ships in Irish folklore of spectral ships of an even stranger nature. For instance, a ghost ship was recorded in the year 1161, but in this instance it was observed not in the sea, but in the sky over Galway! Similarly, an aerial ship was also recorded in 1798 and seen by hundreds of people at Croaghpatrick, Mayo. Writer W.G. Wood-Martin believed that the vessel was in fact a reflection of a fleet under the command of Admiral Warren, which had been sailing off the west coast of Ireland.

... AND AN ELUSIVE SUBMARINE

In the 1970s there were a couple of odd cases regarding alleged phantom submarines. On 24 April 1974, the *Daily Express* reported very briefly on the sighting of a mystery submarine, which had been reported off the coast of County Cork, Ireland. Police had been alerted to the craft but an investigation revealed nothing. This wasn't a unique incident, because the previous month at 4 a.m. on 30 March, the master of a boat named *Rathmines* contacted coastguards on the Irish coast of Limerick to report a mystery submarine. Crew on the boat shone a searchlight on the black object before it disappeared. Around the same time, there were also reports of a phantom helicopter in parts of England. Were these sightings simply created by hysteria, or were there really phantom subs and choppers around?

Stranger still, a mysterious object turned up on the beach at Holyhead, Anglesey on the night of 4/5 February 1974. The story was reported by the *North Wales Chronicle*, who claimed that the craft – resembling some type of plane, or winged submarine – had been found beneath the cliffs at South Stack and measured 9ft in length with a wingspan of some 5ft. The body of the craft was black aluminium and pretty heavy, and no one seemed to know where it had come from. Suggestions put forward were that it was some type of advanced submarine object that had drifted ashore, while others commented that the craft had been a form of aerial ship that had crashed into the water before washing ashore. The RAF and Aberporth Range Establishment stated that the object did not belong to them, and so a description of the object was passed on to the navy underwater research department based at Portsmouth. Why no one actually took photographs of the object seems to be the biggest mystery of all and, despite the stir the object caused, it seems as if it was simply left to rust on the beach. A bomb-disposal squad took a look at the object and declared it to be safe but, rather oddly, local coastguards were told not to comment on the craft. Eventually, the mysterious 'plane' was filmed for a television documentary but by the time cameras had begun to roll, souvenir hunters had already started to dismantle it.

2

GHOSTS AHOY!
SOME HAUNTED BOATS

THE DEAD ON DECK

Reports of phantom ships seem confined more to folklore than anything remotely factual. As we've already observed, the tales, usually connected to an anniversary of a tragedy, make for great yarns told around a crackling campfire on a blustery beach; but for every so-called genuine encounter with a spectral vessel, there seem to be so many that are nothing more than urban legend. However, how do we then account for tales of supposedly haunted boats?

One of the strangest cases of a haunted ship comes from Bridlington in East Riding, Yorkshire. A fishing trawler named the *Pickering* was believed by its crew to be cursed, and many a foray out at sea to catch fish to make money proved frustrating, as time and time again problems would plague the ship. Some people may argue that anything mechanical being battered by rough seas may be prone to faults, but for the *Pickering* it was a case of high strangeness to the extent that skipper Mick Laws felt the boat was jinxed. This was confirmed when, time and time again, Chris Clark, a sonar radar engineer, would be called out to tend to malfunctioning dials and peculiar wiring defects, the like he'd never seen before. On one occasion, the boat came back to shore and Chris was called out. He reported:

> I went to the automatic pilot – when we asked it to go to starboard it would go to port. I changed the wires around but later on that day the polarity going to these two wires had been reversed. This is against the laws of physics. I've never come across anything like this before.

Whilst boats may be prone to mechanical faults, no one could explain why certain spots of the *Pickering* were icy cold, but again, sceptics may argue that out at sea it

Haunted boats galore! (Neil Arnold)

would only be natural for areas of the trawler to be chilly. Then, things got very spooky. One night, Mick Laws was lying on his bed when suddenly the side of the mattress went down, as if somebody had stepped on it in order access the top bunk. Shortly afterwards this happened again and so Mick decided to investigate; but there was nobody else in the room. At the time, Mick believed that another crew member had been messing about; but they assured him that they had not been. Then, on another night, a crew member named Barry Mason was on deck alone, on watch. The rest of the crew were downstairs when suddenly Barry noticed a figure resembling a fisherman standing up ahead. Barry visited the rest of the crew but went as white as a sheet when he realised everyone was present and no one had ventured on deck.

Eventually, the crew of the trawler found themselves without any work because due to the recurring problems with the boat, they rarely were able to get in a good fish. One afternoon, Mick had visited the local Jobcentre and told the man at the desk about the strange occurrences on board the *Pickering*, and although Mick was expecting the man to laugh, he was startled when the assistant suggested speaking to a priest, and said he knew just the man. Reverend Tom Wallis, official exorcist to the Archbishop of York, was contacted by the *Pickering* crew and he visited the boat one afternoon. To their astonishment, the reverend had done a bit of historical work and discovered that the boat – previously known as the *Family Crest* – had been built in

Ireland on 1 December 1977. Whilst on turbulent waters shortly afterwards, a crew member had fallen overboard and drowned. The owners sold the boat immediately.

Reverend Wallis blessed the boat, paying special attention to areas where alleged paranormal activity had taken place, and the next day the crew reported an immediate effect, with no further problems since. This case echoed that of the coaster *Somersby Dyke*, a British ship docked at Hartlepool in 1973. Reverend Anthony Hodgson, Vicar of St Oswald's, paid a visit to the coaster in the hope of finding the spectral stowaway. Revd Hodgson told the *Hartlepool Mail* that the sailors, who appeared as 'normal' and 'intelligent', had 'seen phenomena on board the ship that they could not explain'. Revd Hodgson spent an hour on the boat performing a blessing and no further ghosts were said to have manifested. Similarly, on 24 January the following year, according to the *Daily Mirror*, a 'Muslim priest went aboard the Malaysian freighter *Bunga Orchid* at Liverpool' to exorcise the apparition of a woman that several crewmen had reported.

On 16 February 1910 the *Pembroke County Guardian* of Wales had shown an interest in a reputedly haunted ship, HMS *Asp*. According to the anecdotal accounts from past files, the ship, a mail packet, had docked one day whilst on a voyage from Port Patrick to Donaghadee, when several crew members found a dead woman in the Ladies' Cabin of the passengers' quarters. Ever since this macabre discovery, there have been reports of a ghostly woman dressed in white aboard the boat. The ghost story had been so potent that the *Asp* lost its trade for a time, although service was resumed in 1850. One night, at around 10 p.m. when the boat was travelling off Queens Ferry Dock in Chester, the captain and first officer were startled from their reading by a sound coming from the Ladies' Cabin. The two men rushed to the room but when they opened the door there was no sign of any struggle. A couple of weeks later, when the boat was anchored at Martyn Roads cove, the door leading to the captain's cabin burst open and in rushed a horrified quartermaster who stated, quite matter-of-factly, that he'd seen a woman on deck pointing skyward. Yet when the captain, a Mr Alldridge, went to investigate, there was no sign of the mystery female. Shortly after this a steward reported seeing the same woman, again pointing skyward, and the incident was said to have unnerved him so much that it aged him ten years.

As in the case of the *Pickering*, a clergyman was called to HMS *Asp* and after a thorough investigation concluded that there was indeed an entity present. This was confirmed to the captain one night when he was disturbed from his slumber by the feeling that a hand had rested upon his leg. The inexplicable happenings increased, and in the end many crew members left and the captain found it more and more difficult to recruit new staff: they had all heard the rumours and feared the ghostly presence. Then, one night in 1857 when the boat had been docked at Pembroke for repairs, a guard sounded the alarm for he too, like so many others, had seen the floating form of the woman in white. Worse still, on this occasion the wraith glided straight through his body. Another sentry saw this frightful encounter and set off in pursuit; he observed the woman as she drifted toward the cemetery on the hill that overlooked the harbour.

The ghost then halted at a vacant grave and, according to the witness, vanished on the spot. Those who tell the story of the haunted ship claim that not since then has there been a spiritual disturbance aboard HMS *Asp*.

A slightly differing version of events states that the boat, when previously known as *Fury*, had been the site of a murder. Whilst docked at Portpatrick on the Irish Sea, the passengers had gone to shore and a stewardess, making her way to the Ladies' Cabin to clean it out, got the shock of her life when she found the body of a woman whose throat had been slit. This is almost a reversal of the story I've told, but either way it seems that the ghostly woman was indeed the spirit of a lady who had been found dead in the cabin.

In 1985 a 600-ton freighter named *Nannell* was purchased by a firm of scrap metal merchants. The name of the boat was changed and her first job, according to author Richard Garrett, was 'to transport twenty-eight miles of surplus cable from Southampton to a port in Kent'. There were quite a few paperwork problems regarding the ship, and so for some time it sat at Southampton. It was here, in the November of 1985, that various members of the crew reported ghostly goings-on. A few of the hands had reported seeing a slim figure in a boiler suit that drifted along the dark corridors of the freighter. Others reported a rather unpleasant feeling in some areas of the ship, and garlic had been hung up to deter any malicious ghouls. Again, like HMS *Asp* and the trawler, *Pickering*, the port chaplain was called in and he in turn contacted the Bishop of Winchester's adviser. Before any investigation could take place the boat was sent out to sea, headed for Kent, but immediately all manner of problems prevented a smooth ride. The diesel engines began to malfunction and the boat had to be sent back to Southampton. In February 1986 the freighter was ready to go again but the destination of Kent had been changed and *Nannell* was now bound for Northern Spain. Thankfully no more ghost sightings were reported by the crew.

HMS *Glory* was undergoing restoration in 1955. The aircraft carrier was situated at Fife's Rosyth dockyard when, shortly after the festive season, a painter had a supernatural experience. It was a cold and frosty morning when he approached the cabin where he stored his overalls. The corridors of the boat were extremely dark and so to venture any further the man would have required his lamp, which he kept in a nearby locker. Having retrieved the lamp, he entered a cabin to plug it in when he was startled to see a man in pilot's attire standing near the dressing table. The painter immediately recognised the pilot as an RAF man; 'Possibly a member of the ship's naval maintenance staff,' he thought to himself. However, things took a turn for the weird when the painter asked the airman if he'd had a nice Christmas, and the figure didn't reply. With that, the painter turned away to get something else from the locker but, upon looking back, was stunned to see no sign of the airman. The painter was so frightened that he dropped his lamp and fled the cabin, running into a workmate of his to whom he explained the bout of strangeness. Both men ventured back into the cabin but in the gloom could find no one. So perturbed was the painter by his experience that he was taken off his shift. At the time of the alleged haunting it was suggested that the ghostly pilot may well have been the spirit of an airman who crashed on the flight deck one Christmas during the Korean War.

Another haunted boat was said to be the square-rigger *The Lady of Avenel*, which was docked at Leith, Scotland in 1933. The boat had quite a history and had been all over the world. After an Arctic voyage it had been renamed the *Island*, and it was at this point that the boat became haunted by a phantom woman. It seems that, due to the bouts of high weirdness, no one wanted to board the boat and so once again the name was changed, this time to the *Virgo*. Nevertheless, on her final voyage a sailor claimed to have had a very peculiar encounter: one night he was reading in his bunk when the bed opposite began to shake violently. On another occasion, a crew member reported that his lamp had grown suddenly dim, and every time he adjusted the lamp it would dim again and again. Finally, the man decided he could not be bothered with the oddity and instead snuggled down to sleep. But when he gave one last glance back to the lamp, he was shocked to see a ghostly figure, which outstretched its arm and reached for the lamp and turned it up. It seems that the spectre on board the ship enjoyed tampering with objects that emitted light. One night a sailor, who often kept his torch under his pillow, dozed off when he was startled awake by the beam of his torchlight. He thought at first that maybe he had somehow flicked the switch, but when this happened for several nights running, he realised something eerie was afoot. This eeriness was confirmed when shortly afterwards the skipper heard footsteps on the deck above him, and then the voice of a woman. When the ship docked at Leith again it remained inactive for a long time. A watchman, employed to keep an eye on the ship, claimed that whilst sitting in his bunk reading one night he'd seen a ghostly woman. So unsettled was he by the spectre, he was said to have resigned from his post the next day.

Scotland has another haunted ship: RSS *Discovery* is now a tourist attraction maintained by the Dundee Heritage Trust. She was first launched in 1901, and in 1902 reached the Antarctic Circle but became encased in ice whilst stationed at her quarters at Ross Island, McMurdo Sound. The boat remained frozen there for some two years but the ghost, that of seaman Charles Bonner (who died when he fell from the crow's nest), is said to haunt the boat even now. Below the spot where Bonner fell to his death there have been strange sounds reported, but whether this is his apparition or not we will never truly know. Either way, the story is certain to attract the tourists! Just a mile from RSS *Discovery* sits HMS *Unicorn*, first launched in 1824. Remarkably, this boat is still in action, remaining afloat in Dundee, although it never served in battle. Those who experience weird activity on board describe feelings of being watched, the sound of heavy footsteps and items being thrown about. Many years ago a ship-keeper did fall to his death on board the boat, so maybe it is his restless spirit that still loiters.

A Welsh tramp steamer named *Stonepool* was reported to be haunted in the *Entiat Times* of 11 August 1938. The ship travelled from Cardiff to Sydney, Australia, weighed down by reports that there were spirits afoot. Legend has it that many years before, a seaman hanged himself on the steamer and the crew that took the ship to Sydney believed it was the ghost of the suicide victim that was plaguing them. One seaman reported seeing a set of horrible eyes peering out of the gloom, whilst another crew member mentioned that some unseen presence had pulled his arms away from the rigging. Others aboard believed the steamer to be cursed, as several crew members had gone down with sudden illnesses or suffered bad accidents. Whilst on its voyage the *Stonepool* broke down some fourteen times, leaving one seaman to comment that, 'For five weeks we lived on tinned meats, tinned pears and beans.'

SS *Great Britain* – a luxury ocean liner – is considered to be one of the world's most famous ships. She was constructed at Bristol from the design of one I.K. Brunel and is now an award-winning visitor attraction at the Great Western Dockyard. The ship was first launched in 1843 and has travelled far and wide experiencing wear and tear. Now, however, the liner is preserved in an airtight dock, which prevents any corrosion. Some would say that the spirits on board the ghost shop are also preserved, embedded within the framework. When the boat was returned to Bristol in the 1970s many people began reporting paranormal activity. On the promenade deck a security officer reported that a door had begun to swing on its hinges of its own accord when there was no draught present. Locked doors were also heard to slam; but one of the eeriest

Even hardened sailors would not venture into the lower cabins of their boats for fear of ghostly encounters. (Neil Arnold)

episodes concerned two members of staff who were spooked by the sounds of a phantom piano. Of course, in these types of great ship some may be of the opinion that all manner of creaks and bangs will be experienced, yet in the early 1990s a 17-year-old student was positive that, whilst on work experience on the ship, he saw a man sitting on a wooden beam in the bowel of the liner. The witness, named Sonny Graffo, shared his experience some fifteen years later when he reported it to the *Bristol Evening Post*. The witness reported that the spectre was wearing a white-collared shirt and had a grey beard. 'I thought he was a workman and called across to him, but he just sat there staring at me,' Sonny told the newspaper. 'Then I wondered how he could have got there, as there was no way of getting out to the plank.' When Sonny was shown a photograph of one Captain Grey he immediately identified him as the man he had seen on the boat – despite the fact that Captain Grey had disappeared from the boat one night in 1872 when it was on a voyage. It is believed he may have jumped overboard.

Another ghost said to loiter on the liner is that of a small child, seen on a few occasions near the Steerage compartment; whilst other phenomena reported has been ghostly footsteps, and numerous other shadowy figures seen to walk through walls and locked doors.

From the 1930s until the 1970s a barge named *Hygea* (built in 1917) was moored at Gravesend in Kent. The name of the boat was rather apt – *Hygea* in Greek and Roman mythology being the name of the daughter of the god of medicine – because the boat acted as headquarters for a medical officer, treating sick and injured sailors arriving at London. When the boat was eventually retired she moved on to Littlehampton, a seaside resort in West Sussex, and was renamed *Seahorse* by the man who purchased her, a Mr Alan Becker. In 1984 the boat served as a pub – and like a majority of pubs, it had a ghost. One humid night, a watchman employed to keep vigil over the barge was settling into his quarters when he was chilled by a sudden draught. He thought that an upstairs window must have been left ajar and so he ascended the steps, only to find all the windows shut. He returned to his room, which was now quite cold despite the muggy weather, and put a big coat on. Then, suddenly, he felt an overwhelming feeling of horror engulf him. With that, the night watchman, who had been used to spending many a night alone in dark places, felt the need to barricade the door from inside until, over an hour or so later, the feeling subsided and the chill seemed to fade.

This wasn't to be his only encounter, however, because one night he saw hanging pot plants swing violently of their own accord, despite the fact the barge was still. Then came his third and most terrifying experience, which again took place at night. Whilst sitting comfortably in front of the pub fire he was startled to see shadowy figures playing out on the wall before him, and this eerie performance went on for some time until the watchman left the area. Of course, some would argue that if such experiences only concerned the security guard then maybe he was prone to hallucinations, but someone in that type of job wouldn't normally be of unsound mind, but thankfully for his reputation, Mandy Milson, a waitress on the *Seahorse*, also reported a supernatural experience. One night she was sitting in the bar area with some friends when a door at the top of the stairs began to open and close of its own accord. An investigation ensued, but there was no one else to be found. A chef on the boat also reported an unnaturally cold area on the vessel, this time in a section of the kitchen. He similarly saw a ghostly figure at the bottom of the stairwell leading to the restaurant.

One haunted ship most certainly worth mentioning is the now retired ocean liner the *Queen Mary*, which was christened in Scotland in 1934 by King George V and Queen Mary. At the time it was the largest ship in the world, and from 1940 to 1946 was used for military service. The ship left Southampton for the last time in 1967 and sailed to Long Beach, California where it sits today. When the *Queen Mary* took to the sea many years ago she was painted battleship grey as camouflage, giving her the nickname 'the grey ghost'; quite appropriate when you consider the amount of ghostly activity reported from the ship. Eyewitness accounts are said to be in the hundreds, and many concern the spook of a young man who is believed to be 18-year-old John Pedder who was killed on board on 10 July 1966 when he was trapped and crushed when a watertight door closed on him. There is also the ghost of a mechanic in the engine room – he spectre is said to wear a white boiler suit – and the ghost of a man in dark overalls has also been seen below deck. Other witnesses have come forward to report a man of authority on board, and this apparition is said to be that of Senior Second Officer W.E. Stark who, on 18 September 1949, accidentally drank a deadly combination of lime juice and cleaning fluid from an unmarked bottle. Stark thought nothing of feeling unwell but the next day fell into a coma and died three days later.

Ghost-hunters and psychic investigators have boarded the moored ship to try to understand more about the resident ghosts. One medium claimed to have contacted the spirit of Lieutenant Carlo Giovetti, an Italian fighter pilot who was shot down over North Africa by the British in the Second World War. Giovetti was transported as a prisoner of war but died on board and like so many other ghosts on board the *Queen Mary*, he seems trapped in some type of limbo; never to escape the clutches of the 'grey ghost'.

There is a reference to two haunted boats, en route from Liverpool, in the 7 February 1888 edition of the *Dubuque Daily Herald*. In a lengthy article written by one of the witnesses, an 'English brig called the *Charles*', which was due to travel from Merseyside across the world to Boston in the United States, is mentioned. The boat was said to have been haunted by a chap named Jack Wallace; a sailor who was shot on board by the captain. Before his final breath he vowed to haunt the ship and it would seem that he stuck to his word. 'I'm blessed if he didn't begin the haunting business that very night,' commented the author of the article, adding: 'On getting into Boston every man but the second mate deserted her …'. When a new crew was put into place for the return journey to Liverpool, it seems that the spirit was intent on making their lives a misery, too, to the extent that the second crew deserted; opting to escape from the spectre mid-ocean on small boats. A fortnight later the *Charles* was due to visit

New Orleans but news of the entity on board had spread like wildfire, with newspapers also covering the haunting. Again, when the boat reached its destination the crew fled in terror and, according to the author, '… the vessel was left in the hands of the consignees at the drop of a hat. I found her two weeks after this with a load of cotton all aboard her and her sails bent for sailing'.

To get them on board the crew were offered double the wages they were already on, but the article's author (who was employed as first mate) and the captain laughed off talk of a ghost on board. When a crew had finally been assembled the *Charles* set out to sea and all seemed very calm. However, one night when a majority of the crew were having cat-naps, the first mate had an extraordinary experience. He wrote: 'I was pacing the deck with everything very quiet alow and aloft, when my attention was attracted to the sight of a sailor coming aft.' The figure approached the port rail as if to head for the wheel and this unnerved the first mate, who added: 'It was a breach of discipline for a foremast hand to appear on the quarter deck without a special errand or without saluting.' But the most unusual thing about the man was that he seemed to glide across the deck and his feet made no sound.

The first mate decided that something odd was afoot. Thinking that the figure was maybe a trespasser on board, as he headed for the man at the wheel, the first mate picked up a rope's end and followed the intruder. However, the figure suddenly disappeared when he reached close proximity of the man at the wheel, who for some reason now began to stagger, despite not seeing the mystery sailor. Immediately the alarm was raised and investigations were carried out in case someone had fallen overboard – but there was no sign of the sailor. The captain was angered greatly by the report and grilled the first mate for creating such a story, but then found out that the man at the wheel had in fact seen the figure and, worse, described the mystery sailor as smelling of death. The terrified witness also described how the figure, when close, appeared young in the face and expressed a mournful groan before gliding over the stern 'as softly as a leaf falls to the ground'.

The captain accused both men of dreaming the whole event but on the third night, at around 11 p.m., the second mate who was in charge of the captain's watch also had a strange encounter. According to the report, 'His watch had just been trimming the yards, and could not, therefore, be charged with dreaming. All of a sudden a figure appeared among them.' One of the men on board spoke to the figure, not realising it was an apparition, and as it glided away the witnesses' nostrils were filled with the stench of death. Four other men saw the figure, which remained in view for a full four minutes as it stood with its hands pressed firmly against its side, all the while rocking side to side. One of the crew members, a man named Will Ketch, shouted to the figure, 'If you are playing a trick on us, look out for yourself!', and with that picked up an item from the deck of the boat and cast it toward the figure, which then vanished into thin air.

The captain was incensed by the commotion, but this time had difficulty in berating several crew members who had all claimed to have seen the wraith. The crew refused to keep their watch, even when the captain pulled out his gun; they said that they would rather jump into the sea than face the ghostly figure. The captain's right-hand man then confirmed what the other crew members had seen, when he went into the cabin and returned as white as chalk, claiming that the 'thing' was down there. Several men, including the captain, descended the steps into the gloom and there, standing in the cabin, was the same figure. After a short while the captain, tired of what seemed to be nothing more than hocus pocus, pulled out his revolver and fired at the figure. The crack of the bullet was met by a tired moan but there was now no sign of the sailor. After this curious incident the entire crew slept on deck: from then on too scared to nap in the darkness of their cabins. The article's author added, 'We were laughed at and ridiculed as a crew but it is a matter of history that the *Charles* never made another voyage'. After a few years the brig was left to rot.

The *Charles'* first mate also spoke of another English ship, called the *Homeward*. He wrote, 'I shipped on her at Liverpool for a voyage to the Cape of Good Hope and return,' but just as in the case of the *Charles*, things were not to be plain sailing. As the boat was ready to sail, the first mate caught sight of a man who he took to be a deserter. As the man ran away, the first mate managed to clutch at his collar, but the alleged deserter broke free of his grasp and shouted back, 'Aye, but I'd sooner sail the sea in a coffin'.

The first mate didn't think anything of the odd remark, especially as he had found that the man was a deserter, alongside another handful of men who, for some unknown reason, had all fled the ship. Four days later the ship was out at sea and only boarded by a handful of men, including five sailors, the cook, steward and cabin boy. Eventually,

another eleven or so men were given to the ship when it docked again, but although the captain was, as expected, sober, these were completely drunk. The first mate was quick to speak to the captain about the condition of the crew and his response was strange, stating: 'Yes, it's beastly, but we couldn't have got 'em aboard sober, you know. Let a whisper get out about a craft and sailors act like fools,' and with that the captain walked off.

Things seemed to be very strange aboard the ship. Another chap, named Anderson, who seemed incredibly

Seamen often abandoned their boats after witnessing ghosts on board. (Neil Arnold)

reluctant to board, asked, 'Do you think they are very bad?' To which the first mate replied, 'What?'

'The ghosts,' responded Anderson.

'Is this a haunted ship?' enquired the first mate. With that, Anderson told the story of how the ship was meant to be so haunted that at every port the crew would flee, and that for every trip a new captain was employed.

For the next three days nothing unusual happened on board the *Homeward*, but on the fourth night a crew member emerged from below deck to say that there'd been some eerie moans heard and a search was carried out in case there had been a stowaway on board. The hunt proved futile and members of each watch began to worry that there was in fact a ghostly presence on board. To the first mate it was clear that the rest of the crew were petrified of visiting certain areas of the boat, and so one night he decided to conduct a personal investigation, which took him below deck. After descending just a few steps of the ladder, an icy hand was felt on his face and his hair stood on end.

'Someone was sighing, groaning and weeping,' he wrote. 'The sound did not come from any one direction … I frankly admit to you that I was scared.'

When the spooked first mate climbed back up he told the anxious men on deck that the noises probably came from a stowaway and that the next day a thorough search would be conducted, but again, when the hunt was carried out after breakfast, no stowaway was uncovered. This of course put everyone present on edge, but again the first mate tried to quash any fears by stating that the noises may well have been caused by the 'rubbing of the cargo'. 'Why we should not hear them in the daytime I could not explain,' he privately added.

The following night, at about 9 p.m., the noises started up again; by this time all of the men on board were terrified of who or what was sharing the *Homeward* with them. When the first mate entered the cabin the captain immediately told him, 'We must go back to Liverpool. This ship is haunted …'. According to the first mate, the captain then burst into tears and locked himself in his cabin, refusing to visit any other area of the boat for fear of encountering the ghost. It was as if everyone on board, apart from the first mate, was descending into some type of insanity. This was substantiated when, during the early hours, the captain suddenly rushed from his cabin and with a scream leapt overboard into the foaming waters. Immediately the crew rushed a small boat out but there was no trace of the captain and, as the bemused first mate concluded, 'I then put the ship about and carried her into Liverpool, and it was the last voyage she ever made …'.

In 1871 the *Mystic* was built at Yarmouth, a coastal town of Norfolk. The ship was constructed for Captain John Bruce and its maiden voyage, consisting of '18 smart men', was from London to Rio Janeiro. According to the *Morning Herald* of 4 February 1894, 'The *Mystic* began her voyage with favouring winds, but after the third night at sea the crew declared that she was a haunted ship,' and demanded that the boat be put into port so they could escape from the alleged horrors on board. Captain Bruce, being the hardened sailor he was, decided to investigate the alleged bouts of eerie strangeness, which many had described as 'mournful cries'. Again, as in the case of the *Homeward*, the boat was thoroughly searched in case there had been a stowaway on board. Despite the multitude of noises one would expect to hear on a busy, creaking ship riding on a stormy sea, the crew mentioned that the most peculiar was that of someone crying, 'Oh! Lord! Help! Help!', whilst a few others stated they had heard someone yelp 'Go back! Go back! Danger! Danger!'.

The captain, speaking from experience, thought that the groans could be explained by the friction of the cargo but those who had experienced the noises were not convinced, and nor were they sure about the stowaway explanation either. However, the strangest detail about the matter was that every time a thorough investigation was carried out the cries would cease.

'I can do no more than what I have already done,' stated Captain Bruce, who was still certain that a child had somehow hidden away from the prying eyes of the crew. As the days passed, accompanied by the soundtrack of the voices every fifteen or so minutes (or so some of the crew members claimed), the *Mystic* cruised on. But the squad had reached breaking point, and despite the captain offering a wage increase, they were too fearful to carry on. The sailors stated that they would rather return home without earnings than spend another day tortured by those haunting cries. Even Captain Bruce admitted to hearing the noises, but again he still sought a more rational explanation, and eventually he managed to persuade some men to board the ship and take her back to London after reaching Rio de Janeiro. The captain, to prove his nerve to his men, said he was happy to sleep in the allegedly haunted location; yet despite a bribe of tobacco to the sailors, none of them were brave enough to spend more than thirty minutes in the forecastle.

Despite all the hysteria on board, it at one point seemed that, due to the diligent investigations of Captain Bruce, it had been proved that there was no ghost after all. According to a newspaper report at the time, the captain had figured it out that 'the wail was caused by the carelessness of the workmen in sheathing the hold'. He claimed that the floor, which was laid over the ribs of the ship, had two loose planks and that the rubbing together of these pieces of wood had produced the most unusual crying noise. What it didn't explain, however, was the fact that the noise was often heard when the ship was still; indeed, a further investigation revealed no loose planks whatsoever, and a meticulous going-over by carpenters and the like could not find any fault with the ship that would cause such a cacophony. Maybe Captain Bruce had been clutching at straws. As the newspaper report concluded, 'If you wonder why the captain was at so much pains, let me tell you that it is death to a ship to have the reputation of being haunted.' The fear of such tales being spread like wildfire was a captain's biggest dread. Neither a leaky ship nor a terrible captain would deter sailors, but mention of a ghost would see superstitious crew running a mile.

The next voyage of the *Mystic* was to Lisbon and it was understandable that the captain was on edge, especially as several newspapers had mentioned the continuing mournful cries on board. The first few nights of the voyage went without disruption; the usual creaks and bangs being ignored by the crew despite their sulky disposition. However, on the fourth night one of the crew slipped below deck to fetch some tobacco but ran back screaming in terror. All those asleep were awoken with a start and rushed to the man, who claimed that whilst looking for his tobacco a pitiful cry had echoed through the cabin. The captain rushed to the forecastle and found there was no one present, but he too heard the noise he had so many times previous. More men were called to investigate, all reporting that they had heard a muffled voice cry, 'Oh! Lord! Help! Help!'. The voice seemed to be emanating from behind the bulkhead but, as one witness asked, 'Why was not that wail heard in port as well as at sea? Why not on the first, second and third nights?'

The whole affair was becoming one of great intrigue, but it had also instilled great fear into the crew. Captain Bruce still declared that the *Mystic* was a lucky ship and refused to give full belief to a haunting; yet when the ship hit port at Lisbon it was claimed that the captain not only agreed to discharge his men, but paid them not to speak of the alleged ghost. Sadly for him, the rumours spread regardless, and the boat sat for some six weeks without a crew to take it on to New York. When a team was eventually found they were next seen out at sea sending out a distress signal as they

The mysterious stench of death attributed to a ghostly presence on board a ship was eventually solved when a dead rat was found behind some barrels. (Neil Arnold)

were so spooked by the ghostly noises. An American man-of-war picked them up, and the captain of the US ship demanded that the crew of the *Mystic* return to their boat, but fifteen days later the reputedly haunted ship was found, empty, floating in the breeze. The crew had jumped ship, leaving the mournful wails behind. After being abandoned the boat was removed of its masts and despite sceptics dismissing the reputation of the ship, the ghostly cries were never explained.

In 2005 a team of paranormal investigators looked into the mysterious happenings on board the *Ross Tiger*, a trawler which since 1992 has existed as a National Heritage Fishing Centre at Alexandra Dock, Grimsby. Staff and visitors have reported strong smells of tobacco, unusual cold spots and phantom footsteps. The investigation revealed nothing of importance, however.

Not all unusual events aboard ships can be blamed on ghosts, however. For instance, a long time ago one unnamed vessel was said to be haunted by its limping cook. Shortly after he died several crew reported seeing the ghost but, according to author T. F. Thiselton Dyer, 'It was found however that the cause of the alarm was part of a maintop, the remains of some wreck floating before them …'. Dyer also speaks of another amusing case, in which several sailors aboard a ship reported smelling a rotten ghost. For this the captain, so enraged by such tomfoolery, ordered the men to be lashed a dozen times each. However, the pungent odour still wafted across deck until it was found that a dead rat had scurried behind some beer barrels, got trapped and died a slow death.

WE ALL LIVE IN A HAUNTED SUBMARINE

On 17 August 2009 the *Daily Mail* reported on, 'The ghost of U-Boat 33', with journalists Christian Gysin and Alun Rees commenting on the possibility that the wreck of a German U-boat sunk in 1918 could become dislodged from the seabed after passing vessels had disturbed its dormant state. The U-boat – which had sunk at least thirteen vessels during its rampage across the English Channel and North Sea – finally met its maker off Dover. It is now said to sit some 80ft below the surface. Such a craft may make for an eerie sight, should it suddenly rise to the surface after being disturbed by a passing tanker or ferry. This brings me nicely to the tale of the haunted German U-boat *UB-65*, which in the same year cruised the waters of the English Channel in search of targets. The U-boat was plagued by disaster, for a week after its launch all manner of malfunctions and disasters took place on board – but by far the most noted oddness concerned the vessel's ghost. According to a researcher named T. Duplain, during January 1918 'The U-boat's starboard look-out on the conning tower, viewed an officer positioned on deck almost exactly under him, despite the fact that all hatches were battoned down.' The look-out screamed in terror upon realisation that the figure was in fact the apparition of the U-boat's previous second officer, who had died in an explosion that took place on the *UB-65*'s first voyage.

The captain of the U-boat rushed to the aid of the look-out and was just in time to see the wraith disappear. However, this wasn't the first time a ghost had been seen on board. Before *UB-65*'s maiden voyage three crew members died on board when they were consumed by fumes in the vicinity of the engine room. Then, when the U-boat set off on its maiden voyage one crew member fell overboard and was never seen again, and on another occasion the second officer was killed when the U-boat torpedoed. To say that this was an unlucky vessel was an understatement, and so it seems understandable that many people were hesitant to board it, especially after rumours of a ghost.

There had been continued sightings of the ghostly officer and eventually a commodore was enlisted to investigate the eerie reputation. Despite initial scepticism, the commodore could not dispel what he took to be a myth as too many people of high rank were reporting the paranormal activity, and eventually the U-boat was made redundant. Rumour has it that whilst docked in Belgium, a pastor was called in to exorcise the craft and eventually, with a new, hardened captain on board, the *UB-65* was put to work again. Bizarrely, when the sceptical captain was replaced, the high strangeness returned with several crewmen saying they were being driven mad by the resident spectre. The ghost stories were eventually put to bed – the sea-bed in fact – when the *UB-65* exploded after coming under attack from an American submarine. Thirty-four crew members went down with the U-boat, which had literally torpedoed itself to death.

The Dover coast – where a cursed and haunted submarine finally perished. (Neil Arnold)

BEWARE OF THE BUOY!

If you thought the tale of the ghost-infested submarine was strange, then consider the following brace of tales – some of the weirdest British sea-related stories I've heard of. The first story comes from 1875, the location being Hoy Harbour on the north-east coast of Scotland. At the time, superstitious fishermen were beginning to talk about the Glendough buoy, which sat out in the water to mark a particularly dangerous spot. However, the jagged rocks and turbulent waters were the last thing the crew of the fishing boat *Braemer* were worried about one soggy spring night. The weather forced the *Braemer* and its crew to be extra vigilant as they combed the coastal water at Hoy Harbour. Those on board could only see approximately 50yds in front of them as the thick mists rolled in, and so the importance of the buoy was heightened; to hear the sound of the bell was a reassuring, albeit dull, echo. The crew were used to hearing all manner of peculiar and eerie noises at sea – from birds to howling winds – on this particular night, however, there was something very alien about the sound they heard: it was the sound of a human in distress; a melancholic cry above the waves that seemed to merge as one with the dull sound of the bell. Captain MacDonald, helmsman of the *Braemer*, ordered his men to be extra vigilant and to slow the boat, hoping that they may see their quarry. After a few minutes they did, but it was not what they expected. Clinging to the bobbing metal buoy was the figure of a woman – and then the true horror of the sight confronted them. As they neared the 20ft-high buoy they could see the tatty white garments of the figure and the long, black, matted locks; yet this was no woman in distress, but a stranded skeleton, hanging on for dear death. MacDonald instructed his men to have the small boat ready, but as the *Braemer* turned and came back around to the buoy, there was no sign of the skeleton.

When the crew returned to the shore, they were in deep shock. So many of the men had stood, transfixed at the sight before them, and yet somehow the dead woman was now not there at all. When news spread of the experience many were quick to scoff, suggesting that the crew had simply seen a large sea bird or a pile of rags that had become attached to the buoy. However, the veteran fishermen stuck to their story and a few days later their encounter was corroborated by the crew of another ship that had come into the harbour. No one on board had heard the news of the skeleton but they, too, heard the mournful cries and witnessed the clinging wraith. From then on, fishermen who trawled the coast refused to go anywhere near the reputedly haunted buoy.

Coincidentally, or so it would seem, months previous a local fisherman – known for his rather aggressive manner – had had a terrible row with his wife of eight months and she had seemingly disappeared over night. The fisherman, named Angus McBride, had told friends that his wife, Maggie, had walked out on him. When Angus went to look for her, he could find no trace and so he assumed Maggie had stormed out and gone to stay with her parents who lived a few miles away. The mystery deepened, however, when, during a search of the area one night, a shoe was found – it had

The haunted buoy. (Illustration by Neil Arnold)

belonged to Maggie. Police began to suspect something fishy was going on and so questioned Angus, who stuck to his original story. The months passed without event until rumours began to circulate that the missing woman had in fact been seeing another man behind Angus' back. Then, one night, a Danish trawler was anchored within the vicinity of the Glendough buoy when a crew member reported hearing cries coming from the floating marker. The captain of the vessel had a lifeboat lowered and men journeyed out to the buoy, and there they could see, clutching to its side, a woman dressed in white who was crying for help. As the lifeboat neared, the captain shouted to the woman to jump into the boat, but her response was something the crew never forgot. The skeletal figure screamed, 'I am the wife of Angus McBride and I curse him … ', and with that the figure vanished into thin air.

   The next day the captain of the vessel contacted the local reverend about the spectre, but he was sceptical, claiming that people had simply seen a large gull or some other sea bird. However, when the captain told the reverend what the woman had said, the reverend was shocked to the bone. A few days later, the coastguards were instructed to go to the buoy and dismantle it, and inside they found a skeleton. The body, still adorned in tatty clothes, was missing a shoe. The remains were of Maggie McBride.

On 1 June 1875, Maggie McBride was interred in the Kirk at Gary Head. Three days later, Angus McBride threw himself from the top of a cliff. He left a note explaining how he had murdered his wife and concealed the body inside the buoy when it was on shore being repaired. The following night, Angus towed the buoy back out into the water.

The second story concerning a buoy is even weirder and comes from the files of ghost-hunter Elliott O'Donnell. He wrote of a man named Paget Hickman who, whilst staying at a Kentish seaside resort one summer, decided to investigate a buoy that had come ashore. The buoy was high and dry, and clearly hadn't been used at sea for a while. Paget rested himself against it and took in the blistering sun before dozing off. What seemed to be only seconds later, Paget woke with a start and found himself standing at a garden gate, which had the nameplate 'Dr Horace Crawley' inscribed on it. Paget walked up to the door of the property and knocked, and within a few seconds was welcomed by an attractive lady.

'I am so glad you have come,' said the woman. She added: 'You are very prompt. He is dead.'

Hickman found himself responding with a smile and commenting, 'When did he die?'

'Two or three minutes before I rang you. I want you with me when the doctor comes,' she said.

Paget was taken into the house and to a back room on the first floor, where a grey-haired man sat in bed. Hickman walked over to the man when suddenly the woman rushed from the room, shut the door and locked it with a click.

'You've been caught,' the woman mocked. 'You poisoned him with that drug you purchased in Brazil. There is some of it in your clothes in your wardrobe; I put it there, now for the police.'

Hickman rushed to the window and peered out; realising there was no escape as there was a sheer drop below. He opened the window and looked down again, then, without further hesitation, climbed over the sill and jumped.

From the house he could hear the woman shouting, 'Eustace, Eustace, he's getting away!' And with that a heavily built man gave chase to Hickman, all the while screaming 'Murderer!'. Hickman scrambled through gardens and down alleyways, and when he looked back he realised that several members of the public were now chasing him, too. Soon he was at the seafront and there, in the distance, he could see the buoy. Hickman sprinted towards it, opened the lid and clambered inside, shutting the cover behind him. Outside the men were banging on the buoy, trying to prize the lid open but to no avail; inside Hickman, completely parched, was breathing heavily, unsure of what to do next.

'What would be worse,' he thought to himself, 'being caught and then hanged by my pursuers or dying of suffocation in this buoy.'

Hickman's fear of confined spaces began to set in, and he decided to force the lid open and try to make a run for it. Suddenly, however, he felt the buoy move and realised, due to the sound of lapping water that he was now at sea. The heat within the buoy was proving to be too much to stomach and with that he passed out.

The next moment Hickman was awake, his back against the buoy on the beach, the sun beating down upon his sweat-laden brow. Had the bizarre experience been a dream? It seemed so, but soon afterwards Hickman made enquiries as to why the buoy had been present on the sands. He was startled to discover that, many years before, a married businessman had visited the resort and become the secret lover of an attractive woman – the woman Hickman had met in his nightmare. The woman had phoned the businessman and asked him to come to her house as her husband was extremely ill. The businessman turned up at the house and, exactly as Hickman had experienced in the dream, he had been accused of poisoning her husband and had to escape the house from the window. The poor man had, like Hickman experienced, run to the buoy and locked himself in. As O'Donnell concludes: '… fortunately for [the businessman], a workman who had been repairing the buoy had left his wallet in it, which brought him back to the beach. The workman found the man unconscious, overcome by the lack of air.'

A strange story indeed, and one that ended with the attractive, yet despicable woman and her accomplice escaping punishment.

Mr Paget Hickman had a supernatural experience pertaining to a beached buoy some years ago in Kent. (Neil Arnold)

3

UNIDENTIFIED OBJECTS OUT AT SEA

SOMEWHERE, BEYOND THE SEA ...

For more than half a century, debate has raged as to whether unidentified flying objects (UFOs), in the extra-terrestrial sense, exist. Ever since pilot Kenneth Arnold observed a peculiar set of craft over Washington, USA in 1947, 'flying saucers' have embedded themselves into the human mind-set. Every year, thousands of people from all over the world claim to have sighted a UFO; but in the majority of cases these can be explained as either hoaxes, misinterpretations of natural phenomena, or terrestrial craft. However, a very small percentage are not so easily explained, and what these things are, we will probably never know. To many, the thought that alien beings from another planet are visiting this realm is ludicrous; but how then can we explain the reliable reports made by police officers, airline pilots and the like, who describe seeing disc-shaped craft that travel beyond a speed any conventional aircraft is capable of?

Over the centuries the UFO mystery has spiralled out of control and spawned several sub-mysteries, such as crop circles, alien abduction and sinister cattle mutilations. But until we can finally prove once and for all that a supreme race of beings is infiltrating our void, the other mysteries will remain just that: mysteries. Some UFO researchers are of the opinion that extra-terrestrials and their craft have been recorded for thousands of years, and researchers often point to ancient texts and images, which seem to mention peculiar flying objects. In my opinion, I doubt very much that UFOs are operated by so-called aliens, and would consider a more earthly option: in that the military are testing out advanced technology. Even so, everyone has their own opinion, which makes the subject of Ufology so intriguing and longstanding.

UFOs and their alleged alien occupants may simply be part of that weird procession of archetypes that have long plagued the nightmares and folklore of mankind. This spectacular menagerie of weirdness would also include the likes of fairies, monsters

UFOs have been reported plunging into, and emerging from, the sea. (Illustration by Neil Arnold)

and possibly ghosts, but are these manifestations the product of the human psyche, or complex apparitions that step through a tear in the fabric of time and appear only to those susceptible to them?

In my 2012 book *Shadows in the Sky: The Haunted Airways of Britain*, I looked at various mysteries pertaining to the UFO enigma, and with this chapter I'd like to explore a more obscure theory regarding such craft. I have long been interested in reports of UFOs seen, not just out over the sea, but emerging from the watery abyss and also hovering just feet above the waves. Whilst it may be easy to dismiss reports of a blurry light thousands of feet up in the sky, can we be so sceptical when it comes to observations regarding weird lights shooting out from the sea? There are some UFO researchers who strongly believe that aliens do not originate from some other galaxy, but in fact have always been with us: possibly as a race that existed on Earth long before humans; or that such beings are in cohorts with our governments, which I believe is highly unlikely. Even so, all theories, however bizarre, must be looked at, as it is a mystery still far from having a satisfactory explanation. It is also worth noting that some investigators are of the opinion that UFOs do come from the sea; that the waves hide many secret civilisations, which can come and go as they please.

Can all reports of water-related UFOs be explained as boats, low-flying aircraft and meteors? Judge for yourself …

When researching stories pertaining to sightings of UFOs under water, I found that in the UK reports are in fact scarce. This flummoxed me, because there seemed to be quite a few reports of underwater craft from elsewhere in the world. With sighting locations ranging from the United States, Greece, Cuba, Norway, Canada, Italy, Spain, New Zealand and parts of Africa, I wondered why such 'flying saucers' were not as interested in visiting the shores of Britain, but I was still intrigued by the few reports made concerning our seas. It seemed that in the last decade or so, unidentified flying objects had preferred to emerge and enter Italian waters – was this because there had been a secret government or military base there; or were real flesh-and-blood aliens in the neighbourhood? In some parts of the world, reports of UFOs – or what some researchers like to term USOs (unidentified submerged objects, or unidentified submarine objects) – seemed relatively consistent, which in turn made me wary of those scant reports from the UK over the last ten years. For instance, on 19 February 2004, the National UFO Reporting Centre listed a strange experience. It had been related by a man who had been watching a golf video, at an undisclosed location in England, when he saw in the background of the training video an object travel across the screen at great speed. When the video was slowed down, he was stunned to see that the flat, circular object had emerged from the sea in the distance. According to the witness, 'The object left the sea at about 30 degrees and when zoomed in you are able to notice that the object is shedding water.'

What are we to make of such a report? Could the object have simply been a fly that zipped across the screen, giving the impression it had emerged from the sea? Possibly, but then this was something the witness originally considered when he first saw the object. Maybe, just maybe, the object had been some type of top-secret military craft; but this does not explain the sightings that took place in October 1983 at Orford Ness, on the Suffolk coast. UFO researcher Jenny Randles filed several reports, which were made above an area of forest, but one report stood out from the rest. On 7 October three fishermen watched in amazement as a great ball of light, consisting of green and yellow colours, hovered above them in the sky over the coast at Sizewell, and then seemed to fade to nothing. Eight days later, at 5.30 a.m., one of the fishermen saw a green light that appeared in the sky but then with great speed zipped towards the sea and plunged beneath the waves. The fisherman reported that even when it had gone into the water its eerie glow was still visible.

Sceptics at the time claimed that the object must have been a meteorite, but a month later more fishermen claimed to have seen a similar object off the coast at Felixstowe, and they stated quite categorically that the object did not behave like a meteor. For instance, a meteor would not change direction suddenly and, as in most of these types of weird cases, witnesses report how the unusual light hovers for quite some time, then may change direction, before heading down into the sea.

Is it possible these sightings were simply down to a lack of observation skills? Had the witnesses seen coastal flares, or possibly a shooting star? We can debate such reports until we are blue in the face, but for every brief British sea-related UFO reported, there appear to be hundreds of other cases worldwide. The River Mersey, which flows into the Irish Sea, stretches for some 70 miles. In the March of 1990, a fisherman was angling with his two sons when they observed a brightly lit object that appeared under the water. Although the mysterious light was some 800m away, its movement was unlike any submarine or man-made object they had seen before, especially when it zoomed away at great speed and then left the water and headed toward a low-lying cloud. At the time, the airport (now the John Lennon Airport) at Speke had received numerous reports of strange lights in the sky moving at great speed. Some witnesses believed that the Ministry of Defence should have done more about such sightings, although it is fair to say that such a body would only act if an object was a threat to national security.

Two years previous, in the May of 1988, a group of fishermen set off into the estuary at Seaforth one night. The only light that illuminated the area was that of the lighthouse. As midnight approached, one of the men pointed to a light in the sky: a banana-shaped craft coloured orange. The object slowly descended and then, to the amazement of the witnesses, plunged into the water. Seconds later more objects followed, all dropping to the abyss beneath the Mersey. The fishermen packed up their gear and made for home. They considered reporting their sighting to the police, but didn't think anyone would believe them.

In 2009 a truly astounding encounter took place in Liverpool and concerned a warship, HMS *Daring*. During June of the said year, several people had come forward to report seeing UFOs over the seaside resort of Southport in Merseyside. The orange balls of light were originally dismissed as Chinese lanterns, but were in fact reported as travelling at several thousands of miles per hour. The *Telegraph* picked up on the story, which seemed to cause a snowball effect: as next an ex-military source came forward to make the amazing claim that the British navy warship, HMS *Daring*, whilst docked in Liverpool, had been alerted to the passing UFOs and tracked them on radar. According to some of the sources for the story, the ship was within seconds of firing on the unidentified objects, but thankfully an interstellar conflict was avoided! Of course, it seems highly unlikely this would have happened, but then just what were the objects seen over Southport that summer?

According to one unnamed source, the UFOs could be explained: in that a plane had flown overhead and 'dropped countermeasures', which are flares used to confuse infrared systems – but these do not travel at high speeds. And what about the even weirder account related by a woman in 1995, who claimed she'd seen a strange object in the shape of a bell, hovering over the River Mersey and sucking up water? The woman was not alone in her sighting, as a further six people came forward to report the same dramatic event. Over the next months there had been a UFO flap around the area, and all sightings seemed to match: a large, bell-shaped object. But what was it doing with the water it was allegedly sucking up?

UFOs have been reported over and in the River Mersey. (Neil Arnold)

Such an incident would no doubt provoke more theories as to the motives of these 'extra-terrestrials'. Over the decades many witnesses and investigators have come to the conclusion that the aliens in question, wherever they are from, may well be depending on us; existing of our energy, or our elements. As one chap said, 'they don't have these type of things where they come from …', but how on earth would he know that? As in the case of ghosts, UFOs are very much guesswork when it comes to humankind sussing out their requirements. The more complex the sightings, the more complex the theories become. Long gone are the days when investigators rambled on about how aliens are visiting our planet to warn us about our destructive ways. Now it seems the aliens do not care about our welfare, but simply want to draw on our energies as if we are some type of cashpoint for them! When we throw together the supposed reports of abduction, cattle mutilations, crop circles etc., there appears to be no sense at all; but instead a crazy, surreal set of scenarios that have embedded themselves into our culture and folklore. It is also fair to say that over the decades the so-called ETs have even changed guise and craft structure. In the early 1900s, such beings apparently spooked us with their phantom airships; and then we had the saucer-shaped objects; whereas in the 1950s the aliens threatened us in the guise of Men In Black (MIBs); and since the epic Spielberg movie *Close Encounters of the Third Kind*, they've become harmless, albeit intrusive, bug-eyed critters who like to take us aboard their giant spaceships to probe us.

There is no real consistency to the UFO enigma and so reports of such objects emerging from the sea seem to make no true sense either. We can only speculate.

WHAT A LOAD OF OL' BALLS …

In 1997 a Merseyside woman named Nikki Limb, who had started a UFO investigative group, told the newspaper the *Wirral Globe* that 'We get a lot of reports of objects rising out of the Mersey …'. Such a statement could lead one to think that Nikki's beliefs were rather far-fetched, and let's face it, there is no such thing as a UFO expert. Then again, can we dismiss so many reports, and also the handful involving coastal areas?

From the year 1067 – yes, that's 1067 – there exists a report from the files of one C.E. Britton who, in his *A Meteorological Chronology to A.D. 1450* (1937), writes of a fantastic phenomenon, which was also chronicled in the twelfth-century work *L'Estoire des Engles solum la Translacion Maistre Geffri Gaimer*. The phenomenon, seen by many people at Northumbria, was recorded as a fire which then spiralled, ascended and then suddenly dropped into the sea. On its remarkable journey the flaming object scorched trees. Was it a meteorite? Again, it is unlikely that such a form could change trajectory. And what of the 'fiery exhalation that came from the sea' and proceeded to set fire to hay with its blue flame, as chronicled from the Tremadoc Bay vicinity of North Wales in 1693? The first mention of the object is recorded in a letter dated 20 January 1694 and published in the *Philosophical Transactions*. The male witnesses who observed the phenomenon reported that they did their best to put the fire out and were of the opinion it was not as a normal fire, as they were able to walk into it without harm. In the same year, Tremadoc Bay was visited by another anomalous object, which could only be seen at night and soared out from the sea before travelling along the coast for several miles. The burning manifestation was so ferocious that not only did it set fire to hay and woodland but it also killed several animals in its path. Once again, the most bizarre aspect was that witnesses who were present at the time reported that they felt no damage from the blue flames, and many a time people had ventured through the flames to rescue their livestock. Stranger still, the furious entity was only put to rest when locals fired guns and blew horns to deter it – certainly not the usual way one would react in order to halt a raging fire.

One theory I would like to put forward to explain such a phenomenon is ball lightning. This is a natural, albeit not yet fully understood atmospheric condition that usually arises before, during or just after a severe storm. Witnesses often describe seeing a glowing ball of red or orange light that gives off great heat, and can pass through houses scorching objects before dissipating. These amorphous balls can vary in size and shape and make a crackling or fizzing noise. Ball lightning has been put forward to explain some sightings of UFOs. In fact, ball lightning is a UFO in the truest form, in that it is an unidentified flying object, but in most cases these balls do not appear as anything more than a few feet across.

Mystery lights are also reported from marshy areas of the UK, where they are known as spook lights, or will-o'-the-wisp. These small, often white or bluish lights are said to be the product of atmospheric conditions, but many years ago when such forms were less understood they were perceived as fairies or trickster spirits, said to appear on dark pathways of a night to a lonely traveller. Legend has it that many a rambler would follow such lights and be led to his death, or, in some cases, enticed out of treacherous fog or swamps to safety.

Peculiar lights have been reported around coastal areas and emerging from the sea, but are these the same as ball lightning and the likes? In the case of the wood-scorching fireballs, I wonder if such apparitions can also be connected to the alleged reports of phantom sky ships, as reported in a previous chapter. Is it possible such lights are misinterpreted forms of natural phenomena witnessed by folk who are without knowledge of such forms?

One night in 1783 a massive ball of fire, described as the size of the moon, was seen to emerge from the North Sea and travel across Edinburgh. As it did so, blue sparks fell from the object and witnesses described how, during its passing, everything became as light as day. At the same time, a similar ball was also reported from Ostend, a city in Belgium. Although bizarre and terrifying, a number of these types of reports can be explained. For instance, in April of 1910 crew aboard the SS *Trafalgar* reported a strange shaking of their vessel and a loud explosion whilst in the vicinity of Lizard Point, Cornwall. Seconds later, a large fiery object hit the sea with a loud fizzing noise and disappeared from sight. The second mate on board, who was holding a steel rod at the time, reported that he had received a tremendous shock at the impact, and the compasses of the boat also went awry. Captain Davies at the helm of the ship stated that, had the object struck the *Trafalgar*, it would have literally been curtains. This rather fantastic sighting of a meteorite does leave one asking: could the mysterious disappearance of some ships at sea have been caused by such a wonder? Interestingly, in the same year a sea vessel was affected by a meteor in the same area, which rendered the ship useless and set the masts aflame. The object, as reported in the *Indianapolis Star* of 27 February 1910, was described as 30–40ft in length and hitting the sea some 20ft away.

TERRIBLE VISITATIONS

On 11 May 1910, the *Irish Independent* newspaper reported 'Ulster Fishermen Affrighted', after a terrible visitation from the sky, described by the witnesses as a 'celestial visitant'. Although coastguards gave a more down-to-earth explanation, stating that the object was a balloon, the newspaper claimed that those fortunate enough to observe the phenomenon at first 'thought it was a foreign steamer coloured blueish-grey coming from the North Atlantic', and such was the speed of the craft that the fishermen expected an imminent crash. The object then moved at pace some 2ft above sea level, occasionally dipping toward the ground before heading over the beach. The object was said to have resembled a torpedo boat in its form and to have had a vaporous hue, but the most curious part of the encounter was its ability to wreck any boat that appeared under its path. The object was eventually lost to sight as it headed out to sea over Culdaff Bay.

Such a form brings to mind the phantom airships reported at the same time around Britain. Many of these aerial vessels were believed to be foreign objects, possibly clever technologies expressed by the Germans, but this was never verified. Although Germany did employ Zeppelins, these were not able to achieve great speeds or travel such vast routes in such a short amount of time, leaving some researchers to conclude that these cigar-shaped craft were in fact of alien design. Some dramatic incidents explain how witnesses had conversations with the crew of these strange vessels, and such occupants did not seem to be of malevolent nature. Airship crew were often described as having olive skin and speaking unusual languages not recognised by the witnesses, but many of these airships also caused great panic, a feeling which seemed justified with the onset of the First World War. However, as stated previously, such ships seemed to display all the attributes of some of the more modern-day encounters; such as destroying crops in their wake, sucking up water or, as in the recent cases, small boats.

In 1913 a steam trawler, *Othello*, was 'buzzed' by a peculiar craft on the North Sea whilst returning to port at Hull. It was 8.15 p.m. when suddenly an object with a powerful searchlight came into view in the distance. The object made a whirring sound and seemed to cover a lot of ground in a short space of time, so that within a few minutes it was very close to the trawler. The captain of the *Othello* was so sure that the two vessels were going to collide with one another that he blew his whistle as an alarm and diverted his boat. With that, the unidentified object circled the trawler twice, all the while keeping its searchlight on the boat, and then eventually moved off to the west. Oddly, despite being unsettled by the airship, the captain saluted it with his siren, to which the sky ship responded; this suggests it was a man-made vessel – unless of course aliens are used to such correspondence!

During the same year at Killary Harbour – a fjord in the west of Ireland – a man was aboard his yacht when he saw a craft resembling an aeroplane drop into the sea. The witness investigated the area and found the craft on the shore with a trio of men inspecting it. The witness assumed that the men were of German origin and so, to be polite, attempted to speak to them. One of the men responded in French, telling the witness he did not understand him and to go away, and he obliged.

In September 1922 another odd object was reported falling into the sea, only this time it took place at Barmouth, Wales. The *Daily Express* of 11 September reported that on the 9th of the month two men, named William James and John Morris – John

Fishermen whilst shrimping on Morecambe Bay observed five flying triangles. (Image created by Neil Arnold)

being the coxswain of Barmouth lifeboat – were standing on the shore when they saw an aeroplane fall ever so slowly into the water. Immediately they rushed to the spot, but there was no trace of the object. Morecambe Bay, which is part of the north-west coastline of England, was similarly the setting for an unusual sighting involving a black, post-like object, which, during the March of 1938 rose out of the sea, disturbing the local bird-life that had settled on the water. The incredible encounter involved a group of fishermen who reported their experience to the *Liverpool Echo* newspaper, which featured the story on 29 September. The newspaper ran the statement of William Baxter, one of the fishermen, who commented, 'Out of the water there rose something large and black, like a big post. It was at least eight or nine feet high, and it rose and fell three times, then disappeared.' A few investigators who have looked back over the case have proposed the theory that the black object was in fact the neck and head of an unknown creature (see Chapter 5 'Denizens of the Deep' for similar reports). Or had the fishermen simply seen a log, or piece of debris from a boat that in the distance had confused them?

In 1992 there were a handful of UFO sightings over Morecambe Bay: one incident took place at approximately 5.30 p.m. one August evening and involved four fishermen who were shrimping offshore not far from the Strathmore Hotel. When one of the fishermen noticed an unusual light formation in the bright sky, all men present agreed that what they were seeing were five distinctive flying triangles. The following day the men returned to the shore and this time spotted ten triangular objects, which eventually 'blinked out' one by one. Three years later, on 18 April at 9.30 p.m., one of the fishermen had another spectacular sighting, this time whilst in the company of three friends at Carnforth. Meanwhile at Bare, a civil servant named Pieter Smit reported seeing a massive object, measuring approximately 200m in length, in his back garden. The awesome craft hovered just 150m above his head and then, after a few seconds, slowly glided off towards the west.

The year 1995 was proving to be an active time for UFOs over Morecambe, because in the August a man and his daughter observed a large, black triangular object that hovered over the bay, its lights lit up the sea. The scary aspect of the sighting, which deeply unnerved the witnesses, was that it moved towards them and came to within about 30m before speeding away to the south. The sightings continued into 1996 when several witnesses reported the mysterious triangles. One astonishing sighting seemed to involve some thirty or so objects alongside one intensely bright craft. The thirty objects seemed to form a triangular formation and then completely vanished. A huge black triangle was later allegedly photographed, some 1,500m off the Thanet coast, in 2009. This was the second time a mysterious black triangle had been snapped; the first case involved what was believed to be a UFO off Ramsgate. The object was thought to be more than 100m in length and casting a shadow. The *Thanet Times* commented that it was 'unlikely to be a ship or aircraft'.

On 28 December 1962 at 7.55 p.m., as registered in The National Archives, a civilian pilot flying from Renfrew to Manchester, whilst over Morecambe Bay, reported seeing a light three times brighter than a star 1,000ft below him. A motorist at exactly the same time reported to police and the coastguard that he had seen a green, flare-like object whilst travelling at Levens Bridge, Harrow.

Five years after the 'black post' incident, an RAF captain was flying his bomber over the English Channel when he saw an orange ball hovering over the sea. The object, also witnessed by the rest of the crew, was not another plane or anything they had seen before, despite many years of flying across Europe.

NORTH SEA STRANGENESS

Many pilots of reputable status have reported strange encounters over our seas. In several cases, pilots have been hesitant to report their sightings until many years later when retired, for fear of not only ridicule, but of bringing the name of their employer into disrepute. Pilots who have witnessed so-called UFOs may not always be willing to come forward, but such sightings are certainly not scant; in fact, during the Second World War many fighter crews reported seeing unusual lights in the sky: weird orbs that seemed to tease and toy with their planes. These objects became known as Foo Fighters. The pilot encounters seemed to be the most impressive, as these were people one would expect to be able to identify all types of flying phenomena. After all, pilots rely heavily on having exceptional eyesight. So what exactly were they seeing?

One of the most dramatic encounters involving a pilot and a UFO concerned a Captain Schaffner who, in September 1970, took to the skies over the North Sea after the radar operator at Saxa Vord, in the Shetlands, reported that contact had been made with a craft travelling at 630mph at a height of 37,000ft. Those who went in pursuit of the object reported that it disappeared from view many times, something which was confirmed by the radar operator, but 90 or so miles east of Whitby something very odd happened. Captain Schaffner, an experienced pilot, reported seeing a very bright blue light that was so intense it hurt his eyes. The light seemed to emanate from a conical-shaped object, which was then accompanied by a strange glass craft Schaffner reported as being the shape of a large soccer ball. Schaffner attempted to stay with the objects over the North Sea, all the while in contact with the radar operator, but after coming close to one of the objects all contact with the pilot was lost.

When contact was resumed some time later, Schaffner seemed bemused and dizzy; unsure what had happened. Then, rather mysteriously, he was told by the operator to ditch his craft. Schaffner assured ground control this was not necessary and that he was able to bring the plane in, but minutes later all contact was lost and Schaffner's plane was reported as hitting the sea.

No one knows what Captain Schaffner saw, and the really bizarre twist to this strange encounter is that, upon investigation of his plane, there was no sign of the pilot. Some have suggested that he ejected from the cockpit, but this was never proven. As many UFO investigators have commented: why on earth would a man in control of his plane ditch it and then jump into the icy waters of the North Sea? Had Schaffner been in contact with a UFO? The whole incident is one of great controversy; a story that no newspaper or UFO investigator has been able to follow up due to the amount of dead ends and doors shut in their face by the Ministry of Defence and the like. Some would argue that Captain Schaffner, despite his experience, may simply have crashed; there were those who stated that he had seen stars and due to some confusion didn't realise how close to the water he was. But what this doesn't explain is the strange, fetid smell reported from the cockpit, or the rumour that the ejector seat later investigated was not the original one.

Had this been a case of a very close encounter with two unidentified objects over the North Sea, or had UFO researchers jumped the gun and reached ludicrous conclusions to explain a simple accident and error of judgement? One thing we do know is that the North Sea has long been considered a hot area for UFO activity. Researcher Nick Redfern mentioned that in 1999 a UFO investigator named David Ledger spoke to a former RAF employee, who was stationed at Saxa Vord in the 1960s. According to Nick, from David's correspondence: 'During the winter of

1964–65, radar operators at the base tracked a stationary object sitting at a height of 20,000ft above the North Sea that defied all rational explanation. Lightning jets were scrambled from RAF Leuchars.' David adds that his source hinted that 'the object seemed to become aware of this fact and what happened next surprised them all. The object just proceeded to go vertical, rapidly, directly up and up until it was lost on the height finder.'

In early 1998 both the *Daily Mail* and *Daily Telegraph* covered the story of the 'giant UFO' that had been chased by British and Dutch jets over the North Sea. The RAF radar station situated at Fylingdales in North Yorkshire were the first to detect the anomalous craft, which they estimated as measuring some 900ft in length. The UFO eluded its pursuers, probably because it was said to have sped off at some 24,000mph! The *Munster Express* also covered a story of an enormous UFO from around the same time, seen over the North Sea during February. The year before, on 12 February 1997 at 2.55 p.m., a man taking a stroll along the beach at Mabelthorpe, Lincolnshire, had an incredible sighting of a small, triangular UFO, which to him appeared as if it were being escorted across the sky – flying low over the North Sea – by an RAF tornado jet interceptor.

On 18 September 2005 a woman named Marcela Krystkova was on a flight from the Czech Republic to Scotland when, over the North Sea, she looked down and spotted seven unusual objects that appeared to be floating on the water. At first the woman thought the objects were lifeboats but not only were they moving very fast but also as one, suggesting these circular objects were part of one bigger vessel. 'I tried to have a better look at what it was,' Marcela said, 'but suddenly there were two white clouds bursting out of two of the circles like an explosion, and all the formation, like one body moved forward with great acceleration …' Marcela was unnerved by her sighting and was made all the more scared shortly afterwards when she observed a huge aerial ship 'as big as a ferry'. Thankfully for her, she was soon to be at Edinburgh airport. In July of 1961 it was rumoured that a UFO had crashed into the North Sea after the crew of a pilot cutter radioed that they had seen the object descend off Walton-on-the-Naze, a seaside town in Essex. As in so many of these types of reports, when lifeboats were sent out to aid the vessel there was no trace of it.

The following year a similar incident occurred, this time west of the Shetland Islands, when the Aith lifeboat was called out to investigate an object that had fallen into the sea. Again, there was no sign of any wreckage. In the summer of 1966 a 21-year-old man from Aberdeen reported that whilst getting ready for work at 5.30 a.m. one morning he gazed out of his flat window, which overlooks the beach, and to his astonishment saw a flat, grey object, around 15ft round, just 30ft away that headed towards the sea. The man, who had been a complete disbeliever in UFOs, was even more shocked when in the newspaper the following day there was an article that mentioned how a dozen people had seen a UFO going into the sea.

MORE CLOSE ENCOUNTERS OF THE COASTAL KIND

There are a few hundred eyewitness reports of UFOs seen over the North Sea, and these have been compiled in numerous books, but they won't be included here, as I'd like to mainly focus on reports of craft going into the sea, emerging from the sea or being seen very close to the surface. The North Sea is not, though, as exceptional an area of water as one might think. Consider the next batch of sea-related tales. The first comes from the county of Kent, Broadstairs to be precise, where on a Saturday night in the August of 1971 a couple were sitting in their car on the cliff top at Joss Bay. Keith Young and Linda Catt were doing what most courting couples do at such an hour, when suddenly from across the English Channel came a glowing red light. The object, rather to the concern of the canoodling witnesses, then began to head in their direction. However, as the red ball got to within just a few feet, it exploded. The impact was felt by residents some 3 miles away, though, thankfully, the witnesses were not harmed. The *Kentish Express* covered the story and reported how local police had explored the site but could find no wreckage of a crashed plane or any other object. A police spokesperson commented, 'In view of the mysterious nature of the incident we can only log it as an unidentified flying object.' All investigations by local coastguard and the like drew a complete blank. Nick Redfern, however, notes a rather unusual twist to the story: 'Further information obtained by the *Kentish Express* revealed that the Atomic Energy Authority was launching a "full scale investigation" that would possibly involve scientists from the Harwell facility inspecting the scene of the encounter.'

In today's climate, there seems to be a lot of finger pointing at similar operations and military projects with regards to alleged UFO activity. Redfern concludes:

> Whether or not Harwell did have a role to play in this particular episode is still to this day unclear; however, the newspaper learned further that in the days that followed the mysterious event, Atomic Energy Authority personnel 'were busy collecting statements from eye witnesses' in the vicinity.

This incident seemed rather worrying; how many UFO sightings could be put down to covert operations? If such objects are not of alien origin, and cannot be rationally explained, then it leaves a lot of reports suggesting that our authorities are involved in some very strange clandestine operations. It is also fair to say that in some cases, especially the Broadstairs incident, people's lives are being put at risk by those the *Kentish Express* described as 'officers with special responsibility'.

In 1997 another alarming encounter took place, this time at Otter Cove in Devon. Two young men were enjoying an evening swim and decided that, before it got too dark, they would make for the shore, get dressed and go home. One of them suddenly spotted something peculiar out at sea: a green light that appeared to be under the water. The man called to his friend who also saw the light, which had now come to the surface and was shining brightly towards them, to the point where the brightness almost blinded them. With that, the men turned and swam for home.

Things then got even more peculiar, because at around the same time there had been a report on the nearby cliff top of an extremely large cat; not a robust domestic cat, but something resembling a wild animal. But by far the strangest thing about the creature was the fact that it seemed to be illuminated. Even more peculiar was that, at the time, a dead whale had been found on the shore; its carcass intact except for a round incision in the genital area. This bore startling similarities to the cattle mutilations that have plagued farmers and ranchers in the United States, who on a regular basis, particularly in the 1980s and '90s, were finding their cows dead and sporting odd wounds. In most cases the genitals had been removed, but in such an extraordinary surgical manner to suggest that the incision had been made with a tool so advanced as to be unknown in human technology. Investigators at the time surmised that the cattle mutilations were the work of extra-terrestrial visitors, and that the animals had been sucked up into the craft and then operated on – for reasons unknown –then dropped to the ground, only to be found next day completely stiff and harbouring the grisly wounds.

The big problem with this theory, as in the case of so many so-called UFO mysteries, is that we need to prove the existence of such beings before blaming them for such sinister operations. A more preferred theory regarding the mutilations is that the

The Orkney Islands were subjected to eerie activity when a number of decapitated seals turned up on the shore. Some researchers blamed aliens for the grisly deed! (Neil Arnold)

government/military were carrying out such operations to test out their technology. Why mainly cattle would be the culprit is unknown but, especially in the case of the American mutilations, there were often sightings of mysterious black helicopters around the ranches at the time. Another theory put forward is that the cattle are always cut around the mouth and genital/anal area so that the assailants can test levels of possible radiation, or some similar form, in the soil. Whatever the truth, if some terrestrial yet cold-blooded killer is responsible, it would be no doubt more than happy for aliens to be blamed in order to hide its own actions. In the United Kingdom several cases of strange animal deaths have sparked great controversy. Officials who have looked at the carcasses of mutilated animals – ranging from ponies to sheep – concluded that the kills were the result of Devil worshippers or predators. Even so, no one could explain why a whale had turned up on a West Country beach with the same macabre incision as the cattle thousands of miles away. If the military or some secret government group were to blame, what was their objective? Due to the lack of answers, UFO investigators began pointing their wayward fingers at the aliens.

A couple of decades ago, *Wildlife on One* looked into the possibility that released mink were responsible for several strange sheep deaths, which resulted in the carcasses being bereft of head and harbouring a neat puncture wound to the throat. Mink were also held responsible for more than 180 seagull heads found on the Scilly Isles, although it is highly unlikely mink would have swam all that way. It is also worth noting in relation to mysterious mutilations how, on the beaches of the Orkney Islands a few years ago, a great number of seals were found headless; a bizarre string of killings, which, according to UFO researcher and ex-policeman Tony Dodd, 'baffled police and animal welfare officers'. The heads of the seals had been removed with surgical precision, ruling out sharks or killer whales. A member of the Orkney Seal Rescue commented, 'what is baffling, is that in a small community where people usually know what is going on, nobody has come forward with a clue.'

Was there some sinister yet earthly killer on the loose targeting seals, or were those wicked aliens up to no good again? Tony Dodd added, 'It is interesting to note that residents of certain Scottish islands have reported UFOs in the days just prior to the discovery of the seal bodies.' A coincidence? The other peculiar aspect to the story was the fact that around the bodies of the seals there was not a trace of blood, suggesting they had been killed elsewhere and dumped, which also echoes the cattle mutilation saga.

Researcher Nigel Wright, who investigated the case of the whale carcass in Devon, commented:

The first thing that struck me as I looked on at this scene was how perfect the carcass was. There was no decay or huge chunks torn from it. Then, as I wandered around it, I noticed that there was only one external wound: in the area of the genitals, a round incision, the size of a large dinner plate, was cut right into the internal organs of the mammal. The sides of this incision were perfectly formed, as if some giant apple corer had been inserted and twisted around. From the wound hung some of the internal organs. I quizzed the official from English Heritage, who was responsible for the disposal of the carcass. He informed me that no natural predator or boat strike would have caused this wound. As I looked at this sight, the first thing that came into my mind was how this looked just like the cattle mutilation cases of recent times.

Weirder still, it seems that around the same time a fishing boat off Lyme Bay had reported seeing an unusual light. Wright added:

No precise date can be given for the evening when a fishing boat encountered a strange light over Lyme Bay but, since this was told to me by the skipper of the vessel concerned, I can vouch for its authenticity. The vessel in question was five miles off Budleigh Salterton. The crew became aware of a bright, white-blue light which hovered some distance from the boat. At first they thought it was a helicopter but they heard no engine sounds, nor saw any navigation lights.

According to Nick Redfern, 'Wright was told by the captain of the vessel that the night had been "bright and clear" and that if the object had made any noise, it would certainly have been "audible for miles".'

Wright concluded, 'The light remained stationary for about one and a half hours. Judging by the mast of their vessel, which is twenty-eight feet high, the crew estimated that the light was not much higher than that. It then very suddenly disappeared.' After this curious set of incidents the sinister mutilations seemed to escalate, as did the sightings of UFOs, which were investigated by Wright and, along with fellow researcher Jonathan Downes, put into a book called *The Rising of the Moon*.

In the summer of 1997 two people at Braunton saw a 'spherical bright yellow light flying inland from the Bristol Channel' but these type of incidents in Devon were nothing new. The *Exmouth Journal* of 13 October 1951 had reported on a 'flying saucer' seen by several witnesses as it travelled across Exmouth's sea front at 8.30 p.m. on the previous Sunday. The object was described as a cone of brilliant light blue, which vanished into thin air. A week later, however, the newspaper featured a front-page follow-up with the headline, 'Flying saucer was a guided missile'; a secret project built by British scientists and able to travel 'at a speed of 2000 miles per hour'. However, Jonathan Downes in his booklet *UFOs over Devon* was quick to note that 'There is no evidence whatsoever that the British Government claimed the Exmouth sightings were of their guided missile'.

Three years later, two men from Torquay reported seeing fifteen balls of fire over the coast of Babbacombe. A newspaper reporter interviewed the men, who said that they were looking out to sea towards Weymouth when the balls of fire, which were 'orange yellow', climbed very rapidly into the sky. These were confirmed when several witnesses reported to the *Herald Express* that they had also seen the 'fireballs' over the sea. One witness, a chap named Mr Stines, was on the Esplanade at Exmouth when his son told him to look at the round objects floating above the sea. A Mrs Bean told the newspaper that her mother and brother were on the beach at Babbacombe when they, too, saw the balls of light.

The case of the whale beaching, mutilation and general Devonshire phenomena you have just read may sound like a scene from a far-fetched science fiction film, but the fact that such incidents appear numerous throughout Britain's chequered history could well suggest that something very eerie is indeed going on. I'm not sure what's worse: the possibility that alien invaders are visiting our planet and carrying out bizarre experiments; or the other option, that the government/military are hiding behind some mask of deception and doing the dirty deeds themselves; or, as one UFO researcher once told me, 'the horrifying fact that the two are in cohorts ...'. It is clearly something we are never likely to find out, but if you are sceptical then there is clearly nothing to worry about! I am just not sure one should be so completely dismissive over such activity.

An interesting event took place on 26 October 1996 at 4.10 p.m. in the vicinity of Port Ness, Isle of Lewis. A strange object with a smoke-and-fire trail was seen heading across the sky out to sea when it suddenly exploded, the debris descending to the icy waters. Lifeboats quickly arrived on the scene expecting to find the wreckage of

In 1996 a strange object exploded over the Isle of Lewis; the debris dropped into the icy waters. (Glen Vaudrey)

a plane, and yet nothing was to be found. At the time, an RAF spokesperson commented, 'We remain puzzled by what could have caused this.'

Local people and shipping vessels were ordered away from the area by the authorities, who claimed that a navy exercise had taken place; but fishermen were quick to report the swarm of military submarines, ships and aircraft that flocked to the scene of the crash. Rumours spread that the authorities had plucked a mysterious wreckage from the bottom of the sea, and this seemed to coincide with the fact that, four months later, a peculiar substance had washed ashore at Tangusdale Beach. Had a UFO in the truest sense crashed into the sea, or had the fizzing ball of light simply been a meteorite?

On 5 October 1996, police at the seaside town of Skegness reported to the Yarmouth coastguard 'strange red and green rotating lights' over what is known as the Wash. The object was picked up on radar at Kinloss in Scotland; staff reported no aircraft in distress but did contact RAF Neatishead on the Norfolk Broads, who also picked up the 'blip'. It is worth bearing in mind at this point, as researcher Dr David Clarke commented for *Fortean Times* magazine, that 'Neatishead is the most important air defence centre in southern England', so it would seem that operators were hardly people prone to flights of fancy regarding alien space craft.

The UFO, or whatever it was, had appeared stationary over Boston and did not emit a signal in response to radar query as an aircraft would have. Before anyone could get excited about the prospect of a flying saucer hovering above the town, rumours were quashed due to the fact that the object had remained in the same position until the next day – some nine hours later. Afterwards, several investigations controllers came to the conclusion that the object had simply been a 'permanent echo', which, as Mr Clarke stated, was 'generated by ground features like tall buildings' such as the almost 300ft-high Boston Stump (better known as St Botolph's church spire). But it didn't explain another blip that had been picked up on radar at RAF Waddington in Lincolnshire, or the fact that crew from a tanker, the MV *Conocast*, had seen unusual lights over the North Sea. The lights were described as stationary; red, blue, white and green; and flashing; which had appeared from the early hours until dawn.

Despite all the fuss, the police officers who had seen the peculiar lights came to the conclusion that they had in fact observed a star! PC Dave Leyland filmed the object from the police force control room – it was white in colour and didn't move. Surely a white, twinkling object in the sky that remains stationary will always be a star unless it suddenly vanishes or speeds away? How could so many people be confusing natural phenomena with alien spacecraft? The Royal Greenwich Observatory commented that on that particular night the planet Venus has been extremely bright; the strange rotating lights of varying colours were explained by astronomer Ian Ridpath as Sirius, the brightest star; while the lights seen by the crew of the tanker were said to have been Vega, another star. However, as David Clarke added, '... these mundane explanations came far too late to kill the excitement the sightings had generated,' especially as the 'UFO' sightings had been made by credible witnesses such as police officers. UFO researchers quickly commented that there was no way stars could be suggested to explain the sightings, as surely these stars would be there most of the time!

In March of 1965 the 70-ton trawler *Star of Freedom* collided with an unidentified object, which the captain believed was a surfacing submarine. The boat had been travelling 15 miles east of the island of Barra when its bows were lifted from the water, leaving a hole that the crew tended to once they beached at Castlebay harbour. The *Daily Mail* covered the story, mentioning the peculiar twist that skipper George Wood was convinced a submarine had been to blame, despite the fact British and American naval authorities stated, quite categorically, that their submarines were not present at the time.

Two years previous, as reported in the *Northern Echo* of 22 November 1963, 'The Aberdeen collier *Thrift* arrived in Blyth at noon yesterday eight hours overdue after an unsuccessful search off Girdle Ness for a mystery object which disappeared into the sea three miles astern of the ship.' According to the report, the boat had been heading south before 6 p.m. when the captain and three other crew members observed a flashing red light, which passed port side within a mile of the ship and only 30ft above the sea before disappearing 'three mile astern'.

The captain of the *Thrift* manoeuvred the ship towards where the light had been seen and, despite the fact two objects were detected on the radar, a three-hour search proved unproductive. A Shackleton from RAF Kinloss and several lifeboats were called into action to aid the collier but again, despite several flares being sent up to illuminate the area, there was no sign of the red light or any wreckage. The most peculiar aspect of the sighting, according to the ship's captain, was that '… it made no noise at all, yet we could hear the Shackleton when it was miles away. It seems that whatever was there must have sunk before we could get to it.'

One of the most fascinating books to look at the underwater UFO angle was written by Peter Paget, entitled *The Welsh Triangle*. This book, published in 1979, covered bouts of high aerial strangeness recorded from an isolated stretch of Welsh coastline – Pembrokeshire to be precise – and also suggested that the extra-terrestrials involved were inhabiting an underwater base at Stack Rocks. At the time, Paget was an editor for a leading UFO magazine, and was very much of the opinion that the newspaper reports being written about the recent Welsh saucer flap were nothing more than journalistic exaggeration. But the more Peter delved into the mystery, the stranger things became. It all seemed to begin in 1977 when several witnesses came forward to report seeing unusual aerial phenomena around the Bristol Channel. Some witnesses described weird planks of light; others metal cigar-shaped objects. Were all the witnesses hallucinating or simply misidentifying terrestrial craft? And so the activity spiralled out of control, with opinion that some of the old smugglers' caves littered along the St Brides Bay area were in fact secret bases; or maybe, just maybe, these hidden places were being used by the military rather than those pesky, slim-lined,

In the 1970s the Pembrokeshire coastline was rumoured to conceal alien bases. (Simon Wyatt)

bug-eyed beings. Either way, witnesses began to report silver-suited humanoids emerging from hidden doors in some of the rock faces. Two witnesses, named Billy and Pauline, told Paget that they had seen a disc-like craft near the rocks and that 'twice they had watched the strange craft actually dive underwater close to the rocks and not reappear'. Paget also interviewed a number of scuba divers from the area, who told him of many deep-sea caves along the coastline. One diver had a slightly stranger story and reported that, in certain areas beneath the sea, strange humming noises had been heard.

Paget, who had mapped several possible flight paths of such craft, commented, 'West Wales is important, because it is on a particular orbital path that crosses not only the United Kingdom but most of Scandinavia, the majority of the Soviet Union and South America.' In other words, a UFO in Wales, travelling beyond the capability of a terrestrial craft, could easily end up on the other side of the world within minutes. But surely tales of secret alien bases were laughable? Not so. In 2010 a Shrewsbury-based UFO group, calling itself the UFO Investigations and Research Unit, told the *Bangor & Anglesey Mail* that Puffin Island, situated to the east of Anglesey, was a hot-bed of UFO activity and that 'Many witnesses, some ex-military and professional people, have witnessed unconventional lights entering or leaving the sea around Puffin Island'. There are strong echoes here of Peter Paget's investigations. Mr Phil Hoyle, who ran the investigative group, claimed that the unusual sightings began in January 1974 when a group of witnesses reported seeing a large, structured craft emerging from the sea. The most incredible detail, however – so Hoyle claimed – was that alien abduction victims, when interviewed, stated they had been taken by humanoids from Puffin Island.

If tales of unidentified flying objects are not enough to move your sceptical soul, then reports of alleged alien abductions will most certainly rattle your cage. Alleged witnesses claim that whilst sleeping in their beds or driving their cars, or even walking in their local woods, they are able to be abducted by aliens. In most cases, abductions take place at night and the witness will describe seeing a bright, blinding light and the next minute finding themselves on board a spaceship occupied by spindly figures with large black eyes and bulbous heads. In a majority of cases, witnesses report being strapped to a bed or table and being probed by the aliens, who have been known to insert microchips into the victim's body to track their movements; or extract from them bodily fluids; or in some, more extreme cases involving women, to remove a foetus. Of course, none of these claims can be verified, and one wonders if such witnesses are prone to terrible nightmares akin to the classic night terrors known as sleep paralysis. Alien abduction seems to be quite a modern phenomenon, although when regressed some victims claim that such extra-terrestrial probing has been going on for many decades, if not centuries.

On 24 February 1975 a man was walking his dog on the East Anglian coast in the vicinity of Sizewell power station (Sizewell, don't forget, has already been mentioned this chapter when the fishermen observed a UFO), when a greenish light approached from the sea. The object came to within a few feet of the stunned witness, who reported a 'warm and tingly feeling' and a pungent acidic odour. The man's dog was cowering behind him and then, in terror, fled the area, only to be found an hour later a mile or so away. This type of incident echoes so many others in that witnesses, in whatever situation, describe seeing a bright light but often claim to have lost time, or to have found themselves away from the area they first saw the object.

For example, on 17 August 1995 a man residing at Westcliff-on-Sea in Kent dozed off to sleep at around midnight and woke with a start at 3 a.m. At first he thought he may have been disturbed by a noise, but upon searching the house realised he must have dreamt it. After several failed attempts to fall back to sleep, he decided to go downstairs for a cigarette and watch a bit of television. The man still felt rather uncomfortable and had the nagging feeling that he had been awoken by a noise; he was determined to find the cause of the problem but again found nothing. Eventually he came back into the living room where his attention was drawn to a light outside the window operating as a searchlight would. Immediately the man jumped to the conclusion that the police were out, but there was no noise of a car or helicopter and so he decided to look out the window, which overlooked streets leading to the sea. He could not now see any lights but his curiosity got the better of him and he decided to take a proper look outside, and so put some jogging bottoms and a jacket on.

Once outside he could see no sign of the light and so walked down to the sea, when suddenly the light reappeared over the sea wall. The man quickly went into a sprint and headed towards the light but the next minute he was waking up with a pounding headache. He said:

> I couldn't open my eyes at first, but I could feel the heat of the lights. It was the talking I noticed first. It was just a quiet mumbling interrupted by a high pitched clicking. I opened my eyes and the light blasted into them, I tried to cover my face but my hands were tied.

That's when he started to panic and in his anxious state began to swear aggressively, demanding to be released; but the dozen or so figures he saw around him did not listen. One of the figures, which had a large head and narrow eyes, smothered the man's face and the next moment he came to, lying on the sand at Westcliff-on-Sea with the sun about to break through the clouds:

> All I did then was run home … My keys were still in my pocket and I let myself in, not knowing what the hell had happened. The first thing I did when I got in was to check myself over. Although I appeared to be in an alright state, my eyes were very bloodshot. I had been out of my flat for just over two hours.

The next few days for the victim were spent in a trance-like state and eventually, with time passing, he was able to wrench himself from the horror of that night. But still, to this day he cannot make any sense of what happened to him on the beach.

One of the most peculiar attempted abduction cases comes from the year 1912, and was first documented in 1937 by author Alasdair Alpin MacGregor. Two young brothers were playing on the coastline of the Island Of Muck – the smallest of four main islands in the Small Isles, which form part of the Inner Hebrides – when they noticed a strange boat approaching the shore. On board the boat were two beings dressed in green attire accompanied by a tiny, rat-sized dog. The beings seemed very friendly and spoke to the boys in both English and Gaelic, and offered them some bread, which the youngsters took and ate. The figures in green then told the boys that they had to go and asked them if they would like to come with them, but the youngsters declined. The entities then told the boys that similar beings would come in the future and to wait at the water's edge and watch the boat until it reached a certain spot out at sea, and only then could they go home. The boys stood and watched until the mysterious boat and its even stranger occupants disappeared in the distance. Shortly afterwards the boys' sister came to the beach and saw her brothers standing, in a trance-like state, staring at the empty sea.

This is a rather creepy, or to some comical story that seems like the work of pure fiction; but it also does not seem too dissimilar to the Westcliff-on-Sea case. The odd detail of the case was the offering from the green men of bread to the boys, which

Inner Hebrides – in 1937 two young boys had a bizarre encounter at the Isle of Muck.
(Glen Vaudrey)

may have put them in the trance. I find this incredible story a little hard to swallow
but fascinating all the same, especially the almost eerie quality of the boat's occupants who, although appearing benign, seemed keen to transport the boys to some
faraway place for goodness knows what. This case reminds me of the Christmas Day
1945 encounter, which took place on the west coast of Scotland and involved a man
who was waiting on the shore for a boat during a furious snowstorm, when a metallic dome descended from the sky and perched itself on the waves. The witness stood
stunned as the vessel lifted and, to the soundtrack of its own drill-like whir, made its
way to a nearby field and crushed two cows as it landed. Two beings dressed in black,
rubber-like suits emerged from the vehicle: one of them walked out into the sea and
placed a phial; whilst the other humanoid, in true sci-fi fashion, blasted a nearby cow
with a ray-gun, zapping it dead with a red beam. This disturbed a dog belonging to
a local farmer, but when the dog began to bark at the entity it became hypnotised
and then, in a trance-like state, ambled on board the craft. It was then reported that
several more craft appeared over the sea accompanied by a strange mist, which the
beings and craft floated into. One of the beings looked back at the startled witness
and waved at him as the craft disappeared. The farmer came to the witness's aid and,
although bereft of his dog, warned the man not to speak of his encounter.

In 1998 a Mr Kevin Round took a series of startling photographs of an arrow-
shaped object over the Bristol Channel. Mr Round had been walking along the

coastline of Brean Down with his partner when they saw the UFO, which flew overhead and then became stationary over the sea. The photographs, which are relatively clear, show the silvery-grey object at a distance of approximately half a mile. Kevin reported, 'I saw no method of propulsion and it made no noise, except for a low-pitched hum, like an electric transformer.' The witness did not jump to conclusions that it was an alien spacecraft, but theorised that maybe it had been some type of smart missile undergoing trials. The photographs appeared in the March/April 1999 issue of *UFO Magazine*, who commented that the object could be 'an unusual and dynamic aeroform' possibly being 'test-flown by the Ministry of Defence or one of its principal aerospace benefactors'.

In the January of 2003 one Richard Thomas had a UFO sighting over the Bristol Channel. Richard was with his father and younger brother at the time and travelling along Mumbles Road in Swansea Bay, when they stopped at a traffic light. Richard looked at the cloudless sky and saw an object, which at first he thought must have been an aeroplane but which, rather bizarrely, was moving up and down. Richard pointed the object out to his father and brother, and they watched it for a short time before it completely vanished into thin air.

In February 1961 a handful of newspapers mentioned an extraordinary incident that took place on the 27th of the month, out at sea between the Inner and Outer Hebrides. Harold Harrison, skipper of the Fleetwood trawler *Boston Gannet* described an object that billowed smoke, 'corkscrewed' over his boat and then crashed into the sea. A search of the area between Lewis and Harris, which involved three ships and a plane, revealed no trace of the craft. Four years later, in the same month, two RAF helicopters, a Shackleton and a lifeboat were called out to investigate a 'ghost plane', which had plummeted into the sea on the North Devon coast at Minehead. A witness, one of four who first saw the 'plane', reported that it 'was so unusual that it attracted our attention. There was definitely something abnormal about it. It did not seem to be distinct, but had a misty appearance, yet there was no mist or fog about.' The 'plane', or whatever it was, soared only 100ft above the ground and made no noise before heading out to sea.

In the August of 1965 a grey, misty ball-like object was seen off the coast of Eastbourne, in Sussex. The strange craft skimmed across the surface of the sea and at 10 p.m. the inshore rescue boat conducted a search of the area after someone observed a 'long white object' that was floating above the water, but as usual nothing untoward was found. This odd sighting has echoes of a similar incident from the 1950s, when a round, flying object was reported as skimming up a stream towards the Solway Firth. The UFO caused a splash and then zipped upwards out of sight.

A further fascinating account of strange objects being seen out at sea comes from the files of the *Australian Saucer Record* of 1956. The publication recorded that in 1954 a submarine commander had seen 'flying saucers' floating on the sea 11 miles off Lundy Island, on the north Devon coast. The commander, a gentleman named Captain

In 1965 a peculiar object was seen skimming over the sea at Sussex. (Terry Cameron)

Chelwan, told his admiral of his experience. The files that contained the reports were eventually confiscated, with Chelwan being told that the information may be released at a later date and that the sighting had to be treated as a military secret. It seems, however, that before all the cover-up, a newspaper had heard about the incident and interviewed Captain Chelwan who in his account stated that 'two discs' first thought to be the sun reflecting off the water, had been seen floating on the sea. Another crew member had been alongside Chelwan and vouched for the authenticity of the sighting; both men stating that the objects were 'shaped like a disc slightly elevated in the middle and had no windows, portholes, or other apertures. The elevated middle portion was stationary, but the flat outside portion, surrounding the middle portion like a collar, rotated slowly on the water.'

The most startling aspect of the sighting was the size of the objects, which the commander estimated at some 100ft across, and although the sighting only lasted for half a minute the objects were viewed through binoculars. The discs emitted a buzzing noise, which heightened as the experience wore on until they rose from the water to a height of approximately 300ft and zipped away at an estimated 2,000mph. As they zoomed off into the distance the captain could see they were surrounded by a reddish glow.

The big question now is: where are those records the admiral confiscated all those years ago?

Interestingly, a year after the Lundy Island sighting there was a report of an orange ball of light seen plunging into the sea off Cardiganshire in Wales. Suddenly, those weird cases investigated by author Peter Paget don't seem that uncanny after all. On this occasion, the object was seen on 24 March 1955 at 7.15 p.m. and moved erratically on its flight path. A lady and her daughter saw the spectacular object, which had a zigzag movement about it and a black smoke trail behind it. When the orange ball crashed into the sea, the glow of it could still be observed from where the two witnesses were standing. Some researchers believe that the witnesses saw a meteor but, rather oddly, on the same night there were similar reports from Newcastle, Devon, Glasgow, Shropshire and Staffordshire.

In the October of 1955 an object of blue/white colouration emitting a blazing red trail was observed by fishermen at Mevagissey on Cornwall's south coast. As the object struck the sea it made a sizzling noise, as sometimes reported in meteorite accounts.

It would be nigh-on impossible, and incredibly time-consuming, to list every British UFO sighting that has taken place over the sea (and that's without mentioning the cases involving strange craft seen over rivers, reservoirs, streams, lochs and lakes), as it is such a vast body of water. But I hope that those stories I have included have shown you that there is something very strange going on. As stated earlier, the seas of Britain are not as active as, say, the salt waters around Italy or the United States regarding UFO activity, but peculiar sightings do occur. When thumbing through my files I found literally hundreds of cases of strange lights being seen, ranging from the coasts of Folkestone and Dover in Kent, Clacton-on-Sea in Essex, Eastbourne and St Leonard's-on-Sea in Sussex to Cromer in Norfolk, and the list goes on; from the south of England to the most northerly stretches of Scotland. I'd like to finish this chapter, however, with a short mention of spook lights. I often ask the question, when is a UFO not a UFO? I think that over the decades a majority of people have come to the conclusion that the term UFO applies to an extra-terrestrial spaceship, but this isn't really the case. UFOs can vary in size, shape and colour; they can appear as tiny pin-pricks of light or vast ships, but the term UFO is so loose that any unexplained light can fit into this bracket. The ghost-hunters of today often speak of orbs, which they believe are the first form of a spirit. This has been dismissed by scientists who have proved that, in the digital camera age, lens flare has caused much of the phenomenon, but what about those eerie coastal flares and will-o'-the-wisps seen out at sea with the naked eye?

SPOOK LIGHTS

Spook lights have been mentioned in folklore for more than a century but not all of the reports are confined to the distant past; for instance, on 14 October 1974 the *Sunday Mirror* reported on the 'ghost SOS flares' seen off the Kent coast. On several occasions lifeboats, inshore rescue teams and coastguards were called out after distress flares were seen over the Channel, but when the crews reached the location there was no sign of any person or boat. Police began investigating the reports, thinking that smugglers had been operating elsewhere on the coast and sending out flares to divert authorities away from their nightly rendezvous. A Dungeness lifeboat coxswain named Tom Tart commented at the time:

> On both times we were called out last month, visibility was perfect, but we never found trace of anyone in distress. The danger is that while we are chasing mystery flares, there will be a genuine disaster and we shall not be able to cope with it.

The distractions had distinct echoes of those smugglers from many years previous, who would tie 'phantom lights' to the legs of horses and cows to divert the course of ships. A spokesman from the Department of Trade and Industry stated, 'Some of the recent calls cannot be explained … they are a mystery.'

More coastal flares were reported from Skegness earlier in 1974. As stated previously, Skegness had a UFO flap in the '90s, which was explained as a false echo; but the peculiar flares seen on the Wash on 30 April were very much moving objects. They were subsequently investigated by the local lifeboat service, who could find no trace of anyone or thing when they arrived at the spot. Much of the activity focused on the Lynwell area of Skegness. A coastguard spokesman believed the lights had been part of a flash-bomb exercise carried out by the RAF – but what about the coastal flares seen at Norfolk on 16 July of the same year? Again, lifeboat crews were called out and they patrolled the sea whilst police and coastguards waited on shore. After a two-hour search the authorities concluded it must have been a hoax; but the lights were definitely there, for some of the red objects were seen by coastguard Brian Coleman.

Peculiarly, just days later, a similar set of mystery lights appeared off Souter Point lighthouse in Northumberland and, again, a two-hour search found nothing. Stranger still, a majority of the locations where such 'flares' were being reported coincided with areas of reputed UFO activity. For example, areas of the Welsh coast have been plagued by the lights for several decades; Anglesey and Dyfed, in Wales – both notorious UFO hot spots – have similarly been plagued by phantom lights for many years; and Haverfordwest, in Dyfed, was at the centre of a fireball frenzy in the mid-1970s, despite the fact that radar screens at RAF Bawdy could not detect anything untoward.

In his excellent work *The Ghost Book*, Alasdair Alpin MacGregor devotes a whole chapter to 'phantom lights'; many having been seen throughout Britain but not just over the sea. From lochs, rivers and streams to inside houses, ghost lights seem to be everywhere, but are they all and one the same thing? For example, in one case from the Isle of Skye there is a report of a doctor who, while staying at a public house in Broadford, decided one evening to go for a stroll along the shore. Upon arrival the

The coast of the Isle of Skye – haunt of a ghostly light. (Stuart Paterson)

doctor noticed a bright light hanging in the air over the sea and at first thought it to be some sort of flare released by local fishermen. After staring at the light for a few seconds, the doctor then realised the light was moving smoothly towards the shore. Within a few seconds, the mysterious orb reached the shore where the tide had begun to lap but was suddenly extinguished, then, for a split second in its place, appeared the figure of a woman holding a baby. To his astonishment the ghostly lady ran across the beach and then vanished into thin air.

This particular account proves how some mysterious lights can flit between vary-ing phenomena, in this case as a UFO at first, followed by some type of spectre. The doctor was so intrigued by what he'd seen that he spoke to the inn-keeper about it and was told that, a few years previously, a ship had run aground on that exact spot of the shore and a woman and child had been killed. So, suddenly, a possible UFO story becomes a potential ghost story and also melts into ghost ship folklore, too.

The Island of Lewis has long been considered a place of high strangeness where phantom lights are seen regularly by those on board ships. One particular place on the isle is said to be haunted by an Irish pedlar who was murdered, and his spirit is said to take the form of a glowing light. The maritime village of Sandwick in Stornoway also has a weird spectral light story attached to it. Many years ago now, a group of young boys were playing on a marshy area when they came across what they at first took to be a log. As they pushed the log into the water a flare seemed to spring from nowhere and illuminate the area.

It seems that a majority of spook lights are confined to isolated spots. For instance, MacGregor speaks of a man named Mr Millar who resided at Wick, 'in distant Caithness'. Mr Millar would often visit relatives who lived 'at the seaward end of the village of Latheronwheel', and one New Year's Eve the villagers had been unnerved by the appearance of a strange light, which nobody could explain. The following day, a terrible storm arose and two boats were engulfed at sea, never to be seen again. When the storm had passed, villagers visited the cliff top in the hope of finding the dead on the beach below. Indeed, in the exact spot where the light had been observed, lay the body of a man. Local men managed to climb down to the water and hoist the broken body of the victim up the cliff. Further examinations revealed that the corpse was of a young fisherman from Lybster. From then on, every time the light appeared over the sea locals would cower in fear, awaiting the next calamity.

Why so many phantom lights have been recorded from the highlands and islands of Scotland we will probably never know, but they seem to act more as portents rather than alien craft. 'Ghost lights are likewise seen on shieling sites in the island of Harris,' writes MacGregor. Harris is the southern and more mountainous part of Lewis and Harris, but although many people call it such, it is not strictly an island. In 1944 many locals of Harris ventured out into the darkness in order to pursue a ghostly light,

Harris – the haunt of coastal lights. (Glen Vaudrey)

which would always vanish as they reached its apparent location. MacGregor added, 'A couple of scientists holidaying in the locality immediately suggested marsh gas, but this explanation did not go down too well with the islanders.'

The township of Manish has also been haunted by a spectral light, known over the years as the Manish Light. The form is said to travel for miles, sticking to the rocky outcrops of the rugged coasts. The village of Kilberry, situated on the western coast of the district of Knapdale, is another settlement with a weird spook light story attached to it. One night, a man named Mr MacArthur, his brother and a friend had been fishing at Tiretigan Point, situated on the Kilberry shore, but due to the blackness of the night the men got separated from each other. Mr MacArthur decided that he would take a shortcut and wait by a roadside gate, in the hope that the other two would soon turn up. As Mr MacArthur looked across Carse Bay he saw an eerie light, which drifted down the pathway, disappeared behind some trees, then re-emerged at a spot where a man was said to have drowned a short time after.

In the Morven district there is said to be a remote spot on the north shore haunted by an eerie light. In 1933 a couple were walking along an isolated path when they saw a light, which resembled a lantern, hanging in mid-air. Seconds later the light burst, expressing vivid colours before fizzing away. Ghost lights have also been reported from Scapa Flow, the Orkney Islands, the coast of Mull, and also at the resort of Oban within the Argyll and Bute area.

Fairy lights, corpse candles, jack o'lanterns, graveyard lights, spook lights *et al*; it doesn't matter what you call them because, like UFOs, ball lightning and other anomalous glows, orbs and spheres, they all play their part in an increasingly complex puzzle that has baffled mankind for centuries. Whether all these mysteries are connected is something we can only guess at and debate. Dennis Bardens, in his book *Ghosts and Haunting*, illustrates this point of confusion when he mentions 'A traditional Welsh ghost called Cyhyraeth', which takes on the form of a spectral light but also emits mournful moans and ghastly shrieks. There are also reports along Britain's coastlines, particularly from Norfolk and Suffolk, of eerie lights that transform into the spectral form of a ghastly black dog, which goes by varying names, the most well known being 'Black Shuck'.

Just like spook lights, the appearance of a hellhound is said to presage a death. For several centuries these shaggy-haired, fiery-eyed dogs of death have been reported, but they, like the spook lights and UFOs, are not confined to coastal areas. Like many supernatural manifestations they have no limits to their territory and often appear to lonely travellers. On occasion they have even been known to burst into a ball of fire or vanish into thin air, leaving behind a sulphuric odour.

It has long been theorised that UFOs are living creatures, and not some sort of metallic, alien-made craft, but each theory put forward is simply another ingredient in the cauldron of mystery. Whatever these coastal anomalies are, it is not confirmed if it takes a certain type of person to trigger them, or if they loiter in dark places all the

The Norfolk coastline – where ghost lights and demonic black dogs roam. (Joyce Goodchild)

time, waiting for an unsuspecting coastguard, pilot or fisherman to spot them. Perhaps they are completely without motive, but instead something that we have a need to classify: so when a light is seen in the same location of a shipwreck or a death, we immediately connect the two. I'm of the opinion that we should not attempt to solve the riddle, because somehow the supernatural realm has a tendency to lead us on a merry dance until we find ourselves going round in circles in our quest for the truth; a truth that is never likely to be found.

Whilst it is important to present these types of uncanny events, I can only leave them for you to judge, because I gave up trying to pigeon-hole these esoteric forms many years ago. There's no denying we all love a good mystery, but when we consider that we know more about the moon than the frothing seas of our own planet, it should give us a good idea as to how unfathomable these mysteries are. And now for another set of coastal anomalies …

4

GHOSTS ON THE COAST AND OTHER MYSTERIES

One of my favourite horror films of all time is John Carpenter's atmospheric 1980s classic *The Fog*. I'm not a fan of more recent horror films, preferring the almost low-budget quality of the older flicks. If you've not seen *The Fog*, then I'll give you a brief plot outline. Basically, a small coastal town in California is invaded by a sinister fog, which just so happens to bring with it a horde of ghostly mariners who perished in a shipwreck a century previous. The undead take to the night adorned in seaweed and armed with fishing hooks as their chosen weapons, and begin bumping off the locals until an ancient curse is lifted.

For me, *The Fog* is a real spine-chiller and certainly the movie that inspired me to write this book. After watching the movie again I felt the need to cover stories pertaining to sightings of ghosts among the waves and on haunted coastlines, cliffs and beaches. Ghoulish fishermen, ghostly seamen and even the occasional spectral smuggler wouldn't seem out of place in the 1980s film, and I doubt they would seem out of place here amongst those spooky ships: so enjoy this selection of some of my favourite coastal ghosts.

SHADOWS ON THE SEA

The following story is one so strange that I'm sure it will give you nightmares, should you think about it too much! Just before the outbreak of the First World War, supreme ghost-hunter Elliott O'Donnell went for a spot of fishing off an islet at Dalkey, a seaside resort in County Dublin. The day had been relatively productive with fish active around the bay, and so even as the evening drew in and the weather worsened to a heavy drizzle, Elliott stuck to his task at hand. Then, suddenly, there seemed to be an eerie silence; a strange atmosphere that appeared to affect the fish, who were no longer frequenting the water. Elliott felt frozen to the spot, consumed by horror and

A ghostly sailor looks out to sea. (Illustration by Neil Arnold)

paralysed with fear. Looking out to sea, Elliott then saw a weird circular glow, yellow-greenish in colour, which became brighter and brighter. Within it, a seething mass of bubbles and churning began, when suddenly a whirlpool appeared, swirling hard around a black hole in the centre.

Elliott knew that he had to get away from this place but something forced him to stare at this turbulence, and soon his eyes were met by another set of eyes, staring blankly from the middle of the foam. The ogling eyes then formed within a face; a face Elliott recognised as belonging to a dear friend who had drowned at sea. Elliott managed to blink, hoping that the ghastly image would fade, but it remained there at sea, swirling and growing until, what seemed like hours later, the face began to fade, disappearing beneath the waves, leaving Elliott horror-struck and calling out to the boatman who had taken him to the islet.

Elliott sat in the boat wondering why the entity had appeared to him. He asked the boatman if he knew of any extraordinary experiences that had taken place at the spot. 'Every year on this day at about this time,' the boatman whispered, 'us Irishmen that is –

who are destined at some time or another to die unnatural deaths, see the spirits of the drowned.' Elliott ran cold all over, the image of the face now embedded in his memory.

Many years ago in 1873, a fisherman named Ranold – a widower – was working on a fishing boat at South Uist when he was given the task to keep night watch. As the night grew long, Ranold began to drift off to sleep and slipped into a deep dream. In it, he heard the voice of his deceased wife shout, 'Ranold, Ranold, dear Ranold, get up quickly and kindle your light. If you do not do so immediately you will be all lost!' With that, Ranold leapt to his feet, just in time to see a large ship approaching on the waves. He hastily lit a candle and, to his relief, the ship managed to see the signal and alter its course. Otherwise, Ranold's boat would have been smashed to smithereens.

In the Western Isles there is a ghost story that concerns a man named Allan Campbell, who was the son of a Stornoway merchant. According to author Francis Thompson, 'One morning in the spring of 1786 he left Stornoway to go to the island of Scalpay to see his betrothed, Annie, and to go through the ceremony of the marriage contract with her.' However, Allan did not expect to be hit by a raging storm that eventually destroyed the boat, killing all on board including himself. A few days after, Annie Campbell, in such a state of grief, killed herself. Her body was put into a coffin and loaded onto a ship for burial at the southern tip of Harris. However, as in the case of Allan's boat, a storm raged on this journey, too, and the coffin fell overboard and disappeared among the waves. Those who were present reported that they had seen

The Western Isles have several sea-related ghost stories. (Glen Vaudrey)

the spectre of Allan take the coffin. Later it was found out that this place in the sea was the spot where Allan had perished. Days later Annie was found, at the exact location where her lover had died.

There is another Scottish tale concerning a sailor who murdered his love, for some unknown reason, and in order to evade arrest joined the crew of a ship due to set sail for a port on the other side of the world. It seems, however, that the Scotsman could not escape his deceased wife. One night whilst at sea he spotted a strange light in the distance that was approaching the boat. He called the other crew members to ask if they could see it and they confirmed they could, but as the form rose to meet the boat it took the shape of a woman with golden hair wearing a white gown. The spectre came aboard the boat and accused the man of killing her. The man stood, eyes popping from his sockets, as she took his hand and dragged him overboard into the waves.

One story of note, which brings to mind those escapades involving phantom flares, was reported on by the *Sunday Mirror* of 5 August 1973. A man named Derek Vine, an experienced coastguard, was looking through his binoculars over Eastdean, at Eastbourne in Sussex, when he spotted a man facing the cliff with the waves lapping at his feet. Derek gave his binoculars to a police officer who confirmed that the man was there, and so two coastguards and a lifeboat were called in to action. When they arrived at the spot, however, there was no one to be found. The odd thing about the report was that the location the man was seen at was considered 'un-climbable'. For Derek, this observation proved embarrassing, especially when the theory of a ghost was put forward. He commented, 'An Excise man was lured to death by smugglers in the eighteenth century …'. Maybe this had been the same man, treading cautiously among the rocks before being swallowed by the waves.

On a more surreal note, on the night of 28 October 1988 a trawler off Dorset contacted the local coastguard to report that his vessel had been covered in a peculiar, sticky substance resembling a cloud of candyfloss! After the boat passed through the weird haze, the crew reported that the apparition had continued northwards. The coastal candyfloss was said to have measured some 30 square miles!

PHANTOM FISHERMEN

During the 1990s there was a fascinating case of a haunting involving a man named John who lived in Plymouth on the south coast of Devon. By day John was a taxi driver, but he also believed himself to have a psychic ability. One evening, at 5 p.m., John walked into his kitchen and was met by a very strong fishy smell. At first he thought that maybe there was something gone off in the fridge or there had been a problem with the drains but, rather strangely, this smell would only waft into the room at 5 p.m. each day. Just to check he wasn't imagining things, John asked his two children and several friends if they, too, could smell the fish; and they could.

One weekend a neighbour of John's named Peter was asked to look after the house whilst John enjoyed a short break away. He too reported the pungent odour. Eventually, John confided in a friend called Mandy who suggested that he get in touch with a contact of hers named Peter Bower, a spiritualist medium. Mr Bower told John that he would be happy to help and said he would come round one evening at 7 p.m. At this time on the arranged night, John and Mandy were sat waiting for Peter's arrival when there was a knock at the door. John went to answer it but there was nobody there. Minutes later the door was knocked again but, once more, there was no one to be seen. Mandy believed that the knock had been made by the phantom that had somehow caused the fishy smell and so, rather bizarrely, decided to 'invite' the spectre in. Mandy opened the door and welcomed the invisible presence, which was accompanied by a strong smell of fish that wafted over to a chair, suggesting the present spectre had indeed sat down.

Shortly afterwards, Peter Bowers arrived at John's house and confirmed that there was a spirit present. He said that it was a man, approximately 60 years of age, short in stature, and with grey hair and a miserable expression. The ghost gave his name as James Goldsworthy and gave the date of 1759. According to Mr Bowers, James had been a fish merchant who would walk from the shore, collecting fish, and take them to sell in the village. His route at the time would have taken him through where John's kitchen now sat! Mr Bowers believed the phantom was somehow trapped and so opened some type of spiritual vortex for him to move on to the light. The stench was never experienced again.

At Sleat in Skye there is a ghost story pertaining to a phantom fisherman. Many years ago a lady had recently been made a widow and was in some distress that her husband had not left her any money. One night as the woman dozed off to sleep, she was awoken by a thunderstorm. By the light of a thunder bolt, she then saw the door open and her husband walk in. The ghost strolled across the room towards the fireplace and then mimed removing a certain brick, before bidding his wife farewell and vanishing. Minutes later, the woman went to the spot and tried several of the bricks until she found a loose one and removed it. Within the wall cavity she found her husband's life savings.

There is an incredibly weird little tale of a spectral fisherman from East Sussex. At some point in the 1800s it was said that a fisherman resided in Hastings, but he was not your average man. It is claimed that he sold his soul to Satan in order to gain supernatural powers. These powers would enable him to turn into wisps of smoke in order to enter a room via the keyhole!

Another tale of a phantom fisherman comes from an undisclosed location somewhere in Britain. The spectre was witnessed by three teenage boys who, one afternoon to relieve their boredom, took a stroll down to their local beach. When they reached the shore the boys sat on the rocks to rest and chat when they suddenly heard a man shouting. The boys looked across the beach and noticed out at sea a man waving his

Skye – haunt of a ghostly fisherman! (Stuart Paterson)

arms as if drowning. As the tide rushed in it brought the man ashore, and so the boys ran towards him – only to see him stand up and stare into space. The boys questioned him, asking him if he was okay, and they noticed he was dressed like a fisherman and that his garments were quite tatty. Suddenly there came from behind them several voices and so the boys all looked round, but when they glanced back at the man he had completely vanished. Strangely, there were no footprints on the sand to suggest that anyone apart from the boys had been there. A few seconds later a lady, who had been shouting, appeared on the horizon and came down to the beach to speak to the boys. They asked her whether she'd seen the fisherman but she replied in the negative, stating that the reason she had shouted was to warn them away from the water's edge.

On 12 February 2012 the *Daily Mail* newspaper ran the headline, 'The ghost on the locked pier', after a student photographer named Matthew Hales claimed he had snapped a mysterious figure on Clevedon Pier in Somerset. The photo was taken at 6.45 a.m., a time when the pier was locked off to the public. Some believe the ghost could well be that of a fisherman, and over the years the man has appeared to some of the anglers who have taken to the pier, which overlooks the sea. Peculiarly, the newspaper article stated that fishermen were allowed on the pier twenty-four hours a day and seven days a week, which would suggest that the man in the photo was nothing more than a flesh-and-blood angler, rather than a ghost. A month later paranormal investigator Richard Case, a former special policeman, was featured on the website thisissomerset.co.uk, claiming to have experienced spectral mists and eerie voices on the pier, but a majority of anglers didn't seem convinced by the vague reports.

SPECTRAL SAILORS AND SEAMEN

Cornwall and Devon have many coastal ghosts and one of my favourite tales concerns James Bottrell, who as a young man served aboard a privateer. He was often haunted by the apparition of a shipmate who had drowned at sea. It began one stormy night: James had settled down at home to sleep but a few hours later he was awoken by three loud knocks on his window. As James looked up he saw the pale, miserable, drenched ghost of his comrade John Jones; within a minute or so the figure faded.

When James woke the next day he tried to convince himself that the wraith had been a nightmare, but every night as he dropped off to sleep, again the ghost would come, staying longer each time. During the day James tried to sleep, knowing full well that the spectre would come at night, but even then, by the light of an afternoon, the house was plagued by weird occurrences: unexplained noises and fleeting shadows. James became extremely paranoid, especially as the spectre was casting him a deep frown, and so eventually he confided in friends. They initially scoffed at such a thought but then, due to the grave look on James' face, realised that something very peculiar was going on and they suggested he try communicating with the spirit. So when one day the spectre appeared to James when he was walking through a field, he decided to address his ghostly shipmate. He asked what could be done so that his spirit could rest. The apparition replied:

> It is well thou hast spoken, for I should have been the death of thee if thou hadst much longer refused to speak! What grieved and vexed me most was to see that thou seemedst to fear thy old comrade, who always liked thee the best of all his shipmates.

'I do not fear you,' James responded. The ghost of John Jones looked pleased and, with that, explained how he had fallen overboard in the Bay of Biscay and that whilst drowning he thought of nothing but his prize-money, stashed in a chest in a Plymouth pub.

The spectre added, 'My son, I want thee to go thither; take my chest to another house; pay what I owe to various people in Plymouth, and keep what remains for thyself. I'll meet thee there and direct thee how to act.' After which, the spook faded away.

The next day James took a horse to Plymouth and on the second night on the road reached his destination. He stayed in an inn up the road from the public house where the chest was stored. As he lay in bed, the ghost of John Jones appeared again, and spoke:

Don't 'e think, my son, that the landlady will make any difficulty about taking away the chest, for she don't know, d'ye see, that it contains valuables, nor that I shipped aboard an Indiaman and got drowned a few weeks ago. But she remembers how – not long since – we wore each other's clothes and shared our rhino, just as brothers should. Tell her I'm in town and will see her before I leave! Tomorrow bring here the chest and I'll direct 'e how to deal with my creditors; and now good night.

And with that, he vanished.

When James visited the inn the landlady was very pleased to see him and was more than happy to be relieved of the old chest. She bid James farewell and asked him to say hello to John – not realising, of course, that the poor man was now deceased.

When all the business was settled, as James had promised it would be to his phantom shipmate, he headed to the dock, where John's ghost then appeared. The spectre told James that he had visited the landlady and kissed her, as only a ghost can. 'My dear Jim,' the spirit said:

I will now bid thee farewell, I'm off to sea again … I know no other way to pass the time. Thou wilt nevermore see me while thou art alive, but if thou thinkest of me at the hour of thy death we shall meet, as soon as the breath leaves the body.

And then the apparition floated to the ship docked at the harbour.

James was sad to see his spectral friend go but livened by the valuables that his shipmate had left him.

On 3 January 1840 the ghost of a sailor was seen by the mother of the Revd Sabine Baring-Gould as she sat in her home at Bratton Clovelly, in Devon. The ghost was that of her brother Henry, who at the time should have been serving with the navy in the South Atlantic. One month later the lady discovered that on the day of her sighting, her brother had died near Ascension Island.

Falmouth Bay in Cornwall has been the epicentre of anomalous phenomena for many years, including sightings of sea monsters (see next chapter) and UFOs. It was at Falmouth in 1940 that a very weird experience took place, involving a woman named Lucretia Kelly. Lucretia had recently met a good-looking young sailor, Alan, who told her he was stationed on HMS *Hunter,* which had docked at Falmouth. They had several dates but on the night Alan was due to leave, Lucretia went to visit him and they took a walk. At one point the couple stopped to look at one another romantically and Lucretia almost screamed: Alan had turned into a skeleton! Lucretia looked away quickly but when she looked back he was back to normal. Lucretia never told her young sailor what she'd seen and they spent the last few hours together as normal, before HMS *Hunter* left Falmouth. On 10 April Lucretia was listening to the news when the story broke that the ship, carrying her lover, had sunk in Norway. Of 156 men on board, only forty-eight survived. Lucretia was sure that Alan had perished.

Lucretia eventually saw a photograph showing all the survivors and Alan was not among them. Many years later she spoke to a manager of a shoe shop about the incident and he told her he knew of the sailor and that he *had* survived! Researcher Michael Williams helped Lucretia investigate the case of the sailor, and wrote to the Naval Records' department on her behalf. He found out that the man named Alan was not a member of the crew, which confused matters, but Lucretia insisted that she had written to Alan whilst he was on board HMS *Hunter*.

It was never known who the man Lucretia Kelly had been dating actually was. Maybe she had confused names? Sadly, Lucretia never kept the letters of the naval man, which served to cloud the waters even more. So the case of the mystery sailor will remain just that: a mystery.

A French sailor is believed to haunt the coast of the Isle of Wight. He was said to have been cast ashore from his wrecked boat and starved to death whilst cooped up in a cave. Golden Hill Fort is also haunted by a sailor. The large hexagonal building is today used by craftsmen, who have reported seeing a sailor who seems to like watching them work. Also in Hampshire, there once stood the old inn known as the White Garter Hotel in Portsmouth. The inn was said to have been haunted by a sailor named Whiskers, who was murdered one night during a game of cards. A group of sailors had been drinking all night when a fight broke out and Whiskers was struck over the head with a glass bottle. The murderer was so scared of being hanged that he struck up

The Isle of Wight coast – haunted by a phantom sailor. (Neil Arnold)

a deal with the landlady of the pub, who agreed that she would bury Whiskers in the garden. Ever since that fateful game, the ghost of Whiskers teased and tormented those who rented rooms out at the inn, until it was eventually demolished. Portsmouth is also haunted by a naval frogman who roamed the Sally Port Hotel. Meanwhile, the Blue Posts Inn, destroyed by fire in 1870, was once the haunt of a spectral sailor who had been murdered in the building. His body was secretly interred in the courtyard; unmarked until 1938 when a headstone was erected in his honour.

Angus Roy was the name of a sailor who served on board a ship that sailed out of the port of Leith in the nineteenth century. For many years he had been bullied by people because of a severe limp. Angus had caused severe damage to his leg when he toppled from the mast of the ship, and so when he came to reside at Victoria Terrace in Edinburgh he became the subject of many cruel jokes, which drove him to an early grave. Some would say that surely in the afterlife Angus would have been free of all pain and able to rest, maybe so; but instead he chose to haunt those who tormented him. Those who have experienced Angus' spectre claim that you always know when he is present because one can hear the sound of his leg dragging along the floor. Those who bullied Angus for his handicap came to regret every minute of their cruel words, and many have themselves now gone to an early grave, haunted by the sound of his cries.

There is another maritime ghost story related to Edinburgh. The ghost of a sea captain is said to haunt Buckingham Terrace, as was reported by members of the Gordon family who had moved into a large apartment there. On several occasions they complained to the porter about the noises coming from the flat upstairs, only to be told that the room was empty. Mrs Gordon claimed that the sounds made were as if furniture was being dragged across the floor, and so frequent and loud had they become that she decided to go above the porter and complain directly to the landlord.

One night, as Mrs Gordon was drifting off into a deep sleep, she was suddenly awoken with a strange feeling that there was a presence in the room. So spooked was she that she reached for her bedside bell in the hope of alerting her daughters, but in her anxiety Mrs Gordon knocked the bell to the floor. At that point, she sensed that the invisible presence had made its way to the door and was heading upstairs, which resulted in loud banging noises. After half an hour the tumult ceased and Mrs Gordon somehow managed to doze off.

In the morning she discussed the dreadful banging with her daughters but they told their mother they had had a perfect night's sleep. As a result Mrs Gordon, being a very level-headed woman, decided that the whole commotion must have been the product of an awful dream. A month passed without any further activity, until one night when Mrs Gordon had gone to stay with friends, leaving her daughter Diana on her own in the apartment. Diana decided to sleep in her mother's room – a bad choice, because as she entered the room for bed some 'thing' ran with haste up the stairs, brushing past her. Despite the overwhelming feeling of dread, Diana bravely gave chase.

She ran up the stairs and opened the door of an upstairs room, only to see a vague shape in the gloom, which appeared to be winding an old grandfather clock. Diana stood still, terrified that the apparition or whatever it was might notice her and eventually it did, turning slowly to meet her gaze. The spectral spell was broken, however, by the call of Diana's sister. Diana rushed back downstairs, told her sister all about what had happened and decided to spend the night in her own room.

When Mrs Gordon came home the following day her daughters were in a terrible state. After another period of ghostly inactivity, however, the spectre was forgotten about. Until, that is, one evening when, as Mrs Gordon lay in bed resting, she noticed the figure of a man standing in her doorway. The figure seemed to have an air of malice about him and in his hands he held a lump of lard and some rags. After a few seconds the figure turned and ran upstairs. This time Mrs Gordon felt so intimidated by the spectre that she decided to take drastic action, and the next day she told her daughters to pack their belongings, for they were to leave the apartment. Despite moving into new premises Mrs Gordon could not rid her memory of the spectre, and so decided to conduct some research. She discovered that the building had been reputedly haunted for quite some time and that it had once been occupied by a retired sea captain, who had become an alcoholic. One night the man became so irate after hearing a crying baby in another apartment that he rushed upstairs and, in drunken anger and realising the baby's mother wasn't present, decapitated the infant. The captain tried to hide his crime and decided to put the corpse of the child in the grandfather clock that stood in the corner of the room. The man was arrested soon after and deemed insane, and a few years later he committed suicide.

At Kenovay, located on the Isle of Tiree in the Inner Hebrides, there is a peaceful and rarely disturbed churchyard said to be haunted by a seaman. According to author J.A. Brooks, the seaman's body was 'seen both before and after his body was washed up on the shore and then buried in the churchyard'.

The village of Sefton in Lancashire once had a weird ghost story attached to it. An inn known as The Punchbowl can be found on Lunt Road in Merseyside. On New Year's Eve in 1972 a member of staff working at the public house observed the ghost of a young man. The spirit was well defined except for his head, which appeared to be surrounded by a mist. The witness to the spectre rushed downstairs and explained to the rest of the staff what she'd seen but when they all went upstairs to take a look there was, of course, no sign of the wraith. The incident was reported in the *Crosby Herald* on 2 February 1973.

After a short while had passed, another member of staff – a waitress – had a spooky encounter at the back of the inn. She had walked into a section called the News Room when she saw a man in a sailor's uniform. The woman screamed and fled in terror. After gathering her nerves – and thinking that maybe the gent had simply been a customer – the young woman decided to go back and take another look, but there was no sign of the sailor.

More and more people came forward to report sightings of the sailor in the same section of the pub, whilst others claimed to have heard ghostly footsteps and found doors swinging with no sign of a person nearby. Things took a rather sinister turn, however, when a young barmaid claimed she was accosted by the spirit. She was about to walk down the stairs when she was pushed. She tumbled half the way but, thankfully, wasn't hurt. Meanwhile, a regular customer of the pub was attacked in the car park by an invisible presence that threw him from his bicycle.

One warm afternoon a man was enjoying a nice pint in the pub when something moving in the nearby churchyard caught his attention. When he looked out the window he was rather surprised to see a man in a sailor's uniform digging a grave and so decided to go and investigate. Despite finding a pile of freshly dug soil, there was no sign of the mariner when the customer got there.

It transpires that, more than five centuries ago, The Punchbowl sat at the edge of the sea and existed as a church vicarage. Ships would often be wrecked off the coast and drowned sailors would be found, quite literally, on the doorstep. Villagers who found the bodies would sometimes bring them into the building and lay them in the area now known as the News Room. Eventually the dead were interred in the churchyard, their graves unmarked.

Nine miles east of Liverpool is Whiston. At Delph Lane in the area, a ghostly sailor has been noted. One night he bid his girlfriend farewell but fell into a quarry and now remains in the area, still pining for his love.

A ghostly sailor is said to haunt an area in Wolverhampton. During the 1920s the young mariner drowned along with two boys that he had attempted to rescue from a pool at East Park. Ian Deakin, in his letter featured in *Fortean Times*, Issue 135 (June 2000), states that in the 1960s his mother and family, who were living in a terraced house in East Park, had an encounter with the sailor. Ian wrote: 'One night, while my mother and her older sister were talking before going to bed, they noticed a figure standing on the landing dressed in a sailor's uniform.' The sailor headed towards the bathroom and then disappeared from sight. Other family members reported seeing child-like handprints on some of the mirrors and also sensed and felt the presence of a child in the house.

A ghostly sea captain is said to haunt the island of Inishinny off Ireland's Donegal coast. During the late 1800s, a small sailing ship consisting of a captain and two men put in to Gola Roads during a severe storm. Islanders at the time, upon seeing the boat on the waves, prophesied some terrible calamity and warned the trio not to return to their boat. Having been stocked up with provisions the seamen, ignoring the warnings, climbed aboard, but the next day their boat was found, ashore, with no sign of the crew. A short while afterwards, a man collecting firewood was walking along the coast when he stumbled upon the body of the captain. The two other sailors were never found.

One night, a group of locals were relaxing at a house on the island of Inishinny when they heard footsteps approach the front door. The islanders knew full well that there was no one else on this isolated land and they waited, with baited breath, to see who was about to enter. Imagine their shock when the door opened and standing there was the captain in all his glory. Most of the islanders were dumbstruck but one, not so affrighted by the figure, said 'Come in', but the figure turned round and headed off into the darkness. All those in the house rushed outside but could find no trace of the ghostly captain.

The county of Kent has a classic ghost story or two about phantom sea captains. One captain is said to make his presence known in an old pub called The Shipwright's Arms near Faversham. The town is ancient, so it is no surprise that ghost stories are aplenty; but it is the Victorian seaman – dressed in peaked cap, reefer jacket and reeking of rum – who is at the top of the town's ghost league. It seems that when his ship floundered somewhere nearby, he used all his might to drag himself across the mud flats but died just as he reached the old, creaky inn.

Admittedly, the remote location and general look of The Shipwright's Arms make it the perfect setting for a ghostly tale or two; in fact, it would almost seem criminal for the place to be bereft of at least one spook. Some believe the Victorian ghostly tale is mere gossip that has embedded itself into folklore, but in 1997 the owner of the pub, a gent named Rod Carroll, claimed that the spectre was still very much active. As in the case of most reputedly haunted pubs, the banging noises, creaking floorboards,

The Shipwright's Arms near Faversham – haunted by a sea captain. (Neil Arnold)

swaying tankards and occasional fallen ashtray are blamed on the ghost. In the 1970s, previous owner Eileen Tester also claimed she'd actually seen the apparition in the bedroom one evening. Indeed, several people have come forward over the years to speak of their encounters with the bearded spectre of a seaman, who clearly likes to get around in the pub. On one occasion an employee at the nearby boatyard reported seeing the captain enter the bar, while in 1995 the haunting was covered by the *Sunday Telegraph*, who stated that the then landlord, a man named Simon Claxton, believed the ghost to be of a Dutch sea captain.

The town of Chatham harbours a historic dockyard: one of Kent's most haunted locations. An American newspaper, the *Edmonton Journal*, on 14 February 1949 remarked, 'Ghost of old sailor seeks haunted house'. The publication claimed that a peg-legged spirit – believed to have fought in the Battle of Trafalgar – was seeking a new residence to frequent after the proposed demolition of his current stomping ground, the barracks at St Mary's. There has long been a rumour that a limping sailor has haunted the Dockyard, but this seems completely unfounded. A few authors have stated that the spectre is Admiral Horatio Nelson; although he never lost a leg, he did lose an eye and an arm. It seems that the dockyard's phantom seaman is simply a tale passed down over the years. Some call him Peg-Leg Jack, simply because witnesses (although I couldn't find any!) claim to have heard his wooden leg knocking on the boarded floors as he walks. Apparently Peg-Leg Jack, or whoever he is, was last seen in 1949 and may well have been a man murdered by French prisoners, but again this has never been verified.

One story I did find rather interesting concerns one of the most haunted parts of the dockyard, the Masthouse. Strange knocking noises were heard here on a ghost investigation and those present believed they were made by a spectral seaman, but what no one could explain was the awful squealing noises, which some believed were from a ghostly baby. The building is constructed out of old ship's timbers (see a later section for more information on this type of haunting) and the ghost could well be that of a seventeenth-century seaman named Abel, who used to keep a pet monkey on board his ship. Maybe the weird scratching and squealing noises are from his ghostly pet.

What about the bizarre story covered by the *Daily Mail* on 5 April 2012 (and was it a belated April Fool's)? The publication ran a story under the heading, 'My haunting goes on: Couple sell house plagued by ghost of Titanic captain who was born there …' Can it get any weirder? According to reporter Jamie McGinnis, a married couple from Stoke-on-Trent in Staffs purchased a Victorian property in 2002 for £35,000, not realising it was the birthplace of one Captain Edward John Smith who, it seemed, had returned to the house after death. Neil and Louise Bonner rented the property out for a decade but constantly heard reports from tenants of paranormal activity taking place, including icy chills in some rooms, a mysteriously flooded kitchen and a unique sighting of the spectral skipper. According to the newspaper article, 'To celebrate the 100th anniversary of the disaster, the couple are now putting the house back on the market for £80,000.'

Two months later, the same newspaper reported 'My replica of the Titanic is haunted by couple who died on original voyage'. An American model-maker from Virginia claimed that, after taking photographs of his precious model, two phantom 'passengers' appeared to be staring from the portholes.

This segment cannot be finished without mention of a ghostly Viking from Essex, as recorded by James Wentworth-Day. The encounter took place at Canvey Island as a man named Charlie Stamp rested one night in his cabin. Charlie was looking out of his window when he noticed a large, bearded man walking up the garden. The man was armed with a sword and had a 'funny owd hat on his head … like a helm that was, with wings on.'

The man came up to the window and, upon seeing the startled Charlie, boomed, 'I've lost me ship, mate. I want to get a ship to me own country. I'm a lost man.' Charlie, feeling like he was in some surreal trance, gave the Viking directions towards 'Grays or Tilbury' and the figure walked off towards the marsh and out of sight.

Although slightly off topic from ghostly sailors etc., Mersea Island, found off the coast of Essex, is said to be haunted by a Roman soldier who frequents the shoreline. Most sightings reported tend to be on 23 September.

A SPOOKY SMUGGLER OR TWO

In folklore, it is often stated that smugglers were the greatest tellers of ghost stories, and their macabre tales were often created to keep trespassers away from their stash of contraband. Little did these criminals realise that whilst they spent their twilight hours fabricating spook tales, they would be shaping local folklore that, centuries later, would still speak of the reputedly haunted spots. As Gay Baldwin and Ray Anker state in their booklet *Ghosts of The Isle of Wight*, 'If all our local smuggling yarns are to be believed there's scarcely a cove or inlet of the Wight where tubs of contraband brandy have not come secretly ashore'. I think it would also be fair to say that, since the time of smuggling there probably is not a coastline in Britain bereft of a ghost story. Who would have thought then that such ghastly smugglers would become one with their tall tales.

On the Isle of Man can be found St Michael's Isle. This desolate-looking place harbours a twelfth-century church with a graveyard believed to be haunted by pirate raiders. The cruel gang were said to have killed the local priest in order to steal his treasure, but when they set sail to escape they drowned not far from the coast. There is an urban legend, which states that if you knock on the wall of the church you can hear the pirates scream in torment. Witnesses have also reported seeing the ghosts of pirates and sailors walking up the beach.

The county of Devon, like so many other coastal areas in Britain, has a smuggling ghost. An area known as Heddon's Mouth, situated between Ilfracombe and Lynton,

Smugglers were said to have created many coastal ghost stories in order to keep people away from their contraband, which they would stash in barrels in caves. (Neil Arnold)

has long had smuggling legends, which is no surprise when one considers just how many of the steep pathways and caves were frequented by such persons. In most cases, people report hearing the sound of creaking oars coming from the sea as if a small boat is approaching; then come the ghostly voices and an occasional dull thud, as if items are being transported ashore. The distinct sound of horses' hooves has also been reported, particularly in the area of Kendall Lane.

Lundy Island, mentioned earlier with regards to ghost lights, also has a smuggler tale. Two male spirits of intimidating presence are said to keep guard over a certain spot, where it is believed gold is buried. A Captain Robert Nutt, described by Peter Underwood as 'a bold and bloodthirsty buccaneer who plundered ships', used to have his headquarters on Lundy Island, so maybe it is his vicious soul that has been reported in one of the caves. Rumour has it that some years ago a journalist travelled to the island in search of the lost treasure. A coastguard was stationed at the mouth of the cave and told the reporter that, should he get into any difficulty or the tide come in too far, he must fire a shot.

The intrepid explorer trudged on in to the blackness of the cave, where his torch beam illuminated a ghastly skull. The brave man probed deeper and his morbid curiosity unearthed two skeletons – possibly victims of the tide as they attempted to recover Nutt's treasure. The journalist explored further into the depths and, to his astonishment, found a rusty chest circled by stones. Rather excited by his find, he pressed forward, but then he heard a noise coming from the darkest corner of the cave and was sure that he had seen something move in the gloom. Was there some type of animal inhabiting the cave or was the treasure being guarded by some ethereal sentry? The reporter sensed that the only way to get to the treasure was to somehow blow the rocks up, but this would be far too dangerous and so, reluctantly, he left the cave and the treasure to the darkness and Captain Nutt's ghost.

An uncanny experience took place at Lee in Ilfracombe a few decades ago now, and concerned a photographer who was taking pictures on the beach during a holiday. When the man returned home he put his photographs in to be developed. When he picked them up was astounded two see in one of the photographs a massive mooring post and, as if imprinted on it, two villainous faces. The heads resembled those of North African pirates, snarling beneath their headscarves. The appearance of these ghostly heads unsettled the photographer so much that he destroyed the photograph. Typical!

Many years after the incident, the photographer was speaking to the curator of a small museum in Ilfracombe about an unrelated topic when the curator brought up the subject of North African pirates. According to the curator, these criminals would lie in wait in the Bristol Channel; it would seem that their souls remain ...

At West Beach, Portreath in Cornwall there is a hotel said to be haunted by a smuggler. The building sits within a few feet of the beach and over the years it has been a fisherman's cottage and private residence. When alterations were made to the building some years back a hidden room was discovered between floors, adjoining the main staircase, and in this room was found a skeleton of a man, wearing a black cloak, who was seated at a table accompanied by an old chest. In the chest was found a couple of coins and some material, and in the hand of the skeleton was a sword. No one is sure whether it is this smuggler who haunts the building but, according to author Andrew Green, the spectre was last seen in the 1960s. A decade earlier, Green had stayed one night in the building and noticed a sudden drop in temperature, which aggravated the pet dog of the property who began growling as if something, or someone, was in the room. The area where the cold spot appeared was next to the wall that hid a tunnel entrance, which in the past would have been used by smugglers.

Dorset also has a ghostly smuggler. His screams have been heard in the vicinity of Worbarrow Bay. It is said that during the seventeenth century a group of revenue officers came upon the smuggler on an unmade road. The smuggler, to avoid capture, ran along the beach but found himself at a dead end and so decided to wade out into the sea, where he was then stoned to death. Is it his screams that can be heard above the howling winds on certain nights? There are some researchers, however, who believe that the ghost of the beach is in fact that of Napoleon; and that it is he who has been seen around the Lulworth Cove area. The figure – who appears as a dark shadow but also in unmistakable garb – was seen in 1930 by a woman who reported that the ghostly figure was accompanied by another person: they walked towards the sea and vanished. The story has been dismissed as legend, despite sightings since 1804.

There have also been phantom screams heard around the area of the beach and these could be connected to Lulworth Castle, which was destroyed by fire in 1929. Twelve maidservants disappeared at the time: some believe they left the castle and were never seen again; whilst others assert that the women had walked along the cliff path but were then swept out to sea. At least five different entities have been reported from the beach, so it could be said that, should one wish to spend a night ghost-hunting, then Lulworth Cove is the place to go. But I suggest you take care on those ragged coastal rocks because, should you suffer the same fate as those servant girls, you too will be confined to the limbo they are trapped within.

Norfolk is also known for its smuggling ghost stories and one such spectral figure is said to haunt Happisburgh. During the early eighteenth century three 'free-traders' had a row over the loot they had accumulated and one of the men was brutally murdered, his corpse hidden. In 1765 a ghost was seen to glide over the salt flats and disappear in the region of Well's Corner. Those who have seen the ghost report that it holds a bundle under one arm, wears a blue jacket, is without legs and its head wobbles in peculiar fashion. A few years after the main hub of sightings, an area of sand on the beach was dug up and a male torso was found. Around its body was the remains of a blue tunic and, according to author Andrew Green, 'a rotting bundle of a man's legs and head were discovered'.

In his book *Ghosts & Legends of the Lake District*, J.A. Brooks writes of a handful of ghost stories possibly created by smugglers to keep people away from certain caves, where their operations were likely based. One such yarn concerned the remote shore at Silverdale, where it was claimed that all manner of boggarts and bogies would be created to ward off trespassers. While a cave at Lindeth was said to be guarded by a woman bereft of a head. How these smugglers managed to spread their ghostly tales is beyond me, especially considering that normal folk would surely have not trusted such men.

The county of Kent is riddled with tales of ghostly smugglers, said to haunt along the coasts. Many years ago the sea would lap away at certain spots, which now seem far removed from the water. Smuggling was rife around Romney Marsh (as are ghost stories) and further inland to villages such as Hawkhurst, so it is no surprise that the phantoms have embedded themselves into local folklore. One of my favourite Kent smuggler tales comes from the Isle of Sheppey, where the coast was once littered with ghost stories pertaining to shadowy figures said to be retrieving their booty from the shore. Several buildings were once said to harbour tunnels that acted as escape routes for smugglers; in the same way some tunnels are said to run beneath Kent churches for the same reason. Of course, a majority of these rumours have never been verified as the tunnels would have been filled in due to health and safety reasons.

The coast of the Isle of Sheppey – believed to be a haunt of spectral smugglers. (Neil Arnold)

A pub in Dymchurch on the Kent coast is possibly haunted by a smuggler. The Ship Inn dates back to the sixteenth century and secret passages have been found during renovations. It is likely these tunnels were used by smugglers. One night the landlord of the pub, a man named Andy Sharp, was awoken by the sound of someone walking about and, thinking it was his daughter going to the toilet, he supposed nothing of it until the sounds continued for quite some time. After a while, Andy decided to investigate but upon opening the door was greeted by total silence.

Many ghostly smugglers haunt Welsh history, too. Phantom pirates have been seen at Llanafan in Dyfed. The ghosts still roam around a cave located at Craig-yr-Rogof where their treasure is said to be hidden.

MORE COASTAL CHILLS

One of the eeriest ghost stories I've heard concerns the fishing village of Llandudno in Wales. Many years ago this remote spot was well away from the prying eyes of tourists and those that inhabited the resort often spoke of, and feared, the Gloddaeth Ghost. Although today the village attracts many visitors, over a century ago it was the perfect setting for a ghostly tale; one sure to send a shiver down the most hardened of spines.

A local pest control officer was called in by local farmers as there had been a terrible problem with foxes nipping away at livestock. One night the pest control officer, a chap named Thomas Davies from Rhyl, set up a hide in a tree overlooking the den of a vixen. As the night grew darker and the air grew colder, Thomas was startled by a horrific scream that came from the direction of the icy sea. It was a sound like nothing he'd heard before – far more bone-chilling than the cry of a fox – and it was coming closer. Thomas looked below him, his eyes scouring the blackness trying to pick out some type of form, when suddenly his eyes met a most fearful sight. There, emerging from the shadows, was a nude figure with the most hate-filled and fiery eyes. Thomas cowered into the branches of the tree as the ghoul fixed its wicked eyes upon him and then it suddenly crouched down low, sniffed the air, and sprang back to its upright position. Davies clung to the tree with all his might, petrified that he might fall into the spindly embrace of this nightmarish spectre, and hang on he did, until the break of dawn when with the coming light the abomination faded from view.

The Welsh island of Ynys Enlli (Bardsey Island) can be located 2 miles off the mainland of Caernarvonshire. More than 20,000 monks are said to be buried there and on

There are many haunted beaches in the British Isles. (Illustration by Neil Arnold)

certain nights, people on the mainland have reported seeing shadowy figures marching along the coastline of the island.

A majority of ghost stories never revel in their horror, but instead often have a moral or are tinged with sadness, suggesting a broken heart or love triangle. One such story from the Cornish coast involves a woman named Sarah Polgrain, who lived at Ludgvan and who poisoned her husband. Legend has it that Sarah was deeply in love with a chap named Yorkshire Jack, who had convinced her to kill her husband, a crime which she was eventually hanged for. At her time of execution, Jack promised her that, three years to the day, after time at sea, he would be with her spiritually. It is said that Jack was so miserable after seeing his lover hanged that every ship he boarded he brought ill luck to, but one particular voyage – which took place three years to the day since Sarah's execution – was to be the death of him. Whilst halfway across the Atlantic, a ferocious tempest swirled about the boat and the crew scurried below deck reporting that they had seen an atrocious female phantom appear in the grey clouds. Those brave enough to stay on deck witnessed a remarkable phenomenon: the evil spirit of her cruel husband in life who had bullied and beaten her. J.A. Brooks adds, 'From the time that this western Jonah was taken away by the lady of his love and the devil, the ship was free from all the strange disasters which were constantly occurring ...'.

Some say that Sarah forever loitered in the shadow of her murdered husband because she had never been baptised in the water of the famous local well; whilst all those who have been baptised will never meet the hangman's noose. Further investigations revealed, however, that Sarah had in fact been christened in a neighbouring parish, and so now the locals believe that in the afterlife she is free from her master.

Another forlorn tale of lost love comes from Porthgwarra in Cornwall, where there is a spot called Sweetheart's Cove. Many years ago, a rich farmer's daughter named Nancy, unbeknownst to her father, was seeing a poor sailor boy called William. They were deeply in love and when William was called away to sea, he promised Nancy he would be true to her and return. Nancy would often sit on the rocks overlooking the sea in the hope that William's ship would return and one night, whilst sitting at Hella Point, the pining woman heard the voice of her loved one calling. She walked to Porthgwarra Cove and was seen by an old woman to perch on a rock at the water's edge and then be joined by a sailor. As the waves rolled stronger around them they did not seem to stir and, worried for them, the old woman shouted to warn them of the coming tide, upon which the figures seemed to drift out to sea. The next day, news arrived in the village that William's ship had been consumed by the waves; the body of Nancy was never found. On certain nights when the tide lashes at the rocks of Porthgwarra Cove you can, if you are lucky, still see the ghostly couple, huddled together braving the winds in their quest for endless love. The rather aptly named Deadman's Cove is also reputedly haunted. In 1978 two witnesses reported speaking to a man dressed in black who then faded before their eyes.

St Michael's Mount – the 'jewel in Cornwall's crown' – is said to be the county's most famous landmark. It can be found at Penzance, jutting out of the sea like some mystical island. The website www.cornwall-online.co.uk states that a Benedictine chapel originally existed there, and that the castle dates back to the fourteenth century. The mount is steeped in folklore, too. It is said that the mount was built by a ferocious giant who would walk through the waves to the mainland to steal cattle and sheep. The spot of the well is said to be where the giant was slain by a boy named Jack: and so was born the legend of 'Jack the Giant Killer'. The 'ghost' from the island, on the other hand, was reportedly a vision experienced in AD 495 by several fishermen, who claimed to have seen St Michael appear over the summit.

Returning to Devon: there is a ghostly woman in white said to haunt a stretch of water at Braunton. The ghost is known as Old White Hat and is said to be the spirit of a female who perished on her honeymoon as she and her groom were being transported across the water and their boat capsized. According to author Peter Underwood, the ghost 'used to be seen walking along the beach of Northside seemingly calling for a passage to Appledore.' This ghost story reminds me of the eerie phantom hitchhikers said to litter some of Britain's roads. Old White Hat is often said to wait on the beach and appear to boatmen, but whoever picks the ghostly woman up is thought to die shortly afterwards. Various female phantom hitchhikers are often

St Michael's Mount in Cornwall. (Dr Chris Clark)

said to loiter by roadsides, waiting to thumb a lift from the people who ran them over in the hope of getting revenge by killing them. In other cases, it is said that the ghostly hitchers are waiting for a lift in the hope of finding the sweethearts they never got to marry; in most instances, researchers and storytellers agree that the spectres are forlorn souls, forever searching.

The main problem with these types of ghostly encounters is finding someone who has actually given a lift to a spectre in their car or boat. Researcher Dan Farson some years ago claimed that he saw Old White Hat on the beach, after he was alerted to her presence by a neighbour. Mr Farson hurried to Braunton Barrows just in time to see a whitish form wearing a white hat perched upon its head disappear into the dusk.

The Woolacombe Sands of North Devon are home to a number of loitering phantoms. One such spook is that of Sir Robert Chichester who lived at Martinhoe, but by far the queerest story concerns a white lady. One late afternoon a man named Taylor was walking along the sands with his small dog. As dusk was drawing in, the man became quite unsettled and hoped that his dog would not keep dawdling. Taylor's dog had a habit of running off into the sea and playing among the waves but this evening Taylor was eager to get home. Too soon, darkness fell. As Taylor reached a certain spot on the beach, the hairs on the back of his neck stood up and a terrible cry filled the air. Immediately, Taylor rushed to the aid of his dog, thinking that maybe he had injured himself on the rocks of the shore, but when he heard the whining again he realised it was further in the distance. All was still apart from the lapping of the waves, and Taylor was now convinced that the cry had not come from his dog. Then, suddenly, just a few yards in front of him appeared a woman dressed in white with her back to him. Taylor stepped back with a start, not expecting to see anyone at such a late hour. The woman gracefully walked on ahead, Taylor never once seeing her face. Taylor watched her intently as she glided towards the edge of the water; she seemed to tiptoe on the sand. He had come to within just a few yards of the woman when he felt a tug at his trousers and, looking down, fully expecting his dog to be there, but was shocked to see nothing. Taylor whistled for his dog but there was no response; just the eerie silence of the night. Turning back to face the woman he was even more surprised to see that there was no one in sight. There was no way she could have run off in such a short space of time; he would have seen her on the long stretch of beach. It was then that Taylor realised something quite shocking. The spot of sand where the woman had stood was incredibly soft, like sinking sand, and it struck him that if he had gone a step further he would have succumbed to the bog. Taylor turned back, changing his direction, and with haste ran home, leaving his poor dog to the night.

The next day, Taylor explored the shoreline and found the broken body of his dog at the water's edge: judging by the injuries it looked as if the animal had been attacked by a large fish. When Taylor spoke to his landlady about the eerie woman she told him that the tales were true and that those who had followed her had perished on the sands. It appeared that the alluring woman had been attempting to lure Taylor to his death. One question did cross his mind: had the ghost of his own dog, who had likely perished at the sound of her howl, saved him by tugging at his leg?

Another peculiar incident was recalled by a young married couple who had once settled down for a picnic one evening on the cliff tops overlooking the sea at Lynton in Devon. The spot, known as the Valley of the Rocks, has always been a rather enchanted place, and on this occasion the couple were drawn to the sound of beautiful singing coming from below them. At first, the couple thought that maybe there had been a boat on the water below but when they looked over the edge there was no vessel. The young lady came to the conclusion that the noise had come from seals but her husband had definitely heard the words of a song.

On 20 October 1964 the *Daily Express* ran the headline, 'Penitent Ghost Haunts Navy Wives', after a sailor asked to be excused from his all-night duty to return home to his wife and son at Seaton in Devon because numerous paranormal occurrences had been experienced. The house, situated in the beachside village, was said to have been haunted by a mysterious figure that wanted to apologise for committing a stabbing. A medium was called in to contact the restless soul, which apparently told the woman: 'I cannot rest until I find my mistress to apologise. I should not have killed her.'

According to the newspaper, 'Twenty-three years ago, a Scottish maid killed her mistress with a carving knife in the house, which the Navy has converted into married quarters.' The sailor – a Mr Smith – was told that his 2-year-old son had been given sedatives to calm him after numerous appearances of the ghost. Judging by the newspaper article, the spiritualists were no more successful in slaying the ghost than the local reverend.

In 1883 a ghostly woman was seen at a location called the Hoe in Plymouth. The wraith was spotted by two 14-year-olds as they took a swim in a pool out to sea. One of the teenagers reported at the time:

> We met no-one on the Hoe but at the bottom of the steps near the bathing houses I happened to look up and saw a woman looking over the wall – looking at the steps at the farther end of the pool. We did not like the water that morning as it was too calm, so we soon returned to the edge of the pool. But instead of running round the pool we thought we would swim across the pool. We both went in together with a big splash, at the point where we had seen the woman gazing. On the way back I saw a hat floating. I brought it in. It was like the hat the woman wore who had been gazing into the pool. Then we dressed and went home for breakfast.

Later that day a policeman got in touch with the teenagers. One of the teenagers was taken out of school and, along with the other who had been at home, was taken to the mortuary to identify the body of a woman. She had been found floating in the pool at the exact spot where the youths had jumped in. Bizarrely, the woman in the mortuary was the same woman the youth had seen overlooking the pool.

The Old Spanish Barn on the seafront at Torquay, Devon, is reputedly haunted by an attractive Spanish girl. She, along with her love, came ashore from the *Nuestra Señora del Rosario*, from the Spanish Armada, whereupon both elopers were taken prisoner and held at the tithe barn in Torquay. Peter Underwood states that she was the first prisoner to die. Her ghost has been seen on the seafront and, on occasion, close to the road where motorists have reported her forlorn form.

A woman in white, often bereft of a head, is said to haunt the north-east coast of Skipsea in Yorkshire. The spectre is of a periodical nature. Meanwhile, between Skipsea and Atwick, there is said to roam another headless wraith. A horseman mounted upon a spectral white horse gallops along the coast and another headless horseman haunts an area between Frodingham and the sea.

We must not forget, either, the terrible tragedy that spawned a ghost story at Staithes on the north coast of Yorkshire. On 14 April 1807 a young girl named Hannah Grundy and her three friends were gathering shellfish to supply to the local fishermen. After a while, they decided to rest underneath a cliff when a sharp stone tumbled from a ledge and severed Hannah's head clean off. To the horror of the other girls, the head of the girl was cast some 30ft away, and ever since this accident a young woman had been seen haunting the beach.

The seaside town of Whitby doesn't escape the realms of folklore either. Not only did author Bram Stoker get inspiration for his classic novel *Dracula* from the town, but there is an eerie coastal ghost story too. In 1907 a local man had an uncanny experience on the West Cliff. At the time, he was in the company of several boy scouts when they noticed something odd on the cliff, just below the monument dedicated to explorer Captain Cook. A whitish, misty figure floated down the face of the rock. Intrigued by the sighting the witnesses ran to the spot where it was due to land, but there was nothing untoward to be seen. Had the witnesses simply seen fog? Well, according to those present, there was no trace of fog or mist that could have accounted for the apparition. Fog also does not suffice to explain the fact that, some seventy-five years later, a woman and her husband walking their dog on the beach also saw a similar form that drifted down the crag. The woman's husband was so scared he left the area immediately and refused to talk about it afterwards.

In the vicinity of St Mary's church there is the grave of a seaman. The weird ghost story from this location claims that a phantom coach travels along Green Lane and then stops at the graveyard. The ghostly passengers alight and, for some unknown reason, stand around the seaman's grave.

There are so many stories pertaining to ghostly women said to haunt beaches. Blackpool, which for the record also has a ghost-infested theme park, has a haunted beach. On the Christmas Eve 1919 a young woman named Kitty Breaks was found murdered on the sand dunes in the vicinity of Lytham Road. The poor girl had been shot at point-blank range three times. Before her death, Kitty (real name Kathleen) had been involved in a stormy relationship with a man named Frederick. It seems that

Staithes on the north coast of Yorkshire – haunt of a headless girl. (Stuart Paterson)

The ferocious coast of Whitby. (Stuart Paterson)

the pair had a terrible argument and Frederick shot dead his partner. He was executed shortly afterwards. Ever since then, a woman has been seen forlornly walking along the beach on Christmas Eve, loitering among the sand dunes and spooking anyone who should be in the vicinity.

A woman dressed in blue is said to haunt Kingsdown in Kent, a stretch of beach known as Old Stairs Bay. The woman is known as the Blue Lady of Romney Codd and has been seen to vanish near the fence of Kingsdown House. Others who have seen this woman have reported how she bends to drink from a spring, suggesting she is rather at ease in her spiritual place. Yet what of the sightings that mention how she moans as if in distress? No one has ever found out who this woman could be, we only know that she often visits the beach at the time of a shipwreck.

Whilst on the subject of Kent, it should be mentioned that one of the most haunted stretches of coastline is said to be Reculver, a few miles east of Herne Bay. Here sits Reculver Towers – a remote spot overlooking the sea where Roman structures have been found. The local ghost story is quite an eerie one, as many ghost-hunters and the like will tell you: on certain nights the cries of babies can be heard, soaring across the sea. Many people believe that centuries ago infants were sacrificed at Reculver, but this may have spawned from the fact that in 1996 archaeologists discovered three small skeletons in the walls of the Roman fort. The size of the skeletons suggested the babies

Eerie Reculver Towers on the Kent coast. (Neil Arnold)

were no more than six months old, and they may have been killed in some type of ritual. On numerous occasions people have contacted local police to report hooded figures; all in all making Reculver one of the county's spookiest locations.

The Giant's Causeway can be found on the north coast of Ireland. It is a spectacular setting of jagged rocks, which are staggered out across the water. The rocks are the result of a volcanic eruption and the area has been described as the eighth wonder of the world. According to the official website, there is a great deal of legend and folklore around the causeway: one story alleges that the structure was built by a man named Finn McCool as a walkway to slay a Scottish giant. There is also a tragic ghost story from the area. In the summer of 1910 the Smyth family of five – consisting of Mr Smyth, his wife, two daughters and their young son – visited the Giant's Causeway for a holiday and took in the awesome cliffs before setting down for a peaceful picnic in the shade from the sun. The Smyths' son Charles liked to think himself as a bit of an explorer and managed to escape the watchful eyes of his sister for a few short moments, but sadly that was enough. The family could not find Charles; the great rocks presented themselves as an inhospitable maze of danger and despite a thorough search, there was no sign of the adventurous Charles, until three days later when his body washed up with the tide.

Those who've encountered the ghost say they saw a small boy in a sailor's suit on the beach. One couple had a frightful encounter with the lost soul when they crossed a serrated set of rocks, only to almost walk into the young boy. They asked him if he was lost but when he turned to face them, they were shocked to see that his skin was pure white and his clothes sodden. Seconds later, he vanished before their eyes.

As mentioned briefly at the end of the last chapter, a creature known as a hellhound has been seen on some of Britain's coastlines. These phantom black dogs go by many names, the most popular being Black Shuck, Padfoot, Bargest, Guytrash and Striker. In most cases, such fiendish creatures are said to have black, shaggy fur, eyes like hot coals and tend to follow lonely travellers. In some instances, such spectral dogs have been known to appear and disappear at will, or burst into balls of flame. Other legends claim that these animals – said to be as big as a calf – appear during bad storms and act as omens of misfortune.

The Black Shuck – the name deriving from *Scucca/Sceocca*, meaning Devil – is said to roam the beaches of East Anglia. Many years ago children would refuse to walk along the coastal pathways in fear of meeting the beast, whilst fishermen were also fearful of the dog. Author W.A. Dutt states that 'he revels in the roaring of the waves and he loves to raise his awful voice above the howling gales'. On some parts of the Norfolk coast the hellhound is said to only have one burning eye and, should you encounter the cyclopean nightmare, then your life will end soon.

No one is quite sure what realm the black dogs of folklore originate from, but such ghouls are not simply ghosts of someone's pet dog that has died. These legends are known worldwide, and the dogs are said to vary in colour and size. In the Hebrides

The fiendish Roy Dog of Dorset folklore. (Illustration by Mark North)

Cave Hole, Portland in Dorset – coastal lair of the devilish Roy Dog. (Mark North)

there sits a spot called South Uist. Here there is a legend of a ghostly dog known as the Faery/Fairy Dog or Mauthe Dog. Those that have seen the animal describe it as white in colour and the size and shape of an Arran collie. It also goes by the name Cu-Sith and has been seen frolicking among the waves.

On the Isle of Mull, locals have a similar creature, but the legend here is far stranger. A man named MacPhee was said to have shipwrecked in the area in 1615 and pulled himself to safety on the shore when he was approached, according to Alasdair Alpin MacGregor, by a 'faery woman' who 'gave him a faery dog, assuring him while so doing that one day this supernatural creature would stand him in supreme stead'. Many years later, it is rumoured that whilst hunting in Jura he was saved by the dog when his own foster brothers tried to murder him.

The footprints of the Mauthe Dog were said to have been discovered on the sands at Luskentyre in South Harris. Men roaming the shore one day came across the enormous prints, said to have been the size of an outstretched palm, which would not really make sense if the animal was only the size of a collie.

In Dorset folklore, there is a phantasmal creature known as the Roy Dog. The beast is said to inhabit a cave at the southernmost tip of the Isle of Portland. When a storm comes in it is said that no one should venture near Cave Hole, because the creature has been known to drag unsuspecting victims into its cavernous lair, which overlooks the sea. There is one story that speaks of three young men who were fishing from the ledges at Cave Hole. It had been such a bad day with regards to a catch that two of the men decided to pack up and go home, but one fellow was of dogged determination and stayed until late. As the shadows crept in, the two early leavers decided to stop off at a local boozer when in the distance one of them saw a massive black hound limping along the pathway. They watched the creature for a short time and realised as it bathed its injured paw that it was in fact the legendary Roy Dog, for it was as tall as a man and had glowing red eyes the size of dinner plates. One of the men almost choked with disgust when he saw that entangled in the fur of the animal was a human eye, which must have been plucked from its latest victim. The men shuddered and made for home.

The next morning word got out that the fisherman who had stayed at Cave Hole had not returned home, and so his two friends walked back to the area to look for him. Once there they found their friend, as stiff as a board, bereft of eyes, perched on a jagged ledge. His fishing rod was still in his hands but his face was contorted with horror, and on the hook of the rod there was a clump of gory hair with a claw embedded into it. A tale straight from *The Twilight Zone* indeed.

It is also worth noting that a giant black hound has reportedly been seen on the beach at Formby in Merseyside. The ghostly dog never leaves tracks.

There are quite a few stories of haunted caves, said to be dotted around the British coast. Elliott O'Donnell spoke of some in his classic book *Ghosts with a Purpose*. One incident that comes to mind featured a place known as Black Head Creek on the Isle of Man, where it was said that treasure had been buried. Several ghosts were believed to guard the cave. O'Donnell writes: 'On one occasion a boat full of people was seen to enter the cave. The boat was subsequently found intact in the cave, but of the people no trace was ever discovered.' Had they been kidnapped by the guardian ghosts?

In Irish folklore there is a horrid creature known as the Pooka. This manifestation is known to haunt stretches of the west and north-west coast of Ireland, especially Galway. In this instance, the beast is said to take on the form of a black horse. Such a beast has been observed crashing through the waves, reminding one of the water horse or kelpie of Scottish folklore, which is said to appear to gullible people who will leap upon its back for a ride only to be taken into the depths of a pond or lake.

Reverting back to Dorset, we find Studland Bay has a ghost story attached to it. A few years ago, a couple were walking along the beach when they spotted a whitish figure walking parallel with them along the shore. The couple walked by a hut and lost sight of the figure, which did not emerge from the other side. This spectral encounter was backed up when a man named William Sargeant reported to ghost-hunter Peter Underwood that one afternoon, whilst walking on the same deserted stretch with his wife, they decided to stop for a nice cup of tea. Whilst sitting on the sand they saw a figure appear in the distance, which looked like a man wearing a white suit. The couple continued drinking and chatting, all the while keeping their eye on the figure. They then realised it was in fact floating. The couple began to pick their things up

Weymouth in Dorset. The esplanade has a weird ghost story attached to it. (Mark North)

and noticed that the figure was now close to the beach hut and then, seconds later, was nowhere to be seen. It seems that a traitor was once found out and killed on the beach. Had the figure been the ghost of an Englishman who was in cohorts with the Germans during the Second World War?

Another Dorset tale comes from Weymouth and was relayed by a Mr Hector D. Campbell, a member of the Ghost Club. He spoke of how one day he was walking along the busy esplanade with his fiancée when his nostrils were invaded by a strong smell of sulphur. Mr Campbell then felt compelled to look towards a seat on the beach and was surprised to see an old woman perched upon it. Despite the fact it was a very hot day, Hector reported how he came over icy cold and when the woman looked back at him, he sensed an air of wickedness about her. Seconds later, Hector's fiancée, who hadn't seen the old woman, asked if they could sit down. When she approached the seat where Hector had seen the crone (which to her seemed empty), he became unnerved and seized her arm, saying abruptly, 'No, no, there is no seat there'. But his fiancée was having none of it, accused Hector of acting crazy and went to sit in the seat. To his horror, as she lowered herself Hector saw the old woman open her arms, as if to invite her. The next thing Hector knew he was lying on the floor with a policeman looking over him. Hector had fainted on the spot. Seconds later, he was told by the policeman that his fiancée had died in the seat.

THERE IS AN OLD LEGEND WHICH SAYS ...

When wild November winds are whirling round the cliffs of North Hill and sailing craft are straining at moorings in Minehead's little harbour, children keep indoors at night for fear of meeting Old Mother Leakey.

This may sound like a verse from a creepy nursery rhyme, but Old Mother Leakey was said to have been a ghastly ghost rumoured to have existed, in the ethereal sense, from the seventeenth century onwards. An old lady named Leakey resided in Minehead, a coastal town of Somerset, during the early 1600s. She was a gentle soul but after she died many people blamed her spirit for odd occurrences, and she was given the nickname of the Whistling Ghost. In life, Mrs Leakey had been the mother of a sea skipper, and in death her spectre was said to be heard whistling through the masts of his boat. So eerie were the moans, and so hideous the activity, that the poor skipper was unable to get a team to sail on his vessel. The Bishop of Bath and Wells, a chap named Sir Robert Philips, was called to the home of Mrs Leakey's grandson after it was alleged that some unseen supernatural force had attempted to strangle him. On another occasion, Mrs Leakey's daughter-in-law was looking in the mirror when a spectre appeared behind her. The ghostly happenings were dismissed by the commissioners, but locals maintained that the Whistling Ghost was very real.

Another ghost considered very 'real' is that of naval air mechanic Freddy Jackson, who appeared in a photograph in 1919 of the maintenance group of HMS *Daedalus*, gathered on the runway at Cranwell in Lincolnshire. Three days before, however, Freddy Jackson had been killed when he fell into the blades of a propeller.

The story of the ghost in the photograph was covered by the *Daily Mail* of 1 July 1996, and everyone who has examined the print believes it to be genuine, with no signs of tampering. An air marshal, Sir Victor Goddard, mentioned the ghostly image in his *Flight Towards Reality* and stated: 'There he was, no mistake, although a little fainter than the rest ... Indeed, he looked as though he was not altogether there; not really with that group, for he alone was capless, smiling; all the rest were serious and set and wearing service caps.'

Without a shadow of a doubt, one of the most unusual and haunted pubs in Britain can be found in Tyneside and is known as The Marsden Grotto. Paranormal researcher Mike Hallowell comments, 'The pub nestles into the limestone cliff face at Marsden Bay on the coast of South Shields.' Several ghost stories are attached to the building: one, which could have been mentioned in an earlier segment, is that of a smuggler who was shot dead many years ago as he tried to evade an excise officer. In the 1990s a television series called *Ghost Detectives* filmed in the pub, and one crew member claimed that an ashtray was thrown at them, possibly by the phantom. The building is also said to harbour two female entities: a mother and daughter.

The Farne Islands can be found off the coast of Northumberland. Some of the most unusual stories are attached to this group of islands. Researcher Alan Robson records that 'Local boatmen and fisherfolk claim to have seen ugly, deformed demons lurching across the rocks ...'. These despicable critters have been known to ride the backs of goats and wolves. It is rumoured the manifestations are the ghosts of people drowned at sea and that, despite being bad people, they were never bad enough to reach the depths of fiery Hell.

An extremely curious tale was once contributed to *Fortean Times* magazine by a chap named Jake Willott, who in a letter wrote of 'a girl at the junior school in Flixton, Manchester who had an interest in strange and paranormal occurrences'. According to Jake the girl, who was only 11 years of age at the time, brought into school a seashell and, like most children, asked the other kids if they could hear the roar of the sea inside when they pressed their ear to it. However, on one occasion Jake said he put his ear to the shell and could hear the distinctive sound of the creaking and groaning of a ship's rigging. Jake passed the shell to his friend who also heard the sound as well as faint drums, which got louder and louder. These were followed by muffled voices and then a piercing scream that was so loud the other people in the room could hear it.

The young girl told everyone present that the shell always acted in this way and believed that the sounds were from the crew of a wrecked ship which had run aground on an island inhabited by cannibals.

The Norfolk coastline has a story concerning a ghost who has become known as the 'long coastguardsman'. In her book *Norfolk Ghosts & Legends*, Polly Howat notes that 'He has not made his presence known for a long time,' and thank goodness because this seems to be one strange character. Local tradition is that the figure, when rarely seen, glides along the coast at midnight on a moonless night and makes itself known by screaming and shouting at the top of its voice whenever there is a lull in the wind. Those who have been submitted to the noises say the ghost emits peals of laughter; but others say they are cries for help. No one has the foggiest idea who or what the spectre is but it does remind one of the spectre known as the Whooper of Sennen Cove in Cornwall. This ghost, if it is a ghost at all, manifests as a strange whooping sound, which drifts through the mist often before a severe storm. The Whooper may in fact be a guardian spirit, protecting not just the cove but fishermen from treacherous weather. Either way, recent legend has it that one night, two determined souls clambered through the heavy mist, broke the spell and the Whooper was no more.

One story that I've always found amusing and intriguing at the same time is related to The Shiant, or 'Charmed' Isles, located in the Minch of the Outer Hebrides. This remote place and its waters are said to be prowled by small blue men, known as the Blue Men of the Minch; a race of supernatural humanoids who have blue-grey skin and bearded faces. These fiends are responsible for the turbulent waters experienced in the channel, which divides the Outer Hebrides from the mainland. The weird race are said to lurk in the waves and lay siege to any vessel that attempts to pass, and so a majority of fishermen tend to avoid the waterway for fear of being captured and then dragged into the caves where the blue men live. Although this story may sound like the *Smurfs* gone wrong, it is a legend said to be based on fact. The book *Folklore Myths & Legends of Britain* mentions how the Norse pirates who invaded the Scottish isles 'used slaves from Moorish ships; these were Berbers who wore blue garments and veils …'.

Almost as strange as the tale of the blue men is the yarn pertaining to Black Eric, a hideous savage who once inhabited the caves around the Shetland Isles, particularly the spot known as Fitful Head. This grotesque wild man would travel across land on a demonic horse, as one does, and steal sheep from the villages. Thankfully, the vile character met his match and died at the hands of a man named Sandy Breamer; who fought Eric, forcing the sub-human over the cliffs to his death. Nevertheless, some say his spectre lives on around the jutting rocks of the bay.

Returning back to Norfolk, I'd like to share with you the haunting of Blacknock, a mud bank that lies about a mile out to sea off what are known as the Stiffkey Salt Marshes. It is the sort of area where people tend to gather in search of blue-shelled cockles. The women who used to collect these shells were known as the Stiffkey cocklers; tough souls who would brave all weathers in search of their quarry. Sadly, due to their persistent nature, one day one of the women who was out on the mud alone didn't see the bank of fog consume the beach and within minutes she was lost. Despite being a hardened woman, in her confusion she began to shout and scream for help. Little known to her, a nearby fishing crew aboard their boat had thankfully heard her pleas. But try as they might, they couldn't find her due to the enveloping vapour and soon the tide drew in and the woman perished in the mud. The next day her body was found on the flats. Her screams can still be heard on mist-enshrouded nights, but no one now dares venture forth onto the mud in case they, too, succumb to the tide.

At Caister-on-Sea there was once a legend that a young girl died from grief after her lover drowned at sea. His ship had run aground on Scroby Sand. The young woman on her deathbed made a rather peculiar request, and asked that her body be encased within a pyramid in the tower atop the church. Nowadays, the 'tomb' is a landmark in honour of brave lifeboat men; rarely is the structure known as the 'Maiden's Tomb', probably because the story is a myth, but a good one at that.

The Isle of Lewis, as well as being known for its phantom lights, is famous for a spectral woman who was seen by two airmen – Donald Paton and Charles Palmer – on the beach as they had crossed the moors from the River Barvas to Loch Barvas. The men had been staying with a widow woman but decided to visit their airmen colleagues, who were situated at the Butt of Lewis. After walking some way the airmen settled down for a bite to eat. When they continued on their way they saw a woman approach along the coastline. She was dressed in all black. The two men turned away quickly to light their cigarettes – made all the more difficult because of the strong winds – and when they turned back there was no sign of the woman.

When the men returned to the widow's house they spoke of the figure and were told that they had probably seen Morag, who in 1895 had lost her husband – who was a shepherd – in an awful storm. Morag went out to search for him, but never returned. Her husband was in fact safe: he'd found shelter in a cave then he managed to get back home to his children, but his wife never came back.

The Isle Of Wight coast is rumoured to be haunted by the poet Alfred Lord Tennyson. In life he resided at Farringford Hall and would often take to the downs for walks. After his death in 1892, Tennyson was still seen walking along the coast, adorned in a dark coat and black, wide-brimmed hat – an arresting sight for anyone on a moonless night.

I would like to end this section with a couple of very mysterious and terrifying tales from Beachy Head at Eastbourne in East Sussex. The chalk cliff is said to be the highest in Britain, at over 500ft, and it is also one of the most common places for people to commit suicide.

As well as being terrified of the sea, I have a fear of heights, and in 1981 at the grand old age of 7 I visited the place with my mum, dad, nan and granddad. I was brave enough to stand about 30ft from the edge whereas my mother, who is absolutely petrified of heights, couldn't even look out across the sea. Admittedly, whether you are afraid of heights or not, there is a certain pull about these sorts of places.

It is no surprise that ghosts are seen around cliffs. Numerous suicides that have taken place at various locations known as Lover's Leap have spawned many a ghost story. (Neil Arnold)

Strangely, the name Beachy Head has nothing to do with the word 'beach'; in fact, the name is a corruption of the French words meaning 'beautiful headland'. In 1274, the chalk headland is noted as Beauchef, but it wasn't until the 1700s that the cliff became regularly known as Beachy Head.

In 1831 a lighthouse was constructed off Beachy Head and was in use by 1834, but in 1999, due to cliff erosion, it was moved 50ft inland. The area around the base of the cliffs does become swamped by mist and so, for safety purposes, another lighthouse was built in 1902.

On average, more than twenty people are said to leap to their deaths from Beachy Head each year. Today there are day and night patrols of the area in the hope of preventing suicides. I've always known Beachy Head for two things: a legend told to me as child that courting couples would jump, hand in hand to their death from a spot known as Lover's Leap; and secondly that one of my favourite films of all time, *Quadrophenia*, had several scenes filmed on the cliff tops. Interestingly, Lover's Leap – a legendary term – is mentioned all over the world in reference to spots where couples have been known to jump to their deaths.

Fairlight Glen in Hastings has its own Lover's Leap. The story in this county is that in 1786 a young sailor named Charles Lamb was in love with a lady named Elizabeth, but her father never approved of the relationship. This went to the extent that, to prevent Elizabeth from seeing Charles, her father put her in a house near the glen under the supervision of a trusted servant. Even so, from the window she was able to signal to the ship that young Charles had boarded and they were able to arrange secret meetings. In some versions of the legend, Charles would allegedly climb the steep face of the cliff to meet his sweetheart.

Those who know the legend cite two different endings: one being that the couple ran away together and lived happily ever after; but the other version states that poor Elizabeth, restricted by her father, jumped to her death from the cliff screaming the rhyme: 'The shells of the ocean shall be my bed, and the shrimps go wagging over my head.' Those who wish for a happy ending to this turn of events claim that, as the young woman jumped her dress snagged on the overhanging branches and she was eventually saved by Charles, but another version tells how both jumped from the cliff, hence the name of the spot: Lover's Leap.

Hastings Castle, now very much a ruin, was built in the eleventh century. There is an eerie legend attached to the area, for it is said that on certain misty mornings, fishermen have seen the original castle, in all its glory, rising from the mist. A ghostly figure has also been seen walking along the cliff edge. But I digress: now back to the horrors of the heights.

I recall many years ago when pulling into the car park of Beachy Head that there was a sign advertising the Samaritans. The sign was erected to try to prevent people from jumping off the cliff. It is said that some of Beachy Head's suicide victims liked to visit the nearby pub for one last drink before jumping to their death. Over the years many people have reported that whilst walking near to the edge of the cliff top they've sensed something very evil lurking nearby. This feeling may simply be the awesome draw of the cliff; in fact, just thinking about Beachy Head makes my knees go weak. Witnesses who have felt the presence describe something unnatural: 'as though there is an invisible path reaching out to the horizon,' commented one passer-by.

A Dr S.J. Surtees studied the increasing fatality rate connected with Beachy Head, stating: 'Personally I feel that it is the publicity of the place that attracts the next victim. It is a question of fashion – one person jumps then others follow suit.' In one peculiar case in point, a photographer was sitting overlooking the cliff when he was approached by a man who asked him if he wanted a good photo, and with that leapt to his death.

Over the years, there have been several sightings of apparitions perched on the cliff edge. One such figure is said to wear black robes and gaze out to sea. Another legend claims that the figure appears at the foot of the cliff and beckons people, whereas other witnesses have described that, whilst walking on the grassy verge, they heard whispering voices and in some cases their name being called. The fact that the area is ancient – it has been used since before Neolithic times – suggests that all manner of spirits could lurk there and some of these may have no relation to the high rate of suicides. One theory put forward is that some spots on the cliff were once used for human sacrifice: where victims were bound at the hands and feet, set alight and then rolled over the cliff. It is said that Roman leader Safo jumped to his death from Beachy Head as he believed it would make him immortal.

Beachy Head is just one of those unusual places, made all the more sinister and negative by the regular suicides. In the past, certain spots of the headland have been exorcised but to no avail: people still report the black-robed figure and also a clutch of wraiths in 'strange dress' that simply walk off over the precipice. In 1952 one exorcist claimed that whilst attempting to bless the place some force tried to edge him off the cliff. The medium, a chap named Ray de Vekey, alleged that he saw the figure of a bearded man wearing a monk's habit. De Vekey was of the opinion that the spirits present wanted some sort of revenge.

The author aged 7, with his grandparents Win and Ron at Beachy Head in 1981. (Paulene Arnold)

Despite the exorcism, a few years afterwards two climbers claimed they were accosted by some type of 'malign presence', which hovered close to them until they moved away from the edge. Several decades ago, a young girl rushed up to a policeman who was on patrol and stated, matter-of-factly, that she'd seen a dark shadow that suddenly enveloped her. Although the sun had been shining brightly, when she became engulfed the woman felt and saw only darkness. The woman managed to break free from the manifestation but then alleged something 'huge and menacing' began to follow her along the cliff top. 'It was as if it was driving me towards the edge,' she reported.

Another of the ghosts about the place is said to be that of a young woman, who walks to the edge, looks around and then jumps. One evening a man named Anthony Lawton was returning from visiting friends at Newhaven when, in the vicinity of Beachy Head, he saw a whitish figure walking extremely close to the edge of the cliff. Anthony called out to the girl as he was worried for her safety but he got no reply; he concluded it must have been a ghost! On another occasion a Mr Ashcroft, from New Zealand, was walking along the road that flanks the headland one night with his son when they spotted a misty figure perched on the edge of the cliff. As they approached, the figure vanished. Another local spirit is that of a farmer's wife who, with a baby in her arms, jumps to her death.

In his book *The Strange and Uncanny*, John Macklin mentions an old manor house situated nearby and points the finger at this building with regards to the strange feelings and dark robed figures seen. He writes that, '... it is from this house that the trouble is said to stem.' It is said that as monasteries were dissolved monks took refuge in other places; one such building was the manor house, the owner of which betrayed the hiding monks. Legend has it that, in response, the monks placed a curse on the man and his property. Is the same curse still in effect, drawing people to the edge and forcing them to the rocks and waves below?

In 1975 a Lionel Geoffrey Jaekel visited the Orkneys for the first time in his life. One Sunday he left Stromness where he was staying and went for an afternoon stroll along the cliffs. There was not a soul in sight as he took in the awe-inspiring sights, including the 360ft-high Black Craig. After walking for about thirty minutes or so, Lionel sensed a powerful force present that gave him a 'feeling of compulsion to go to the cliff edge and look over'.

Despite taking to the cliffs that day, Lionel had always had a fear of heights, and yet something was drawing him ever closer: 'I had literally to fight to keep about ten yards from the edge.' This awful feeling stayed with him for half a mile or so, and then gradually dissipated.

When Lionel returned home he was keen to conduct a bit of research into the area and found out that the spot was reputedly haunted. In 1860, two farm labourers had fallen out over their love for the same local woman and one had murdered the other with an agricultural tool. Then, under the cover of darkness, he had tied his erstwhile rival to a white horse, which he led to the cliff edge. There, he somehow forced both horse and rider over the rim. Ever since then there have been occasional sightings on the cliff edge of a white horse, and the strange feelings are no doubt the awful echoes of that terrible tragedy.

As a quick note, it is worth mentioning, although not sea related, the Cairngorm mountains, which are said to be haunted by an apparition known as the 'big grey man'. This allegedly sinister figure can stand up to several hundred feet tall and instils a feeling of utter dread upon ramblers, hikers and the like. Those who have experienced the spectre note how they feel an oppressive air and also report hearing voices or ghostly music. In a sense, this type of phenomena echoes the trickster spirits embedded in folklore, whether in the form of phantom lights or black dogs, said to lead people astray or to their death.

So, Beachy Head seems to be one of those places best avoided; or is there a possibility that the terrible statistics are false? Folklore researcher Michael Goss contacted Eastbourne police a few years ago to enquire about the suicides and asked whether the stories were true, to which the officer on duty replied, 'Yes. A look in the newspapers will tell you that.'

As we know, newspapers are not always the most reputable source when it comes to alleged 'true stories', and ghost-hunter Elliott O'Donnell, who briefly mentions Beachy Head and its haunting in his *Haunted Britain* book, doesn't give much credence to the legend either. He states: 'A remarkable feature in many of the Beachy Head tragedies, and one that has never been satisfactorily explained, is that when the bodies of suicides have been found, the left shoe has been missing.'

I'm not sure how Elliott knew this and, let's be realistic: if just a couple of people leapt from the cliff to their death, there is probably a good chance that a shoe may come off on the way down or during impact on those sharp rocks. There is also the possibility that the phantom monk, the ghostly woman and the like were all made up; simply being urban legends created to tie in with the alleged regular suicides of the cliff. Even so, on a rain-battered and windy night I can think of far better places I would rather be.

MISCELLANEOUS MARITIME MYSTERIES

Before I move on to the final chapter and bewilder you even further, I'd like to share a small selection of extraordinary tales that I haven't been able to squeeze into the previous chapters.

Phantom plankton and other marine swarms

Firstly, there is the tale of the mysterious green ooze – reported as being the size of Devon – which enveloped the coastal waters of Cornwall in 1999 causing much intrigue. Several British tabloids covered the phenomenon, which appeared as a lush turquoise blanket on the surface of the water. The bizarre carpet consisted of billions of minuscule aquatic plants, which exploded due to the hot weather in the July of said year. Stranger still, when viewed from the space the phytoplankton appeared as a milky white colour.

In his book *Lo!*, Charles Fort speaks of the coast of Norfolk in 1869 being covered by a substance 'of a thick, pea-soup appearance': a peculiar band of drowned ladybirds, 'about ten feet wide, and two or three miles long'. There is also mention that, on 26 July some 60 miles off Lincolnshire's coast, 'columns of aphides' descended from the heavens and gave the air a foul stench.

When I was very young, my family and I would often go on day trips to coastal resorts, zoo parks and other attractions. My mum often tells me the story of how, one summer's day, we visited the town of Ramsgate on the Kent coast and there was a ladybird plague. 'The bugs were literally everywhere,' she said, 'absolutely billions of them that had swarmed in from the coast like some ominous cloud.' I don't recall this incident but looking through files have found several reports pertaining to marine swarms that certainly back this type of occurrence up. An ominous cloud seen over the Channel, moving from Calais to Ramsgate, was reported in the late 1800s. Billions of ladybirds appeared on the coast, and seats, buildings, boats and people were covered in them. According to Fort, 'Ladybird shovellers were hired to throw the drifts into sewers.'

All manner of objects and animals have turned up on the shores of the British Isles.

Fort then records that a few days after, Kent was once again bombarded by a lady-bird swarm and the next day 'an enormous multitude' of new arrivals appeared at Dover. Worse still, the *Field* of 28 August 1869 records how a man, visiting Ramsgate by steamboat, experienced a hideous swarm of a 'bee-like fly', with billions more being reported 'at Walton, about 30 miles north of Margate'.

According to the *Daily Express* of 19 February 1974, thousands upon thousands of 'sea mice' had been found washed ashore on the coast of Southsea, Hants. The 5in-long grey sea worms are rarely seen. In July the same year, millions of spiny crabs were reported invading the coast of Bognor Regis, destroying fishermen's nets and pots. On 5 January 2011 the *Daily Mail* reported '40,000 devil crabs washed up on British beach after freezing conditions gave them hypothermia'. The incredible story was confirmed with a photograph showing Palm Bay at Margate. Meanwhile, www.kent-online.co.uk on 13 January 2009 featured the story of thousands of crabs washed up at Thanet, and then the following year a 'Tide of dead crabs' on Westbrook Bay, also in Thanet.

I must admit, though, the funniest maritime swarm I've seen of late has to concern the thousands of plastic toy ducks which turned up on varying coastlines around the world after falling off the back of a cargo ship (not a lorry this time!) some fifteen years previous. The ducks – all 20,000-odd of them – had travelled around 17,000 miles, some turning up on West Country shores. They were spilled from the hold of a ship in the Pacific on 10 January 1992 and have gradually turned up in places as far and wide as New England, Hawaii and the Hebrides, north-west of Scotland.

It is amazing just how many strange things turn up at sea, and whilst on the subject of out-of-place bird life, I can't leave this segment without mentioning a story from July 2009 concerning an ocean-going budgie who was found off Brixham in Devon on the 5th of said month. The bird was discovered by a team of scuba divers, given the name Captain and then taken to the local RSPCA shelter. Apparently a budgie breeder had lost five birds from his garden, but who would have thought that one of them would end up at sea! And what about the even stranger tale from 1830 of the 'large eagle' that was found washed ashore at Deal? The bird of prey was 'presented to the Canterbury Philosophical Institution', according to the *Rochester Gazette & Weekly Advertiser* of 16 February.

If you thought these avian mysteries were bamboozling, then I'll leave you with two, even more incredible stories – the first from March 1960, off Flamborough Head, Humberside. Fishermen aboard a trawler got the shock of their lives when in their nets they found … wait for it … an elephant! Scoff all you like sceptics, because, sec-ondly, twenty-two years later fishermen off the Aberdeen coast also found an elephant, albeit dead, that was floating some 32 miles out in the North Sea! The mind boggles!

Killer sands
Culbin Sands dominate a huge stretch of coastline in Moray, Scotland. The beach is owned by the Royal Society for the Protection of Birds (RSPB) as it is a haven for

wildlife. In the July of 1955, Bill Macintosh had visited the sands with his wife and family. It had been a glorious day and Bill had lain on the sand and dozed off, high up on the beach. His slumber was disturbed by a North Sea chill. A drizzly mist was now sweeping across the beach, and as Bill got to his feet and looked around for his family, he realised the beach was deserted. There was no sign of his wife and three children, who he was sure had probably found something of interest nearby to pass the time while he slept. Bill shouted out, hoping for some sort of response, but all was still; eerie, almost. 'No need to panic,' he thought to himself, and he called out again before walking across the beach, just in time to see a beach ball bobbing on the waves. At that point, his heart started to beat faster and a cold sweat broke out on his brow. But there were footprints, he now saw, not going into the sea but instead heading up towards the dunes. He followed them until they seemed to stop dead. Despite searching for a couple of hours until dark, Bill never found his family and was completely unaware that they had been taken by the killer sands of Culbin: a cruel beach that for centuries has claimed many victims. Some say an ancient gypsy curse was to blame.

Perhaps this was the same curse that caused the sands to wipe out a village and bury it hundreds of feet below. Rumour has it that in the 1960s two forestry workers discovered a cottage, all but consumed by sand. They found an opening into the building and it looked as if the owners had only just left it. When the foresters returned with another team the cottage had been engulfed again, only the bumps on the beach

Beware the killer sands! (Joyce Goodchild)

now signifying where these remnants had been. Author John Macklin, in writing of the sands, added, 'Nobody knows what brought the killer sands to Culbin, or why they started'. Somehow, this freakish area has the ability, like deadly waves, to wipe out communities and swallow them whole, just as it did to Bill Macintosh's family.

Shiver me timbers!

A few years ago, I was investigating a haunted house and spoke to an antique dealer who was firmly of the opinion that inanimate objects could harbour so-called paranormal energy. The dealer told me that on several occasions he had destroyed items of furniture and even jewellery because it had a bad vibe about it! This brings to mind a couple of sea-related tales.

In 1935 a Mr Rhomer built a house out of the timbers used to construct a ship by the name of *Mauretania*. When the house was built strange things began to occur: odd creaking and moaning noises came from the woodwork, as if the house had become a big old ship on rough seas. Ghost-hunter Peter Underwood investigated the house, known as Little Gatton, situated in Reigate in the county of Surrey. Those who visited the dwelling got a very sombre feeling from it and tragedy seemed to revolve around it, with there being several deaths outside. This included the death of a young woman who had been run over outside, and a fire killing a girl in the neighbouring house. Maybe all this ill luck was simple coincidence, but the house was nevertheless eventually sold and the next owner regretted every minute of being there.

I've often wondered just how many houses, or at least their bowed ceilings, have been constructed using ships' timbers. Could a ship that has experienced a lot of tragedy, such as a shipwreck, transfer its negative energies elsewhere?

In his book *Healing the Haunted*, Dr Kenneth McAll writes of a 'happy, united family' who resided in an 'old, thatched cottage', at an undisclosed location. Despite being very level-headed people, the family always sensed a presence around the house and eventually asked Dr McAll if he could pay a visit. When he arrived, he was extremely impressed by the huge oak beams across the ceiling that 'were obviously old ships' timbers'. The family gathered round and told their accounts of seeing an old man in the house, often in the vicinity of the stairs. Although the man was not malign in his presence, the family felt uncomfortable at him being there and so Dr McAll requested they hold a service to 'release' the spirit, which seemed to work.

The Mermaid Inn, a delightful twelfth-century, Grade II listed building located in Rye, East Sussex, not only has strong smuggling connections (the notorious Hawkhurst gang had their headquarters there in the 1730s and '40s) but some of the chairs have been carved from old ships' timbers. This and the smuggling link could explain why the inn is so haunted and why it was even exorcised in the early 1990s. The village in general is considered one of Britain's most haunted locations and there are a few sea-related phantoms. A house at South Undercliff may well be haunted by an old sea captain who was rumoured to have shot himself in the building. In the

The ghost-infested Mermaid Inn at Rye in East Sussex. (Terry Cameron)

village church there is said to be the spectre of a headless sailor. A ghostly sailor is also said to haunt the Hope Anchor Hotel, although those who have experienced the ghost only hear its footsteps.

Another old inn with similar paranormal activity, which has been greatly investigated, is Jamaica Inn, situated on Bodmin Moor in Cornwall. This building used to be a notorious haunt of smugglers who would go to the coast and with false lures entice ships aground. Numerous ghosts are said to haunt the property.

An even more peculiar case pertaining to a removed part of a ship being haunted comes from St Levan's churchyard in Cornwall. Many years ago a Captain Wetherel perished at sea in the vicinity of Rundle Stone (Runnelstone), described as a 'hazardous rock pinnacle situated about a mile south of Gwennap Head'. Captain Wetherel was interred at St Levan's churchyard and his grave strikes fear into the heart of anyone who should walk by it. Legend has it that beneath the soil the toll of a bell can be clearly heard at the time that marks the anniversary of his death at sea. The bell is said to be the exact same bell used on his ship. One afternoon a group of young people visiting the churchyard reported that, as they walked by Wetherel's tomb, they decided to stop and read the inscription upon it when suddenly a loud ringing came from close to beneath their feet.

A local sailor returning home from sea one day began hearing stories about the phantom bell and assumed it was complete nonsense and simply folklore, but decided that at midnight he would visit the grave to be sure. Two comrades of the sailor decided to go with him but remained in the church porch and waited. As the clock struck twelve, the sailor rushed back to his colleagues and through heavy gasps exclaimed, 'True as I'm alive, I heard eight bells struck in the graveyard and wouldn't go near the spot again for the world.' It is said that shortly afterwards, upon returning to sea, the young sailor drowned. No wonder local people rarely talk about the toll of the phantom bell: for fear, not of ridicule, but of death.

Stanbury Manor, situated in Morwenstow, Cornwall, has a haunted relic. An old chest, which was believed to have been on board one of the ships of the Spanish Armada, was purchased by a Stanbury Manor owner named Mr Ley. He told researcher Peter Underwood that the dealer he purchased it from was 'glad to see the back of it' because there had been an air of the weird about it – probably due to the fact that it had been decorated with depictions of headless bodies. According to Mr Ley, when the chest was owned by the dealer it would cause items within its vicinity to fall off walls of their own accord.

When Mr Ley brought the cedar chest home he placed it in the armoury of the building until he could find somewhere more suitable but, according to Underwood, 'there the first unexplained incident took place'.

The following morning Mr Ley walked into the room and suddenly six guns that had been hanging on the wall near to the chest just fell to the floor. Mr Ley thought nothing of this although it was extremely unusual, and decided that day to move the object into his and his wife's bedroom. Later that evening, the couple were hanging some curtains when a picture fell from the wall and struck Mr Ley on the head, even though he was not close to the frame. The weirdest thing, however, was the fact that although the picture was heavy Mr Ley didn't feel a thing when it hit him.

The next day, Mr and Mrs Ley were in the same room when a trio of pictures suddenly fell from the wall and then, two days later, more pictures dropped to the ground. Then, a couple of days after this, one of Mr Ley's relatives died – but he was hesitant to connect the two. A while afterwards, according to Underwood, 'A former curate of Newlyn West recognised the photo of the Morwenstow "poltergeist chest" and related the following story …': a long time before it had been in the possession of two elderly women who, due to being deaf, could only communicate to each other by writing. Over the years, and due to their reclusive nature, they had accumulated a lot of items – some junk, some valuable – and eventually decided to put them up for sale. When the local curate decided to visit them he found it very hard to communicate, as they expected him to write notes as they did. According to the curate, when the women were youthful they had stayed with some friends and, as they had arrived late, decided to go straight to bed rather than unpack their belongings. The next morning their attention was drawn to the old chest on which they had placed their clothes, not least because it had begun to open of its own accord. The women sat agog as the chest revealed something so apparently vile that it shook them to the core, rendering them deaf on the spot. After this incident, the women never revealed exactly what they saw that night.

Peter Underwood, in hearing the tale, was reminded of a similar chest once encountered by a level-headed and sceptical surgeon in the Midlands. He had gone to stay with a friend one night and was drawn to the object. Upon opening the large chest, he was horrified to find inside the body of a man whose throat had been slit from ear to ear. The surgeon slammed the lid shut but once he had gathered himself, creaked it back open – only to find the chest empty. The following day he mentioned the incident to his friend who told him the grisly tale of a man who had committed suicide, his body being found in the trunk.

Had this been the same ghastly chest that had struck the two old women deaf? Had they seen the suicide victim when they gazed into the blackness? I guess we will never know until someone takes a peek into the sea chest of doom again.

Another reputedly cursed item is that of a model galleon, housed in what is said to be Britain's oldest pub: Nottingham's Ye Olde Trip to Jerusalem. The model vessel was said to have been left by a sailor more than 150 years previous and remained hung from the roof of the pub. The cobweb-ridden artefact is said to be cursed and should anyone attempt to clean or move the boat, then tragedy will befall them. Over the years, three people who ignored the curse are said to have died. In October 1996 the pub closed for a few months of refurbishment and pub manager Marilyn Dare was hesitant to disturb the ship. She told the *Nottingham Evening Post*, 'I have a bad feeling about the galleon being moved. Strange things have been happening over the last few weeks; lights have been switching on and off by themselves and things have been moving of their own accord.' Medium Mallory Stendall was even called in by the brewery bosses to bless the ship, so as not to expose any of the builders to the alleged curse.

More cursed items

According to *Fortean Times* magazine, Issue 256 (December 2009): 'Mike Gilpin was working as a docker on a pier in Boston in 2000 around the time a salvage vessel was landing pieces of hull from the wreck of the RMS *Titanic*.' Mike, eager for a souvenir, grabbed a chunk of the wreckage and took it home and kept it in a jar, but within weeks strange and negative things began to happen. 'I've been divorced, lost my house, I crashed my truck and my motorcycle,' so the *Irish Examiner* reported on 16 April 2009. 'Then I took the piece to my new summer home in New Hampshire and it burned down ...' The only way for Mike to avoid further ill luck was to visit Cork Harbour on the 97th anniversary of the sinking of the *Titanic*, and toss his souvenir back into the depths.

In the September of 2008 an American tourist – as reported in the Scottish *Sunday Post* – visited the isle of Iona and, whilst taking a trip to the thirteenth-century abbey, decided to keep a piece of stone that had broken off from the wall. The tourist then hopped on the boat in order to leave the island but the tour guide asked if any visitors had taken any souvenirs, for, if so, they could expect bad luck. Of course, the American didn't believe in such fate until, moments later, her £250 digital camera dropped into the water. The tourist was initially able to laugh this off, until the next day when, on the plane leaving Dublin, another strange incident took place. The cabin pressure had been malfunctioning and so the plane delayed take-off. Then, when the 'victim' finally made it home, she suffered severe financial problems and also had a nasty fall, resulting in an operation. In the December of 2008 the American decided enough was enough, and posted the piece of stone back to the isle of Iona, requesting it be put back where it had come from.

Supernatural spouts

On 18 July 1967, a lobster fisherman named Bertram Stride was checking his pots 2 miles off Highcliffe in Hampshire when his eyes met a spectacular sight. 'I looked up,' he reported, 'and there it was, a vast curtain of water about half a mile away as high as Salisbury Cathedral.'

Had this been some type of extremely rare natural phenomenon, such as a waterspout? It may be a coincidence and completely unrelated, but around the same time strange lights were seen off the coast by witnesses, including an airline pilot, who saw 'clusters of objects streaming trails of light' that headed towards France.

Even more interesting was the report from August 1974 of a giant waterspout, which was observed near the Isle of Wight and witnessed by the master of the Hull-based ship, *City of Athens*. Skipper Charles Hanson contacted the coastguard after seeing a giant spout, which he believed could easily have damaged any small boats in the area. It was first seen some 6 miles off the coast of St Catherine's Point and headed towards the mainland. 'It was a solid column of water about 20-ft high,' Hanson commented. 'And there was a disturbance in the water around it like a hovercraft would make.' The Meteorological Office confirmed that later that day there had been a similar giant spout seen off Peacehaven in Sussex but a coastguard at Bembridge, Isle of Wight said, 'I've seen only one before. They're like smaller versions of a tornado.'

These types of rare waterspouts have been held responsible for some unusual falls from the sky, in their time. Fish, frogs, snails, hay, metal, blood and excrement have all been known to fall from the sky for no apparent reason, though it seems highly unlikely that a spout could be so selective as to only chose certain species of fish, or sweep up frogs and no other creatures.

A peculiar sea-related fall such as this was reported in the *Metro* of 9 August 2012 under the heading, 'Kelp me if you can … now it's raining seaweed here,' after a Mr and Mrs Overton of Berkeley, near Cheltenham, reported a weird find in their back garden. In fact, a whole street had been covered in seaweed, which a Met Office spokesman named Ian Fergusson claimed had been picked up by a tornado some 20 miles away at Clevedon beach, north Somerset. Why the tornado chose just seaweed seems rather odd, but Fergusson remarked: 'There were several thunderstorms in the area and if one of the funnel clouds touched down on to the beach, making it a tornado, it could have quite possibly picked up the seaweed.'

The main issue with such a theory is that if such a funnel-type anomaly had swept across a beach, then why hadn't it picked up shells, sand and other matter – only seaweed?

Devourer of steel

The *Irish Times* of 11 August 1998 reported on a bizarre 'steel-eating micro-organism' said to be causing severe problems in the port of Killybegs, County Donegal. According to *Fortean Times* who catalogued the snippet, 'The unidentified bug, believed to be a combination of two bacteria, destroys modern steel 20 times faster than ordinary rust.' Bad news then for piers, although a spokesperson for the Department of the Marine in Dublin played down the worry, stating that 'the symptoms were consistent with accelerated low water corrosion, caused by oxygen-producing bacteria' even though the rumoured bug had eaten away several Scottish piers in Shetland and Ullapool.

The Devil and the deep blue sea

The Devil. Satan. Lucifer. Old Nick. Whatever name you know him by, his part in folklore is potent. In Dorset there are two huge chalk stacks, which sit out in Studland Bay on the tip of Handfast Point, and have been eroded over time by the waves. These two white protrusions are known by several folkloric names: Old Harry, Old Harry's Wife and Old Nick's Ground. The rocks were once considered as eerie beacons amidst the crashing waves, and were used to warn ships to steer clear. The devilish associations may have originated as far back as the seventh century, from whence comes a legend that claims the Devil once slept on top of the rocks.

There is also a legend that claims Sir Francis Drake once sold his soul to Satan in order to become an accomplished sea admiral. In his defeat of the Spanish Armada, Drake was said to have been aided by a group of sea witches who conjured up great storms to destroy enemy boats.

Another devilish sea legend comes from the aptly named Devil's Dyke in Sussex. This beauty spot was allegedly formed when the Devil attempted to dig it out in order to allow the sea to flow in to drown god-fearing parishioners. The problem was, the Devil made so much noise that it awoke an old woman who chased him away with a candle.

Interestingly, the Isle of Wight is actually said to be a lump of soil that fell from the Devil's furred hoof.

Submarine dream

There is a slightly unusual story of a prophetic dream in *Lord Halifax's Ghost Book*, which mentions one Countess Chichester, who during the war was visited by a Scottish nurse. The elderly lady told the countess that one night she had had a very strange dream

Old Harry's Rocks.
(Mark North)

The Devil was once
said to have slept on
the rocks off Handfast
Point in Dorset.
(Illustration by Simon
Wyatt)

concerning the Forth Bridge, and that in this dream she had seen black whales with castle-like objects upon their backs. These odd forms were circling the third pillar of the bridge. She ignored the dream until the following night, when it came to her again. So vivid was the dream that she wrote to her nephew about it, as he had been employed to work on the bridge. Bizarrely, he replied saying that the 'whales' were in fact submarines that had been attempting to attack the bridge, and the strange castle-like protrusions were their periscopes. The nephew stated that at the time his aunt's letter arrived much work had been done to protect against submarine attack and every pillar, except the third one, as work was still being carried out on it, had been guarded.

The nephew rushed to his foreman and showed him the letter, which he took very seriously, responding, 'We had better take measures to make everything safe'. Lo and behold, an enemy submarine did try to destroy the third pillar shortly afterwards, but to no avail thanks to the strange dream!

An unusual meal

The *John O'Groat Journal* of 8 September 1855 ran a bizarre story of the 'Kitten Swallowed By A Cod', stating:

> A correspondent in Kirkwell alludes to a recent notice in our Stromness news of a rabbit's leg being found in a ling's stomach, and adds of his own knowledge something more wonderful, being nothing less than the discovery of an entire kitten in

The burning cliff at Dorset. (Mark North)

the stomach of a cod caught not long ago in Kirkwell Bay. These facts show that fish in general are not particularly fastidious in the selection of their food.

I'm now expecting several fishermen to report catching fish with plastic ducks in their bellies!

The case of the burning cliff

I'd like to end this chapter with a strange and peculiar yarn attached to the county of Dorset. Local legend has it that during the April of 1827, the east cliff at Ringstead Bay caught fire for no apparent reason. Researchers Mark North and Robert J. Newland, in their fascinating book *Dark Dorset*, wrote, 'The cause was once thought to be the effects of a lightning strike igniting the oil shale, but geologists later discovered heat generated by the decomposition of iron pyrites ignited the bituminous shale, and black stone.' The cliff was said to have been aflame for many days but eventually died out. Ever since that strange episode a National Trust sign has been erected to indicate the legend of the burning cliff.

5

DENIZENS OF THE DEEP

WHO NEEDS NESSIE?

There can be no doubt that the most famous water-dwelling monster legend of our times is that which concerns Loch Ness in Scotland. For many centuries it has been alleged that a large, unknown creature lurks within the loch – a body of water so vast and deep that it is unlikely to ever give up its secrets. So much has been written about 'Nessie', the leviathan of Loch Ness, and yet to this day no one is any closer to proving whether such a beast exists at all. Even so, it is an endearing mystery set in the most wondrous and magical of locations, overlooked by the ruins of Urquhart Castle, visited every year by thousands of people. In 1996 I was one of those people fortunate to experience the early morning mist, inky black waters and a soundtrack of wheezing bagpipes. I was also amazed at how many tourists became excited by a distant splash or a strange shadow that seemed to loom across the mirror-like surface. I never saw the monster, perhaps because I don't think it exists. I want it to in my heart, but in my mind, the creature that people claim to see is probably a visiting sturgeon, or maybe a large eel or even a big catfish. Of course, to call the enigmatic beast the Loch Ness Catfish would not sell t-shirts, mugs and toys, and so Nessie remains as something it cannot be – a long-necked dinosaur.

There are countless books written about the reputed creature of Loch Ness. Thousands of newspaper articles can be found if one chooses to search for them, and there are even claims that the beast may well have distant cousins in a few other lochs and lakes dotted around Britain. There are even lake monster legends from the other side of the world: the United States and Canada, Sweden, Norway, the list is endless. Of course, it is unlikely that the existence of these alleged monsters will be proven, and that's probably a good thing because it means they continue to have that majestic aura about them. I really can't see a freshwater angler reeling in anything more

Do sea serpents exist in Britain's seas? (Illustration by Neil Arnold)

exciting than a big pike, or maybe an out-of-place Wels catfish or snapping turtle from a lake, but the seas around Britain and those vast, deep oceans of the world could be the place to hide real monsters. Way back in the first chapter I spoke about a few monster eel legends, but the monsters I'm going to be talking about in a moment are not simply overly large yet known species; no, I'm talking about beasts that could well be unknown to science.

Legendary creatures said to inhabit lakes and lochs seem unlikely, but in the deep blue sea all manner of creatures could exist and, judging by some eyewitness reports, they do!

MORGAWR

The name 'Morgawr' may sound like some fetid demon from J.R.R.Tolkien's epic *The Lord of the Rings* trilogy, but it is in fact something far stranger, or so people believe. Morgawr – Cornish for 'sea giant' – may be an anagram of ragworm, but it certainly doesn't resemble one. Morgawr is a semi-mythical monster, akin to Nessie, said to inhabit the waters around the coast of the West Country, particularly Cornwall's Falmouth Bay. Sightings date back a couple of centuries and some people claim to have even photographed the beast. The most famous cluster of sightings of Morgawr took place in the mid-1970s; a strange time for the area as UFOs seemed to be buzzing the local skies and a frightful creature named Owlman (see my book *Shadows in the Sky*) was seen at Mawnan Old Church a few miles from Falmouth.

In the September of 1975 a Mrs Scott and her friend Mr Riley observed Morgawr off Pendennis Point. They described the monster as approximately 20ft in length and having a humped back and a long neck. The monster was said to have dived into the depths then resurfaced with a conger eel in its mouth. Shortly afterwards, mackerel fishermen saw the creature and at the start of 1976 reports flooded in. A majority of these were chronicled in a peculiar little pamphlet called 'Morgawr the Monster of Falmouth Bay', which was written by Anthony Mawnan-Peller. This small work has often been regarded as nothing more than tomfoolery and legend, but it still acts as a brief and quirky guide to the legend.

Mawnan-Peller wrote in 1976:

A hundred years ago a long-necked monster was caught by fishermen in Gerrans Bay. Fifty years later, a Mr Reese and a Mr Gilbert, trawling 3 miles south of Falmouth netted an amazing creature. It was 20-feet long, with an 8-foot tail, a beaked head, scaly legs, and a broad back covered with matted brown hair.

In most cases, witnesses described something akin to a plesiosaurus, a prehistoric creature that became extinct millions of years ago. The plesiosaurus, despite existing in the Jurassic period, is very much alive today according to some researchers. For them, there can be no other creature in the ocean to explain the sightings of a long-necked beast; but can such an animal have eluded science and extinction for so long? It seems highly unlikely that even in the most remote parts of the world dinosaurs still exist, and yet we cannot dismiss every eyewitness report.

In the February of 1976, the *Falmouth Packet* newspaper published two very intriguing photographs, claimed to have been taken by a lady calling herself Mary F. The photos appeared to show a large, dark, humped beast rising from the waters off Trefusis Point, at Flushing. The monster, if it was a monster, had the typical long neck and small head one would associate with a plesiosaurus. The photographs seem to show some 'thing', but whether it is an animate object or not we will never know. One thing is for sure: whatever it appears to be, it seems too far out of the water to be a creature. Still, it added to the mystery of Morgawr.

The other major problem, as mentioned by Anthony Mawnan-Peller, was that there appeared to be a lack of consistency in the reports of the creature, which stated that its 'length varied from 12 to 45-feet'. One report, made by two businessmen in the May of 1976, described *two* creatures at the mouth of Helford River. This particular spot became known as 'Morgawr's Mile', as most of the sightings seemed to take place on the coastal stretch from Rosemullion Head to Toll Point. Mawnan-Peller also states that in the January of 1976 there was a sighting of Morgawr made by a dental technician, who described seeing a large, dark hump in the water, which he took to be a whale until the long neck rose out of the water. The witness claimed the beast was almost 40ft in length and, around the same time, a holidaymaker claimed to have seen a similar thing.

A majority of lake and sea monster sightings around the world seem to describe a large, dark hump in the water that resembles an upturned boat. Some researchers who have analysed photographs, occasional pieces of film footage and spoken to eyewitnesses believe that these monsters may in fact be sturgeon – especially in the case of the Loch Ness critter. Sturgeon do not grow to 40ft in length, but it is known that eyewitness reports are often inaccurate, especially when judging size of an object from a distance. There are some twenty-six species of sturgeon and some of the largest can grow to almost 20ft in length. A majority of sturgeon prefer freshwater, which could explain the sightings in Loch Ness of an 'upturned boat', but such fish rarely venture beyond coastal areas and certainly do not have long necks.

Another suspect put forward to explain sea serpent sightings is the conger eel. However, eels do not reach much more than 9ft. A 210lb conger eel has been caught off Falmouth waters so maybe, just maybe, eyewitnesses are getting it wrong. Over the years, several differing species of whale have turned up on Devon and Cornish beaches. For instance, on 17 February 2010 a 17m-long fin whale was seen floating on the surface of the water at north Cornwall, and a few days later the creature was found beached at Porthowan, some 37 miles away from the first sighting. On 14 May 1998, an amazing spectacle was witnessed when more than 500 basking sharks appeared off Cornwall's coast at Kennack and Coverack. The plankton-eating sharks, some measuring up to 35ft in length, may have been taking advantage of the unusually warm water.

Is it possible that in the mid-1970s witnesses, caught up in the Morgawr hysteria, had seen a species of whale or shark in the distance and wrongly identified it? Okay, so maybe we can sweep all those sightings under the carpet, but what about the strange sighting that took place in the autumn of 1944 and involved fishermen, the sort of people who should know their whale from their eel? On the website www.mevagissey. net, there is a fascinating account that describes an encounter with Morgawr off Fowey Point. The best thing about the sighting, apart from the actual incident involving the monster, was that a short while previous the fishermen in question had observed a whale a quarter of a mile off starboard.

Later that night, the crew had begun to haul in their nets when suddenly the boat seemed to bump on a large wave that had come from nowhere. The four fishermen, almost losing balance, stared into the blackness of the water when suddenly, just

Falmouth Bay – home to a sea serpent or two? (Neil Arnold)

12ft away, an object appeared. 'A 3 to 4-foot diameter object with a ball-like head came straight out of the water and rose to a height of some 12-feet above the water's surface,' one fisherman stated: not the behaviour of a sturgeon, eel or whale. The creature, or whatever it was, seemed to breathe hard and then with grace slipped back vertically into the depths, rendering the witnesses silent until they returned to shore, realising that no one would ever believe their story. Five years later, on 5 July 1949, a Mr Harold T. Wilkins, accompanied by a friend, saw two plesiosaur-like creatures at East Looe, Cornwall. 'What was amazing,' Mr Wilkins exclaimed, 'were their dorsal parts: ridged, serrated, and like the old Chinese pictures of dragons.'

On 1 August 1999 a Mr Holmes, who had worked for the Natural History Museum for some nineteen years, was visiting Gerrans Bay, south-east of Truro in Cornwall, with his wife. Mr Holmes was equipped with his video camera and had been filming his wife swimming in the water when he caught sight of a 'fin-like' object, which emerged 200m offshore. Initially, Mr Holmes thought the creature was a shark, until he zoomed in and realised that the 'fin' was in fact a neck. Just behind the neck a rounded back, measuring approximately 7ft in length, could be seen breaking the surface of the water, and atop the neck was a reptilian head.

The creature eventually disappeared below the depths. When John took his video home and watched it back, he was again stunned by the form. Eventually, he showed it to various marine biologists: one expert ventured that it may have been a distressed oarfish, but all essentially said that, whilst unusual, the footage was too blurry to determine. Oarfish are bizarre-looking fish, which could explain some mistaken sea serpent sightings. They can grow up to 56ft and are the longest bony fish said to exist, but they prefer tropical waters and are rarely seen. Even so, beaching does occur when the fish is sick or dying. In 1866 a 15ft-long oarfish washed up dead on England's north-east coast at Seaton Crew, near Hartlepool in Cleveland. The creature was stuffed and put on display at Redcar's Kirkleatham Old Hall museum and can now be found at the Gray Art Gallery in Hartlepool. In 2003 a 3m specimen was also caught off Cleveland, and in 1981 one was found washed up at Whitby in Yorkshire.

In 2002, two experienced seamen – Dan Matthew and Mike Bedford – had two separate encounters with a creature that couldn't have been an oarfish. Dan Matthew, cox for the St Piran patrol boat, was on a small vessel in the vicinity of Maenporth at 10.30 a.m. on 8 May, when he noticed something 'weird' in the water up ahead. 'As we got to within 100 yards,' reported Matthew, 'its neck was completely out of the water, but when it saw us coming its neck fell from a vertical position and made quite a big splash. It was grey/black in colour.' Matthew was literally stunned by what he had seen, concluding: 'I've boated in the Fal for many years and I've never seen anything like this. I've seen lots of dolphins and whales, but it wasn't either of those?'

Amazingly, four days later, a chief engineer aboard the same patrol boat got talking to an elderly fisherman, who told him that on the same day as Matthew's sighting he was a mile north of Manacles when he had seen an object resembling a large fin, but some 3ft in length, protruding from the water. 'It was too big for a basking shark,' he reported; so what was it? If people were seeing a plesiosaurus, or something of a similar nature in the waters around Cornwall, then the descriptions didn't always seem to match the classic Morgawr reports.

Could sunfish be held responsible for some of the Morgawr 'fin' sightings? The ocean sunfish is an unusual-looking fish that can weigh over 2,000lb. It spends most of its time in tropical and temperate waters, and is recognisable by its long dorsal and ventral fins. On 25 July 2006, *BBC News* reported that some nineteen sunfish had been spotted off Cornwall's south-western tip. 'We only spotted the sunfish lying on their side at the surface,' reported Dr Brendan Godley, a senior lecturer at the University of Exeter Cornwall Campus. 'This is the first time we have spotted them during our surveys.' The fin of a sunfish would certainly confuse a lot of people as it protrudes from the water.

In the September of 1995 the West Country papers were all in a fuss over more Morgawr sightings. During this period, one Gertrude Stevens was at Golden Bank, in Falmouth, when she saw a small head atop a long neck just 60yds away. She described the monster as around 20ft in length with a conical body narrowing towards the tail. The beast then sank out of sight. The latest sighting had triggered the memory of several other witnesses who came forward to speak of their encounters with the Cornish sea giant. On 10 July 1985, for example, a Dr Eric Bird, accompanied by his sister Sheila, spotted the creature off Porthscatho on a very calm evening. They also reported the creature to be approximately 20ft in length and having a 'long muscular tail visible just below the surface'. The same year, Carrie Ham spotted an object resembling an overturned boat in the Helford River but was shocked when a long neck emerged from beneath the water.

According to *Fortean Times* magazine, 'One of the most celebrated sightings was by Falmouth fisherman George Vinnicombe in 1976.' He also reported seeing an upturned boat-like object some 30 miles off the Lizard, and then the head and neck appeared, convincing the witness it was something out of the ordinary. In the same year Doc Shiels, a local magician and showman, had his sighting of Morgawr, but he was hesitant in reporting his experience to the newspaper as he thought that coming from a theatrical background may have led people to believe he had made the whole thing up. Even so, Mr Shiels' wife Christine contacted the *Falmouth Packet* because she, too, along with her children, witnessed the creature, which she described as a 'large, dark, long-necked, hump-backed beast moving slowly through the water, then sinking beneath the surface'.

On 11 August 1976 one Patrick Dolan, whilst sailing from Falmouth to Kinsale in Ireland, spotted a 'worm-like' object some 30 miles north-north-west of the Scilly Islands. 'The neck was about 8-feet out of the water,' he said, 'it [the creature] was about 40-feet long and propelled itself with an undulating movement … I must have had it in my vision for about twenty minutes.'

With so many sightings of Morgawr being reported over the years, sceptics have asked why there isn't more film or photographic footage of the beast. Considering the amount of people who were visiting the coast armed with video cameras and the like, should there not be more?

On 17 November 1976 David Clarke, from *Cornish Life*, visited Helford River with Doc Shiels. Mr Clarke wanted to take some photographs of Mr Shiels with the water in the background, and so they went down the cliff path to Parson's Beach. After taking several photographs, Doc noticed something out in the water, which resembled a small, dark-coloured head, and so several photographs were taken. Sadly, they remain inconclusive to this day. As author Graham J. McEwan wrote: 'the frames were double and triple exposed' due to the slipping of the wind-on mechanism of the camera.

On 27 July 2010 a long-necked sea creature was reported off the Devon coast. Witness Gill Pearce took several photos of the object and reported her sighting to the Marine Conservation Society (MCS). The creature appeared 20m or so off Saltern Cover Bay, at Goodrington (bringing to mind Richard Freeman's story from the first chapter regarding the monster eel) and moved with a shoal of fish. A spokesman for the MCS commented, 'It was reported as a turtle as it had large flippers and what appeared to be a shell, but was also said to have a small head on a thin neck about 2ft long which craned above the surface like a plesiosaur.' An electrician named Graham Oxley also reported seeing the creature in the bay: he said it measured some 10ft in length and was black in colour. The MCS spokesman added: 'The lady thought it might have been a turtle but turtles don't catch fish, so at the moment it is "unidentified".'

Had this been the same creature bothering Cornish waters for more than a century, or was there a more down-to-earth explanation? In 1993 the legend of Morgawr had become so popular amongst locals that a mechanical sea beast named Morgawr was built and put on display as an attraction at Land's End. Whilst Morgawr had embedded itself into local legend, just like Nessie in Scotland, there seemed to be more to the Cornish beastie than just folk tales. Cryptozoological researcher Jon Downes, who spent many years investigating the Morgawr phenomenon, came across a fascinating story from the 1970s that a majority of people had overlooked: Anthony Mawnan-Peller wrote of a 'Strange (and so far unidentified) carcase … discovered on Durgan Beach, Helford River, by Mrs Payne of Falmouth.' Jon added: 'This account has been quoted extensively in books about the subject, but few bother to report the aftermath of the story.'

It seems that, a short time after the discovery, a teenage amateur naturalist named Toby Benham contacted the press to state that the bones were not from a sea monster but from a whale that had been brought in on the storm tides. According to Jon:

> For the past five years the skull had apparently been in the art department of Toby's old school in Falmouth. Eventually we [The Centre For Fortean Zoology] managed to contact the teacher Mr Brown and were told we could photograph the skull whenever we wanted … but we wanted more.

Jon asked Mr Brown if they could borrow the skull of the 'monster' for analysis, to which the teacher obliged. Upon seeing it, Jon realised straightaway it was indeed from a whale.

Of course, for every mystery solved, another puzzle emerges. Prawle Point, a coastal headland in south Devon, was reached in July 1912 by the German vessel *Kaiserin Augusta Victoria* and at the helm was a Captain Ruser. On 5 July at 6.30 a.m., it was reported in the ship's log that a creature, measuring some 20ft in length and of the appearance of an eel, had been seen splashing the waves violently with its tail. Captain Ruser commented that almost all of the monster's body was visible (just like in those strange photographs taken by 'Mary F.'). The previous year a serpent in the region of 60–90ft in length with brown-green skin was observed at Westward Ho!.

In 1934, the *Western Morning News* featured a report of a 10ft-long, 6in-thick 'monster' seen off Whitsand Bay, but the description very much resembled a large eel. It had been observed by a Mr Gunn who, along with three other people, was relaxing on the beach between Tregantle and Freathy when a black object – which they at first took to be a log – appeared in the water some 50yds away. The object then turned and headed towards the shore, moving how a 'caterpillar crawls'. The witnesses were convinced

the beast was not an eel, and the closest creature they could match it to was a boa con-
strictor snake. The following year, a huge black creature was seen off Port Isaac, on the
Cornish north coast. It was said to have been almost 50ft in length.

'But where are the sea serpent bodies?' I hear you cry. Interestingly, the *West Briton*
– a weekly Cornish newspaper of 1876 – covered the story of the capture of a 'sea
serpent', which was found alive and tangled around a buoy by some fishermen who
were pulling in their crab pots. They were around 500yds from the shore when they
saw the creature, which they struck with an oar. When they finally dragged it ashore it
was finished off and thrown back into the sea!

The legend of Morgawr is never likely to fade. Every time an unusual object is seen
off the Devon or Cornish coast, it will become part of Morgawr folklore. However,
the most intriguing aspect about this particular sea giant is that a majority of eyewitness reports seem detailed when compared to a majority of rather vague wakes, plops
and splashes associated with Nessie and other water-dwelling monsters.

Two types of sea serpent are reported by witnesses. (Illustration by Neil Arnold)

The thought of a plesiosaur or two roaming Britain's coastal waters still doesn't sit right with me, but then again, what else can be put forward to explain such sightings? In his classic book *In the Wake of Sea Serpents*, Belgian zoologist Dr Bernard Heuvelmans proposed that the multi-humped monsters being seen could well be primitive whales, thought to have been extinct for 30 million years. But those witnesses who have observed Morgawr have never been of the opinion that they've seen a type of whale. One obscure option is that such beasts are mere phantoms; ghostly apparitions roaming an ethereal sea and still appearing to those susceptible enough to witness them. Maybe the theory isn't so crazy when we consider the amount of reports concerning spectral ships, ghostly sailors and the like; and so until a carcass is found and scientifically analysed, or conclusive enough film footage emerges, I guess every theory is plausible, however ridiculous it may seem. And it is not as if these monsters are unique to Devon and Cornish coasts: indeed, judging by the next batch of reports, sea monsters are all around Britain.

CURIOUS CREATURES OFF THE KENT COAST

Mr Andrew Drew, in a letter to the *International Weekly Journal of Science*, wrote:

> On Monday, August 5th 1879 a number of geologists crossed in the Folkestone boat to Boulogne, to study the interesting formations of that neighbourhood, and, when about three or four miles from the French coast, one of these gentlemen suddenly exclaimed, 'Look at that extraordinary object passing across the bow of the steamer, about a mile or a mile and a-half in advance of us!'.

The crew looked where the man was pointing and saw 'an immense serpent about a furlong in length, rushing furiously along at the rate of 15 or 20 miles an hour'. The object was described as being black in colour with a paler behind, and its elongate body appeared on the surface of the water.

The Kent coast doesn't feature heavily with regards to sea serpent sightings, but it does still feature. One of the earliest reports comes from 1912 when a Mr Stone and two other witnesses observed a creature with a long, sinuous body off St Margaret's Bay, near Dover. Five years later in the July of 1917, a monster was reported to have been seen off Ramsgate. According to a W.H. Lapthorne, in an article submitted to *Bygone Kent* magazine (Vol. 6, No. 9, 1985), the monster was witnessed by the crew of 'an armed drifter', which had been 'attached to the famed Dover Patrol'. The boat had been cruising between North Foreland and Margate when a look-out on the boat shouted that a large snake-like creature had appeared up ahead. The witness, startled by the monster, described it like 'some gigantic conger eel about 15-feet in length, with a long scaly body, a large spiny dorsal fin and dark olive green in colour'.

Strange serpents have been reported off the coast near Dover. (Matt Newton)

As the vessel neared the serpent, the captain ordered his men to fire (which seems a little unusual) and the sixth shell struck the dorsal fin of the beast, causing it to violently thrash about in the waves before sinking in a frothing whirlpool of its own crimson. However, that was not the end of the saga. In 1957 a similar incident took place, this time off the Sussex coast, when some of the local fishermen began to speak of a strange monster out at sea that had destroyed their nets. Those that caught a good enough glimpse of the serpent claimed it was some 50ft in length and bore a large scar on its fin. Was it the same serpent? Then, in 1968, a creature was seen off Seaford, suggesting that maybe a family of these leviathans were loitering off the south-east coast.

In 1934 there were reports off Herne Bay of a 20ft-long monster that had been pursued by motor boats. Even travelling at 40mph, they could not catch the sea beast. A big crowd gathered on the seafront to watch the chase. Some described the serpent as having a dark back but a yellow underside and that, as it arrowed through the waves with an undulating motion, bathers ran for their lives. Sixteen years later in 1950 at Cliftonville, between Margate and Broadstairs, a similar creature was seen by a John Handley. Mr Handley, a Londoner, had visited the seaside resort in the July and was swimming in the cool waters near to the Libido Baths when there was a strange disturbance in the water. Just 200yds away a '2ft long head with horse's ears' emerged from the water. Mr Handley panicked, swam back to shore and never once looked back. Another woman who was sunbathing confirmed what Mr Handley had seen, but neither could identify what the creature was.

In 1999 I was contacted by a Mr Wire who told me of a spectacular incident off the Kent coast. He said:

I was fishing off Folkestone Pier with a fellow angler when in the distance we saw a black object. I looked through my binoculars and saw a huge animal that I can only describe as a sea serpent. The creature was roughly 100-feet long and seemed to be diving and then resurfacing. We both watched it for about 30 minutes and it was so ridiculously large that I laughed and did not tell anyone else about it. The animal had a long neck, moved very slowly and looked all the world like the Loch Ness monster plesiosaur that people talk about. It was massive.

Is there any way Mr Wire could have been mistaken? Despite their stories of 'the one that got away' anglers usually know their species pretty well, but then the Kent coast has had some unusual visitors over the years.

On 14 April 1998, two teenage boys thought they had discovered the carcass of a sea serpent at Greatstone-on-sea, near Romney Sands. Peter Jennings and Neil Savage were strolling along the beach looking for anything unusual when they stumbled upon an 8ft-long decomposing body. The creature still possessed a skull, a series of large vertebrae and rotting body tissue. The story was featured in the *Kentish Express* of 19 April and the *Folkestone Herald* on the 23rd. The boys told neighbour Peter Fender about their find, who in turn told the *Herald*: 'It's a bit of a mystery. The dead creature is dark yellow, and has stripes running the length of it.'

The reporter wrote: 'Mr Fender said it was too big, with a thick spine, to be a conger eel. It is thought the body has been on the beach for a while. It is falling apart, with the tail missing – and it smells.' Zoologist Karl Shuker examined the pictures of the creature in the newspapers, and in his 'Alien Zoo' column for *Fortean Times* magazine, he commented:

As soon as I saw the photos I realised that the carcass was strikingly similar to the famous Hendaye sea serpent corpse of 1951 – conclusively identified by Dr Bernard Heuvelmans as that of a basking shark. All of the telltale features were present – the cottonreel-shaped vertebrae, the long triangular snout, and most distinctive of all, a pair of slender curling 'antennae' projecting from the snout's base. These are in fact the rostral cartilages which, in life, raise up the shark's snout.

Of course, basking sharks don't grow to 100ft in length so did Mr Wire, an experienced fisherman, unknowingly see a whale? In the December of 1763 a whale (species unspecified) measuring 56ft in length was found washed ashore at Seasalter, near Whitstable. Other reports from the time suggest it was 36ft long. Even so, a sperm whale measuring 61ft is recorded from Broadstairs a year previous. Another sperm whale turned up at Whitstable in 1764 at and was said to have measured 54ft in length with a girth at its widest point of 38ft. The *Chatham Standard* of 29 July 1980 commented on the 36ft-long dead whale discovered by anglers at Yantlet Creek.

Whales have certainly been known to come further inland, with numerous sightings over the years in British rivers. The River Thames has seen a few, as has the River Medway; the most unusual being the narwhal that was found at Wouldham Creek in 1949. The narwhal, measuring more than 13ft, was a rare find as such creatures are normally found in Arctic waters, and this beast had only been the fifth of its kind found in British waters in more than four centuries. Mind you, the weirdest creature, and the closest thing we've had to a monster in a Kent river, was encountered in the 1940s in the Medway: when the Pocock family gave chase to a 40ft-long form resembling a 'monstrous eel' that evaded capture and seemed immune to bullets. In 2008 the *Medway Messenger* reported on a similar serpent seen swimming up the Medway towards Strood. If such a monster can loiter in rivers then the sea would be a far more likely lair to hide in, and so it is very likely that, whatever it was, it must have come from the North Sea.

To list even a small portion of unusual (albeit known) visitors caught, found dead or sighted around British waters would be a monumental and exhausting task, and so we must stick to those 'monster' stories and head off to the Scottish coast.

SCOTTISH SERPENTS

Over the years, there have been several reports of alleged serpents in Scottish waters. One of the first ever recorded was in the June of 1808 at Coll, in the Outer Hebrides. A Mr McLean, parish minister of Eigg, wrote to a Dr Neil, secretary of the Wernerian Society, to discuss his encounter, which then appeared in the *Transactions of the Wernerian Society*. In his letter, Mr McLean wrote that that whilst rowing along the coast he 'observed, at about the distance of half a mile, an object to windward, which gradually excited astonishment'. The monster appeared at first as a 'small rock' until it elevated itself above the sea, revealing a large eye. So stunned was the witness that he made sure to steer clear as the beast eyed his boat then plunged with a disturbance into the depths. Mr McLean rowed hard for sure, worried that the animal, or whatever it was, was now on his trail. This was confirmed when 'as we leapt out on a rock … we saw it coming rapidly under water towards us.'

As the serpent reached the shallower waters, it raised its mighty head and then headed off out of sight. Just what type of creature had Mr McLean witnessed? He described a beast bereft of fins that moved with an undulating motion – certainly unlike a whale – and its size was some 70–80ft in length, unlike that of an eel! Mr McLean also mentions in his correspondence that, whilst off Canna, some thirteen fishing boats had seen a similar brute; with one crew member describing the head of it as the size of a small boat and the eyes the size of dinner plates.

In his book *Sailors, Sea Serpents & Sceptics*, Graham J. McEwan lists many Scottish serpent sightings. He includes one from 1822 from the 'Scottish coast' that was allegedly observed by a 'friend of Sir Walter Scott' but, according to McEwan's table, the next sighting doesn't come until the 1850s when a Mrs M'Iver observed a long-necked creature at Greiss Bay, in Sutherland. This sighting was mentioned in the *Evening Telegraph* of 24 January 1893 under the heading, 'The Great Sea

Serpent'. The report speaks of a Mr W.H. Russell who, in writing 'to the *Times*', speaks of visiting Mrs M'Iver in 1851 and receiving a detailed eyewitness statement of the encounter. According to the witness, the creature had been seen in the little bay causing great alarm to the fish population until eventually heading out to sea, where fisherman apparently shot and wounded the poor creature. After this incident, the beast headed toward the shoreline where it proceeded to haul at least 8ft of its body onto the ground. There it rested until the boats came close, and then it slid into the depths.

The most amazing aspect of the encounter, however, was that the serpent left behind some scales, described as 'about the size and shape of a scallop shell'. Mrs M'Iver was said to have been in the possession of some of these scales. The article also goes on to mention another monster sighting, this time from the shore of Dunrobin, as witnessed by a Revd Dr Joess and a Lady Florence Chaplin.

In 1872 there were several sightings around Scotland of a serpent. The *Inverness Courier* commented that:

In the present case, the limit in which the animal has been seen on our coast, is Lochduich to the north and the Sound of Mull to the south, only about a fifth of the space between Cape Wrath and the Mull of Kintyre; and it is in that part it should be most looked for.

In the August of that year the Revd John McRae (Minister of Glenelg, Inverness-shire) and the Revd David Twopeny (Vicar of Stockbury, Kent) reported to the *Zoologist* that, on 20 August whilst travelling in a small cutter from Glenelg to Lochourn, they, as well as two women and a young lad on board, observed a serpent on a perfectly still and sunny day. At first the monster appeared as a 'dark mass about 200 yards astern of us, to the north' but was then followed by another hump, and then another. The creature moved very slowly across the water, then was gone. The next moment, the first 'mass,' which they took to be the head of the creature, reappeared, followed by more humps that suggested the rest of the body. 'There was no appearance of undulation,' reported McRae and Twopeny, who estimated the creature to be some 45ft in length. The serpent came to within 100yds of the cutter and its crew, much to the alarm of some of the witnesses, but the monster then headed off towards Skye.

The following day the serpent – as the creature was believed to be – was seen again. This time it was sunning itself in the rays and looked to be considerably longer. More sightings of the serpent followed. 'We were inclined to think it perhaps might be attracted by the measured sound of the oars,' McRae and Twopeny wrote, concluding in their letter that, 'The public are not likely to believe in the creature till it is caught and that does not seem likely to happen just yet …'. A day or so after these extraordinary sightings others claimed to have seen the monster, particularly in the Loch Duich area.

In 1873, on 17 September, a Dr Soutar reported seeing a serpent at Golspie, Sutherland. In 1886 there had been another sighting of a serpent in the sea loch of Duich, whilst in 1893 a Dr Farquhar Matheson and his wife were sailing one afternoon in the Kyle of Lochalsh, off the north-west coast of Scotland, when they observed something rise out of the water some 200yds ahead. The neck and head resembled that of a giraffe and was brown all over, and despite being in view for a mile or so, the witnesses eventually lost sight of it.

During the early 1900s there were more serpent reports in Scottish waters. One night, three fishermen were off the Isle of Skye when one of them observed a large object that rose out of the water some 50yds or so ahead. The two other fishermen – who hadn't yet seen the creature – began pulling on the nets, hoping to haul in a decent catch. When they caught sight of the serpent, however, they dropped their nets in the water and made for the shore with haste. On a summer's day in 1910 a Mr W.J. Hutchinson had a similar experience. He was out shooting wildfowl with his father and cousin in the vicinity of Meil Bay in the Orkneys when, as they were sailing towards the Skerries, they saw several whales thrashing in the water, as if in distress. Suddenly, the long neck and huge body of a creature appeared out of the water, terrifying the men who did their best to avoid the leviathan. Mr Hutchinson reported that they had a good view of the creature, which was only just over 100yds away, and that its neck rose some 18ft out of the water.

In 1910 three men witnessed a serpent in the vicinity of Meil Bay in the Orkneys. (Glen Vaudrey)

In the August of 1935 it was claimed that a sea serpent had washed ashore at the small port of Girvan, on the west coast of Scotland. The anomaly was said to measure some 35ft in length and had skin covered in bristles. Archie and Gwen Wilson, who saw the decaying lump, reported: 'We saw the thing laying on the beach close to some rocks; it was horrible to look at, like some eerie relic from our past.'

Sceptics often dismiss reports of sea serpents and state that if such creatures existed then surely we'd find remains. This is untrue when we look at the giant squid, which, for all its size, rarely turns up on beaches across the world let alone in fishing nets. Some forms that do wash up on coastlines decay quickly: a creature such as the basking shark, when decomposed, has a bodily structure that resembles a plesiosaur. Many people can thus become confused when seeing animal remains, especially when they are not used to seeing such disfigured and pungent blobs. In July 2011 several newspapers reported that a sea monster carcass had been found at Aberdeen. A dog-walker stumbled across the rotting carcass, commenting: 'It's nothing like we've ever seen before. It almost looks prehistoric.' Of course, the remains were not from some type of dinosaur or dragon; with Rob Deville, marine life expert from London Zoo, commenting that the body was probably of some sort of whale.

There are numerous cases on record of strange animals washing ashore in Britain. Some of these are alien species not native to our waters, but in the case of alleged serpents it is always important to go with the consistency rather than jump to conclusions; all other angles and species must be eliminated first before any talk of serpents can be taken seriously. A prime example of media sensationalism occurred with the case of the Canvey Island 'monster', found washed ashore in Essex in 1954.

On 13 August 1954 the local press ran the headline, 'Fish with feet found on beach', after a Revd Joseph D. Overs claimed to have discovered the creature. The newspaper article, accompanied by a photo of the 'monster', stated that the fish was more than 4ft in length and that underneath its stomach could be found two feet, each having five toes. Sadly, this was another case of witnesses having no knowledge whatsoever of nature. The fish was nothing more than an ugly anglerfish. Bizarrely, some authors and researchers who looked into the story – without actually researching it adequately – sketched their own interpretations, resulting in several hilarious mutants, which didn't in any way, shape or form resemble the creature that had washed ashore.

In Issue 245 of *Fortean Times* (February 2009), a Mr Gary C. Hammond wrote in and stated that, 'Cold and deep are ideal water conditions for anglerfish and Canvey holds the British record for a shore-caught angler, some 68lb, caught in the Sixties.'

In 1990 a peculiar creature was found washed ashore in Benbecula in the Hebrides. A Louise Whitts, aged 16 at the time, discovered the 12ft-long carcass and took a photograph of it. Bizarrely, Louise never presented the photograph to an expert and mislaid the item until 1996, when she finally took it to the curator of the Hancock Museum in Newcastle-upon-Tyne. According to the curator, a Mr Alec Coles, no marine biologist, botanist or zoologist could identify the furry remains, which to

In 1954 an alleged monster washed up on the shore at Canvey Island in Essex. It turned out to be an anglerfish. (Neil Arnold)

this day remain a mystery. The creature became known as the 'blobster' of Benbecula. The story took a rather unusual twist, however, with Louise commenting: 'It was beside some land owned by the Ministry of Defence and there were big notices all over the place saying that if people found anything on the beach they were not to touch it.'

Was the hairy carcass some type of secret experiment gone wrong or, like so many other potential serpent carcasses, nothing more than a badly decomposed whale or other known species? To this day the photo remains intriguing (I understand the last place it was on show was in the Hancock Museum).

On 26 June 1908, the *Daily News* ran the incredible story of the crew of the steamship *Balmedic*, who had dredged up a strange skull north of Scotland and taken it to Grimsby. The skull suggested an animal roughly the size of an elephant, but with huge eye sockets and a leathery tongue some 3ft in length. The *Grimsby Telegraph* of 29 June reproduced a photo of the skull. A Mr Pycraft, from the British Museum, stated that he had never seen anything like it before.

Although not quite a serpent, one of the most fascinating catches to be recorded took place on 17 April 2001 from the waters of Kinlochbervie, Sutherland. A halibut measuring 8ft in length was caught by James Lovie, skipper of the trawler *Enterprise*, and after being weighed (topping the scales at 20 stone!) it was sold to a fishmonger in Aberdeen. This particular fish was more than twenty times the size expected. The biggest fish ever caught off British waters, however, was a sturgeon hooked off Orkney in 1956 and weighing 50 stone! If one of these was to wash ashore and rot, I imagine all manner of strange stories pertaining to serpents would circulate.

On 25 September 1808, a serpent carcass was said to have been discovered on the island of Stronsay, north-east of the Orkneys. The carcass was found at Rothiesholm Head after a local man noticed a large amount of seabirds fussing over something on the shore. As he neared the beach in his boat, he realised that some type of carcass was on the rocks and it appeared to have a long neck and a body length of over 50ft. When the gales blew the corpse to the shore, it was revealed that the skin of the creature was grey and six limbs extended from its body. The neck was over 10ft in length and the head, resembling that of a sheep, had the eyes of a seal.

The remains stayed on the shore and rotted to nothing, but some researchers who looked at the case believed that the monster was nothing more than a basking shark. If this was the case then the measurement of over 50ft is a mystery in itself, because the longest basking shark recorded measured 40ft (caught in nets in Canadian waters in 1851). The average adult reaches lengths of between 20–26ft, so if the Stronsay carcass was simply a basking shark, it was still a monster of one!

On 18 November 1873, a sea serpent was observed in the Firth of Forth by more than 120 witnesses, who described a gigantic, eel-like creature. In 1882 the *Glasgow Herald* of 2 June told the story of a serpent seen off Shetland, 28 miles east of Fetlar. The monster was said to have measured over 150ft in length with a head covered in bar-

nacles. The whiskers on the face alone were said to be 8ft long! Witnesses on board a boat named *Bertie* claimed that the creature was making straight toward the vessel and 'had blown', but not like a whale. The witnesses could see the wide, gaping mouth – a mouth big enough to have swallowed the boat. Thankfully, the serpent merely followed the ship rather than deciding to take a bite out of it. Eventually, so unnerved were they by the presence of the pursuing creature that the crew

Alleged sea serpent carcasses have been washed up on the beaches of Britain. In most cases, they turn out to be nothing more than badly decomposed known animals. (Illustration by Simon Wyatt)

showered it with stones, it nevertheless only gave up the chase some three hours later. When the witnesses came ashore, they spoke of their encounter and a while later were called upon to give sworn statements.

On 13 September 1959, a shark fisherman and his friend saw a strange creature in the waters off Soay. One would have thought that the witness, a Mr Tex Geddes, would have been used to seeing large fish, but on this occasion he could only describe the beast as 'some hellish monster of prehistoric times'.

His colleague, a Mr Gavin, confirmed, reporting:

the head was rather like that of a tortoise with a snake-like cranium running forward to a rounded face. Relatively it was as big as the head of a donkey. I saw one laterally placed eye, large and round like that of a cow. When the mouth was open I got the impression of large blubbery lips and could see a number of tendril-like growths hanging from the palate. Head and neck arose to a height of about 2ft. At intervals the head and neck went forward and submerged. They would then re-emerge, the large gaping mouth would open (giving the impression of a large melon with a quarter removed) and there would be a series of very loud roaring whistling noises as it breathed.

What type of monstrosity had Mr Gavin and Mr Geddes seen? Mr Geddes added, 'The head was definitely reptilian, about 2ft 6in high with large protruding eyes. I would say we saw 8 to 10 feet of back on the water line.'

A number of witnesses reported seeing a serpent in the Firth of Forth in July 1939. The beast was described as having a horse-like head and large eyes. Eight years previous, a man and his teenage daughter were cycling along the beach at the Isle of Arran when they saw a large, upturned boat-type of object lying on a rock out in the water. The curious witnesses approached the object but were shocked when it moved and revealed a head and set of eyes, which were glaring at them. The beast 'wobbled' and plopped into the water, leaving a huge wake. The witnesses described the monster as greyish in colour, heaving a parrot-like head with a strange beak. The general size of the creature was estimated to be that of a large elephant. So stunned were they by their encounter that the witnesses wrote a letter to the *Glasgow Herald*, although it was not featured.

In 1953 at the Firth of Clyde, a fisherman reported seeing a 30ft-long monster. This was not the first time a serpent had been seen there: in 1935 fishermen observed a creature with a long neck in the vicinity of Great Cumbrae.

In 1962 a dog-walker watched in horror as a bizarre beast slithered into the water off Helensburgh, Glasgow. Two years later, two naturalists spotted a serpent through their telescope as it swam in waters off Shuna and the following year, in 1965, one of the most unusual monster sightings took place in the Tayside region, when motorists travelling east of Perth on the A85 claimed to have seen a sea monster on the side of the road! Add this to another fifty or so sightings from around Scottish waters and we have a strong case to suggest there is something lurking in the coldest depths, which is not recognised by science.

The main problem with such reports, however, is that due to lack of evidence they are very quickly relegated to folklore, alongside dragons and the like. Legends of dragons are very much harder to swallow for some, but as a mythical creature the fire-breathing sky serpent of folklore has most certainly embedded itself into British history. One such tale concerns the Arbroath behemoth, which many foggy centuries ago was said to have killed and eaten many villagers before returning back to the depths of the sea. One rumour, which began to circulate at the time, was that local fishermen had caught one specimen – albeit a small one – in their nets, put it into a metal cage and taken it to Dundee, where it drew in the crowds like moths to a flame. Of course, like in all good Hollywood movies, the dragon eventually escaped and wreaked havoc on the area, killing many before it was chased back to the sea. En route, it managed to devour many fishermen and crush their fragile boats. A great story indeed, but it seems that, over the years, the serpents of our seas have calmed down somewhat.

WELSH WONDERS

Wales could well be considered the monster capital: its folklore is drenched in tales of fairies, sprites, giants, mermaids and, of course, dragons. There is something so enchanting about Wales; maybe it is the deep valleys and the remote peaks that overlook those rolling hills. It gives a sense of magic; a sense that there is still a place within the British Isles that could offer us a secret, or hide a monster.

On 3 September 1882, a group of people were standing on the pier at Llandudno looking across the sea when they spotted something unusual in the region of Little Orme's Head. The object was travelling at some speed toward the Great Orme, suggesting it was about a mile away from the witnesses. An F.T. Mott, as recorded in *Nature*, stated: 'It is estimated to have been fully as long as a large steamer, say 200ft; the rapidity of its motion was particularly remarked as being greater than that of any ordinary vessel.' Whatever it was, it had a jet-black colouration and was 'snake-like with vertical undulation'.

In 1805 the crew of the *Robert Ellis* watched in awe as an 'immense worm' followed in hot pursuit in waters between Anglesey and the mainland of Caernarfon. The creature swam so quickly that it soon overtook the ship and was said to have climbed aboard via the tiller-hole. Then, like a snake, it coiled itself under the mast. One crew member was said to have attacked the creature and somehow, instead of battering it to death, they forced it back to the water. Even so, the beast was back in hot pursuit until the ship changed course and pulled away from the critter. Seventy years later, a 12ft-long object, black in colour, was seen by staff at the Minydon Hotel, Anglesey. The creature was spotted at the west of Red Wharf Bay.

Sea serpent legends are rife on the Welsh coast. (Simon Wyatt)

Stories of Welsh serpents are not just confined to foggy archives, though. In the August of 1963 a man holidaying at New Quay, Dyfed, on the west coast of Wales, was stunned to see a 30–40ft-long object that disturbed a seal colony. The description of the monster seemed to match that of a plesiosaurus, with the long neck, small head and a dark body propelled by four flippers.

On 2 March 1975 at Barmouth, six schoolgirls (all aged 12) were walking along the beach at dusk when they saw a 10ft-long monster about 200yds away. The creature had a long neck, green eyes and a long tail. The creature was also on the beach and heading off towards the sea. Around the same time, other visitors to Gwynedd reported seeing strange things out at sea and there was also the discovery of big footprints on the sand. Had this been some elaborate hoax or was there a sea serpent coming ashore?

Barmouth certainly has a history of serpent sightings. In the summer of the same year, a husband-and-wife team were sailing in their 30ft-long sloop 5 miles off Shell Island, when they saw a creature in the calm water. 'As we drew closer we thought it was a huge turtle,' remarked one of the witnesses, 'but it turned out to be unlike anything we'd ever seen.' Although the neck was short like a turtle, the creature was in the region of 11ft in length and 8ft across. Maybe the couple had in fact seen a turtle. Leatherback sea turtles are the fourth largest modern reptile and the largest of the sea turtles, and can grow to around 9ft in length. Coincidentally, the largest ever found was a specimen of over 9ft, found in Wales on the west coast. It weighed 2,020lb!

Is this the skeletal remains of a sea serpent found on the Welsh coast? No, it's just an unusual rock formation. (Found and photographed by Simon Wyatt)

In 2009 a serpent of sorts did come ashore, quite literally. The *Daily Mail* of 5 August reported on the 'Revolting Dr Who sea monster that terrified tourists', after the discovery of a 6ft-long creature, which had washed ashore on the Gower Peninsula. Hundreds of people were said to have flocked to see the ghastly beast and the press had a field day, despite the fact the tubular manifestation was nothing more than a 'seething mass of goose barnacles'. It was likely that, somewhere beneath the mass of barnacles there was a piece of driftwood that the barnacles had attached themselves to, but this explanation did not stop children from having nightmares about it!

Mind you, the Gower Peninsula has featured in many serpent sightings over the years. In his book *Gower Journey*, author A.G. Thompson mentions seeing a 30ft-long creature whilst standing on a cliff overlooking the bay. The monster had the head of a horse, complete with a mane. After staying in view for a short time, it dived into the abyss.

In the March of 1907 some fisherman were trawling off the Bristol Channel when they claimed to have seen a 200ft-long serpent that had four fins, each as large as a sail. On a smaller yet equally strange note, *The Field* of 23 May 1847 reported on a 'Strange Fish' caught alive at Holyhead Bay. The creature, although just 9in long, was said to be 'conically shaped', bereft of fins and scales, and sporting two large eyes. The 'fish' had feelers as long as its body and, according to the source, 'It neither resembled a lobster, crab, nor any kind of shell fish seen on the coast. It is quite a curiosity.'

A baby sea serpent, anyone?

IRISH MONSTERS

In Irish lore there are said to be all manner of sea-, lake- and river-dwelling monstrosities: from super otters to horse eels, and from serpents to dragons.

In 1871 a member of the clergy observed a creature with a horse-like head off the coast of County Clare. Are we to disbelieve a man of the cloth? The monster had a mane of hair and glassy eyes. Was it in any way related to the serpent seen on 26 April 1907 off County Cork? At the time a Sir Arthur Rostron, chief officer of the *Campania*, which was coming in to Cobh, reported a sea monster that was only 50ft from his boat. The head of the creature then raised some 9ft out of the water. Rostron sketched the monster and passed it on to a Commander Rupert T. Gould.

On 31 July 1915, a British ship named the *Iberian* was torpedoed in Irish waters. Legend has it that amongst the debris a monster resembling a crocodile was seen. As the boat exploded, the creature was flung into the air: a cracking story, but most probably nothing more than a hoax. Or maybe not! A couple of decades later a Captain Hugh Shaw and his crew observed a black, shiny, long-necked animal in the River Shannon in Ireland. The creature appeared close to the boat and then turned to head upstream. Several more witnesses observed the monster.

In their book *Mystery Animals of Ireland*, researchers Gary Cunningham and Ronan Coghlan list several sea monster sightings in reference to the Emerald Isle. According to them, on 20 May 1950 the *Nenagh Guardian* reported on a strange sea creature seen a century previous between Dundalk and Sutton in Dublin Bay. It was witnessed by two men, surnames Walsh and Hogan, who whilst sailing at 6.30 p.m. spotted a creature heading towards Howth. The head of the animal resembled an eel but it certainly wasn't one for, according to the men, the beast measured over 100ft!

In the same year, a 30ft-long creature was observed in the Bay of Kinsale as it scratched itself against a beacon! Only the shot of a rifle startled it: the monster jumped into the air with a start and came back down with an almighty splash.

There are many monster legends from Ireland, such as the one from the area of Lough Swilly, an inlet of the sea at County Donegal, which apparently is named after a creature from the Middle Ages. The creature – named Súileach – was said to have many eyes and so was probably nothing more than mere fantasy. County Donegal is, nevertheless, still known for its monsters. As the *Rochester Gazette & Weekly Advertiser* of 12 January 1836 reported: '[the] huge monster of the deep that recently cut the fishing-boat across whereby three men met an appalling death off St John's Point ....' Shortly after the incident, the beast was found dead on the shore. Described as 'one of the largest ever seen in this country', when opened up it had a 'young one' inside measuring 10ft. Sadly, the newspaper does not give too many details, but I am of the opinion this may be some known species of sea dweller, especially considering that 'the produce of the fish will be applied to the relief of the families of the unfortunate sufferers'. I'm sure that, had this creature been some unknown serpent, it would have been photographed or put on display somewhere rather than eaten.

Finally, contrary to popular belief, sharks can be seen around the coast of Ireland. For instance, in 2008 several basking sharks were noted off Cork, and one was later found dead on the shore. Then, in 2009, the *Irish Times* reported 'Half-ton shark caught off the Clare coast', after a 70-year-old man hooked a six-gill shark. The following tale suggests that stranger things are afoot, however. *The Field* of 13 October 1855 records 'Sharks on the coast of Ireland'. It states:

> The fishermen of the coast declare that they have seen several of these monsters of the deep on the coast of Achil Head and Clare Island. Last week a boat proceeding from Achil towards Newport laden with turf, and having a crew of two men and one woman, was suddenly capsized, and the woman was drowned, the men having held on by the boat; the peasantry declare that the boat was upset by one of those leviathans of the deep, and that the woman was carried off.

MORE SEA SERPENTS

Space here does not permit an exhaustive list of British sea serpent reports, and so I'll now present to you instead a clutch of my favourites.

The county of Dorset is steeped in folklore and, according to researchers Mark North and Robert J. Newland, 'one such monster was discovered on Weymouth Sands in October 1752'. The beast was said to have measured over 50ft in length. The monster was then cut up and 'expected to make 120 hogsheads of oil' suggesting it was actually a whale.

In the early nineteenth century, it was recorded that a serpent washed ashore at Chesil Beach. The monster had a long neck and a snake-like head but, despite a lot of interest, the creature turned out to be a camel! Even so, in his *Holinshed's Chronicles* of 1577, Raphael Holinshed recorded:

> In the month of November 1457, in the Ile of Portland not farre from the town of Weymouth, was seen a cocke coming out of the sea, having a great creast upon its head and a red beard, and legs half a yard long: he stodd on the water & crowed foure times, and everie time turned him about, and beckened with his head, toward the north, the south and the west, and was of colour like a fesant, & when he had crowed three times, he vanished awaie ...

And so was born the surreal sea chicken of Dorset!

According to North and Newland, a ship carrying several French monks observed a monster sporting five heads, which flew in the direction of Christchurch. The beast then proceeded to torch the abbey with its fiery breath.

Chesil Beach in Dorset – a monster is rumoured to frequent the waters here. (Mark North)

Dorset's most popular sea monster, though, is said to be called the Chesil Beach Monster after a handful of alleged sightings off Chesil Cove, Portland. In 2009 the *Dorset Echo* reported on 'A monster effort for Weymouth carnival', after craftspeople at Weymouth College constructed a replica of the monster, who is said to be called Veasta. The unusual name *veasta* is believed to derive from the old Dorsetshire dialect, meaning 'feast'. Sightings of the monster date back a handful of centuries and in 1996 a stone monument depicting the beast was erected outside the Ferry Bridge Inn, Weymouth, although the stone seems to resemble a seahorse rather than a serpent.

The county of Sussex, as briefly mentioned in the Kent section, was once said to have harboured a sea serpent. Dragon folklore is rife within the county but tales of sea serpents are few and far between, and those that are mentioned seem extremely dubious. On Good Friday 1906, solicitor Charles Dawson claimed to have sighted such a leviathan in the company of three other people, as it swam in the Channel. The witnesses were on board a steamboat journeying from Newhaven to Dieppe between two and three o'clock when Dawson, through a pair of strong opera glasses, sighted an object some 2 miles away that he at first described as a 'cable-like object struggling about'. Two other people then observed the form and whilst it never revealed a head or tail, it presented itself as a series of hoops. Dawson, in a letter dated 7 October 1907 to his friend Sir Arthur Smith Woodward, of the British Museum, commented:

'I judged that the hoops were fully 8-feet high out of the water and the length 60 to 70-feet …'

Dawson fetched his wife and she, too, observed the serpent until it faded into the sun's rays on the horizon. Although this story didn't properly come to light until 1955, those who knew of the yarn believed it to be a hoax, possibly due to the fact that Dawson – an amateur archaeologist – had perpetrated several previous hoaxes.

One Sussex-related sea anomaly that has intrigued me for many years concerns the case of the Sussex shark, which was sighted in shallow water off Brighton during the September of 1785. The creature was spotted by a man swimming: it allegedly approached him at speed but its toothy attack fell short and the beast ended up beaching itself. Within minutes locals had surrounded the shark and, with hatchets and a variety of other weapons, bashed, hacked and slashed it to death. Then, upon opening up its stomach, they discovered the head of a man.

The shark – said to have been a tiger shark – measured 12ft in length, and its appearance caused great panic for many years after. According to *The Times* of 6 August 1802, 'Nothing of the kind has been heard of since.' Researcher Paul Chambers, who wrote of the incident for *Fortean Times* magazine in December 2009, stated that if this indeed was a tiger shark then it was a most unusual case, as such a fish is 'predominantly a warm water species whose nearest proven occurrence is in the Bay of Biscay, France'. One such specimen was reported from Cornish waters in the late 1960s, and so it seems that, although rare, finding such a species around Britain is not impossible. There is a possibility, of course, that the shark that 'attacked' the swimmer wasn't a tiger shark at all, but something more docile like a basking shark. Sadly, due to the quick intervention of the locals, we will never know for sure.

Another, albeit mythical monster said to haunt Sussex is the kelpie, or water-horse. As reported at Rye in 1926, a courting couple were dog-walking across a misty field when they heard the sound of galloping hooves heading towards them. When they peered into the gloom they saw a horse-like creature with wild staring eyes that then thundered past them. The male witness was so intrigued that he sent the dog after it, but the animal refused to follow and so the man decided to chase it. He then watched in amazement as the monster bounded over a high fence and leapt into a murky pool. To see such a beast is a bad omen; as L. Grant in his *A Chronicle of Rye* states, 'The kelpie is a sly devil, he roars before a loss at sea and frightens both old and young upon the shore.'

Such a beast has also been seen cavorting along the beaches, which are situated just 2 miles from the village. This brings to mind a tale concerning what became known as a 'thunder horse' in the folklore of Scarborough in north Yorkshire. The appearance of the monster was recorded in *Chronicon de Melrose*, compiled by the monks of the Cistercian Abbey of Melrose. The hideous creature was said to have appeared during a great storm over York in 1065 and was seen 'always flying towards the sea to tread it underfoot', accompanied by a terrible soundtrack of booming thunder and crackling lightning.

The great horse was said to have left an enormous impression on a mountain at Scarborough, before plunging into the foaming sea.

Off the Northumberland coast there has long been legend of a sea monster called the Shony. The Vikings used to live in fear of such a creature, as it was known to lurk beneath ships in the hope a sailor or two might fall overboard into its waiting jaws. The Shony has always been the stuff of local superstition and was even blamed for several strange deaths recorded from the twelfth century. Those souls brave enough to venture across the causeway between Northumberland and Holy Island would, according to folklore, be picked off by the bloodthirsty monster. In one incident, several bodies were washed ashore and an inspection revealed that the eyes and innards of the victims were missing. Of course, there is a possibility that the unfortunate dead had suffered such appalling mutilations after being smashed onto the razor-sharp rocks, whilst crabs, and then birds, may have scavenged on the eyeballs. Yet, as is the case of so much other folklore, it is far more enthralling to seek a more dramatic, and in this case monstrous, explanation.

The Shony loiters in the darkest depths of the North Sea, but has reportedly been seen off Marsden Bay more recently. On 17 August 1906 the *Sunderland Echo* spoke of a 'Bather's alarming experience' after a man, noted for his swimming ability, had been in the waters off Seaburn when he was struck by some unseen form, which briefly paralysed his right arm. Whilst nobody ever found the cause, the Shony was held responsible. The following year, on 14 September, the *Western Daily News* covered the story of 'The Sea Serpent' with a letter from an A.C. Mason. It stated that, whilst in the company of a friend perched upon the rocks of Gulla Stern Cove, Tintagel, they saw a 'black object', which moved through the calm water. One theory put forward was that the sightings were of ribbon fish, also known as oar fish, but I'm unaware of black specimens.

Researcher Mike Hallowell, in his excellent book *Mystery Animals of the British Isles: Northumberland & Tyneside*, records several encounters involving the Shony. One incident concerned the crew of a steamer named the *Black Eagle*, who in 1946 spied a long head and neck that raised some 6ft out of the water. Several crew members set out in a motorboat but the creature eluded them. In 1998, Mike Hallowell thought he, too, might have seen the creature. On 11 August he, his wife and his father were travelling in the direction of Whitburn on the coastal road when Mike and his wife, looking out across the water, observed a dark hump that broke the surface and then slowly plunged back into the deep. When Mike arrived home some time later, he found out through the local *Shields Gazette* that the object may well have been a bottlenose dolphin, but the mystery didn't end there. Mike then received a call from a friend who said that, whilst in the local fish and chip shop, he had overheard two men arguing about the identity of a creature, which one of the men claimed was big enough to have swallowed the dolphin that everyone was talking about.

Interestingly, the Western Isles has a Shony, too. In the folklore of the Isle of Lewis the Shony was a god of the sea, and locals would wade into the sea and offer up a jug of ale, in the hope that the seaweed for the coming months would be abundant so as to enrich the ground.

In the December 1750 edition of *The Gentleman's Magazine*, there is mention of a sea serpent being seen off the Norfolk coast. The report reads:

> The creature was about 5-feet long from what could be viewed of it above the water, with a head like a dog and a beard like a lion. The skin was spotted like that of a leopard. It passed in a leisurely fashion finally disappearing beneath the waves to the great amazement of all those watching from the shore …

Some have theorised that this serpent may well have been a leopard seal – a highly aggressive predator usually found in Arctic waters but also known off Australia, Tasmania, South Africa and New Zealand. The body of a leopard seal is dark grey but the throat area is spotted.

In 1912 an animal that clearly wasn't a leopard seal was sighted by Lilias Haggard who, in a letter to her father, author Sir Henry Rider Haggard, commented: 'I happened to look up when I was sitting on the lawn, and saw what looked like a thin, dark line with a blob at one end, shooting through the water at such a terrific speed … I suppose it was about 60-feet long.' One of the more recent sightings of the serpent occurred in 1978 when a holidaymaker taking a stroll on Kessingland beach was astonished to see the head – which resembled a seal – of a large, many-humped creature that disappeared into the depths after a few seconds.

In 1931 there was a report of a monster off the Suffolk coast. The sighting was made by a woman named Sybil M. Armstrong who, whilst accompanied by her children's governess and cook, saw a dark object at a distance of 400yds moving through the calm water. The serpent appeared, like so many others, to have many humps trailing behind a head.

On 1 March 1934 the *Daily Telegraph* ran the headline 'Coastguard meets monster by night', after an astonishing sighting of an unknown creature ashore at Filey in Yorkshire. The witness, a coastguard named Wilkinson Herbert, was walking along the rocks at Filey Brig on a moonless night when he heard the strangest guttural growling up ahead. Mr Wilkinson flicked his torch on and came face to face with a huge neck that reared up some 8ft into the air, and two saucer-like eyes that glared down at him. The startled witness had the sense to shine his torch toward the body of the creature and realised it was some 30ft or so long. So horrified was he that he threw a handful of stones at the monster, causing it to groan and slowly move away. The fiend then plopped into the sea, its eyes reflecting the torch beam brightly. Whatever Mr Wilkinson had seen, it was no ordinary creature. 'I have seen big animals abroad,' he exclaimed, 'but nothing like this.'

Weirder still, the sighting seemed to bring other local folklore legends to life. For many years there had been a legend that a dragon had perished in the local waters and its great bones became the rocks that now sit at Filey Brig.

The seaside town of Skegness in Lincolnshire also has a serpent legend. In 1966 a Mr Ashton was walking along the seafront at Chapel St Leonards when, at a distance of 100yds, he spotted a snake-like head trailed by several humps moving through the water. A few decades previous, a Mr R.W. Midgeley reported seeing a monster during holidaying in Trusthorpe. Whilst peering over the sea wall, he was startled to see a creature some 400yds from the water's edge. Again, there were the semi-submerged hoops, which Midgeley saw before it sunk without a trace.

In 2002 an amateur palaeontologist found the skeleton of a 4m-long 'monster', south of Filey. The bones of a plesiosaur dating back to the early Cretaceous period were protruding from the base of a cliff and they caught the eye of Nigel Armstrong from Doncaster. According to plesiosaur expert Mark Evans, this find was a rather unique one. He remarked, 'We know about early plesiosaurs from the Jurassic period and ones from later on in the Cretaceous, so this new specimen fills a gap in our knowledge very nicely.'

Serpents have been reported off the Thames Estuary, too. One such beast was recorded in 1923 in an area known as Black Deep, which had been closed to shipping for some eight years. The crew of a ship called HMS *Kellett*, captained by F.D.B. Haselfoot, described seeing a long neck that rose out of the water some 200yds away. As recently as 1993 a creature with a long neck was seen at Leigh-on-Sea by several witnesses.

An unusual creature washed up on the Norfolk coastline in the eighteenth century.
(Joyce Goodchild)

Do prehistoric survivors roam the waters around Britain? The jury is still out until a fully formed specimen turns up on shore or in the nets of fishermen.

MERMAIDS FROM THE BLACK LAGOON

The mermaid is a creature embedded in legend and a fantastic being, which, alongside the unicorn and the dragon, remains one of the most celebrated of mythical figures. But what are we to make of the alleged encounters with these denizens of the deep?

Let us hop into a time machine for a moment and drift back to the year 1204, to the small Suffolk town of Orford. It was here that a legend began of a strange humanoid that was caught up in the nets of a fishing boat. Many people gathered on the quay to observe such a hideous spectacle – a wild man of sorts that had come from the depths. The body of the being was covered in hair but its head was bald, and so bizarre was this catch that the governor at the castle was informed. The creature made its way to the castle and was met by the governor, who had the docile creature shackled and secured within the castle dungeon. Despite being housed in such grim conditions, the wild man showed no malice and was happy to feed off fish. Eventually, he was given freedom to roam the castle, although some of the servants and guards on duty were uncomfortable with this and rather appalled by the creature. The fact that he had no way of communicating didn't endear him to the locals, either.

Ultimately, so much friction was caused between the governor (who had grown fond of the wild man) and his staff that those in opposition to him began to bully, prod and provoke the creature. When the governor was away, the Orford merman was taken outside and beaten. Upon his return, the governor declared he was disgusted at such behaviour and became even more intrigued by the beast. He was said to have even taken the merman to mass.

The novelty of the wildman gradually wore off for the governor, though, and the lack of response to his teachings made him feel frustrated. So the governor decided to section off an area of the water where his subject was first captured and allow the hairy creature to return to its watery abode, whilst

The Mermaid – fact or folklore?
(Illustration by Simon Wyatt)

Was a mermaid killed and buried in Benbecula in the Outer Hebrides? (Terry Cameron)

still being able to monitor it. This plan relieved the castle staff and some of the locals but one afternoon the wild-man escaped through a hole in the netting and swam out to sea. Some claim he continued to loiter in the waters around Dunwich cliffs – maybe the creature had become fond of his new surroundings – but gradually the sightings decreased and the merman of Orford became a legend.

There are so many stories of mermaids and mermen, and even tales that claim there have been many inter-actions between them and humans over the years. Another popular mermaid story comes from Benbecula, which has been mentioned previously in this book. In 1830 a peculiar creature was spotted off the island of Benbecula in the Outer Hebrides by a group of people cutting seaweed. The figure, which appeared to be female in form, was cavorting in the waves, seemingly comfortable with the human presence. Several of the male witnesses decided that they would try to capture the being. The creature – a classic example of a sprightly mermaid – eluded its pursuers until some children began to throw stones at it; one of which struck the creature on the head, causing it to sink into the depths.

Sadly, a few days later the mermaid washed ashore in Nunton some 2 miles away. People gathered round to view the weird specimen that was described as having the upper portion of a well-fed 4-year-old child, but sporting an abnormally developed breast. The skin of the creature was very pale, the hair upon its head long and dark, and the lower part of the body resembled that of a salmon but was bereft of scales. In the volume *Carmina Gadelica* it is recorded:

Mr Duncan Shaw, factor for Clanranald, baron-bailie and sheriff of the district, ordered a coffin and shroud to be made for the mermaid. This was done, and the body was buried in the presence of many people, a short distance above the shore where it was found.

The actual spot of the grave has never been found. An alleged headstone found in Cuile Bay proved to be nothing of the sort, but it is possible that the mermaid story may have been fabricated to give the lonesome stone some meaning. Others, in speaking of and researching the legend, claim that the grave is elsewhere, such as the graveyard of the Chapel of St Mary, east of Cuile Bay. Many of Benbecula's inhabitants have been laid to rest in the churchyard so maybe the mermaid was, too. Whatever the truth is, the story of the Benbecula mermaid is classic folklore, though we wish it was more. Maybe there is a grave to be found – but even those who actually believe the story are to some extent of the opinion that the creature was possibly a deformed child or some strange animal.

In the late 1700s there was a mermaid encounter on the Highland's north coast at Sandside Bay. On 8 September 1809, *The Times* featured the eyewitness account of schoolmaster William Munro who mentioned how his attention had been drawn to a nude female sitting on a rock out at sea. The figure seemed to be combing its hair; the light brown hair floating on its shoulders. After watching the figure for a few minutes, the witness was shocked when it dived into the sea. Strangely, in the 1800s a mermaid with a monkey-like appearance was seen by six fishermen and a naturalist off the island of Yell, which is part of the Shetland Islands. The being became entangled in their lines and when observed was described as being about 3ft in length with the top half resembling a human, although the face was like that of a monkey and the lower half of the creature was of a fish and grey in colouration. The creature lay before the stunned witnesses, who noticed how it seemed to surrender to them, emitting a low moan, before the men released it back into the sea.

Mermaids have allegedly been captured quite often. In the 1800s a Captain Eades exhibited one such form in a London coffee house and made good money out of the shrivelled specimen until it was revealed, after some debate, to be a fake. Many alleged mermaids put on display in the last 200 years have certainly been nothing more than ghastly products of the human hand. Such creatures are usually an amalgamation of a monkey (top half) and a large carp (bottom half) fused with wires and papier mâché. These forms may have lost their ability to shock but they have fooled people for many years. In early 2012 I came across a photo of an alleged mermaid that was said to have been housed in a public house in Gillingham, Kent. The *Evening Post* featured several letters from readers in the January of 1969 claiming that such beings were real, with one man demanding that a mermaid had been witnessed by his father who was serving with the Royal Navy in the South Sea Islands. The mermaid had been killed and floated to the surface after a depth charge had been dropped.

In the 17 January 1969 edition of the *Evening Post* a Mr Keightley wrote in, stating that he once owned two photographs of mermaids originating from 1931. 'One photo shows a male merman,' he wrote, 'beside a fishing vessel, and a female, and on the boat a youngster.' The letter provoked a fiery response from a Mrs Bonneywell, who stated quite matter-of-factly that mermaid legends had simply spawned from encounters with dugongs and manatees, which are large marine mammals. Even so, on 21 January a C.R. Taylor wrote to the newspaper, saying they had seen a stuffed mermaid some forty years previous in Gillingham Park: 'the head was partly covered by wisps of red hair, the teeth were pointed and the eye sockets very round. It was rather repulsive … 20-inches long'. It was owned by a man who had a private collection of similar curiosities.

On 28 January a Mr Tubby added his two-pence worth, stating that the 'man fish is a man hoax' and that such specimens were constructed by the 'Chinese in Shanghai about 1920/30 and sold to tourists'. This was confirmed on 3 February when a Frederick Sanders mentioned another exhibit in a Chatham pub. These types of wiry oddities seemed far removed from the angelic-looking sirens of folklore, which were said to sit atop rocks and lure sailors to their deaths.

In Dorset folklore there is mention of a mermaid being washed ashore on Cogden Beach, Burton Bradstock in 1757. It was seen by a local historian, Revd John Hutchins, who in his 1774 volume *The History And Antiquities of Dorset* wrote:

> A mermaid was thrown up by the sea, between Burton and Swyre, 13-feet long. The upper part of it had some resemblance to human form, the lower was like that of a fish; the head was partly like that if a man, and partly like that of a hog. Its fins resembled hands: it had 48 large teeth in each jaw, not unlike those in the jaw bone of a man.

Above the delightful Church Ope Cove there once sat the Mermaid Inn, which is now a private residence. The pub sign showed a rather voluptuous-looking mermaid leaning seductively on a rock. This sign commemorates an incident that was said to have taken place in 1756, when a mermaid washed ashore and eventually died. As Mark North and Robert J. Newland point out, however, 'this incident must have happened many years ago, for the church was abandoned in July 1756 and now lies in ruins.'

The Orkneys have several mermaid legends: one such tale comes from the 1890s at Newark Bay, where a frequent visitor to the shoreline would be witnessed by hundreds of locals as it frolicked amongst the waves. In the same century, in 1833, an Arthur Nicholson wrote that, in the company of three other men, he had hooked a mermaid whilst fishing 30 or so miles off Cullivoe on the Shetland Islands. The creature, said to have measured 3ft in length, 'had breasts as large as those of a woman' but the 'whole front of the animal was covered with skin, white as linen, the back with skin light-grey colour, like a fish'.

In 1913 another mermaid was sighted off the south coast of Hoy and was observed by the crew of a fishing boat who had seen the figure rise from the depths of Pentland Firth. At Burra Firth, Unst, in the Shetlands, it is said that two giants named Herman and Saxie fell in love with a mermaid. She, however, could only offer herself to one, and then they disappeared out at sea never to be seen again.

At Busta there is a fantastic mermaid legend concerning Thomas Gifford, who was said to be the richest man in Shetland. One afternoon in 1748, his four sons were in a boat

Sign from the now demolished Mermaid Inn in Dorset. (Mark North)

Church Ope Cove – a mermaid was said to have washed ashore here a few centuries ago. (Mark North)

rowing to the inlet of Busta when suddenly the boat stopped. The men looked at each other in worry and muttered a prayer, and were thankful when the boat began to move again. But suddenly all the men present became entranced by three creatures, which swam astern of the boat and then faded out at sea. The next day, three of the men climbed back into the boat to visit a relative. The fourth man, who was scared by the previous night's encounter, had refused to go with them and said he would ride his horse instead. However, when it transpired that his horse had vanished overnight, he agreed to set sail with his brothers. Shortly afterwards all four men drowned when the boat swayed violently and capsized, despite the fact it had been a calm day. Had this been a mermaid's curse?

In the county of Caithness there is a tale, often told, of a local fisherman who fell in love with a mermaid. So besotted with the man was the fish woman that she bestowed upon him many jewels, which in turn he gave to human females he admired. Naturally, this upset the mermaid who, as an act of revenge, took the man to a cave where she was said to hide all the treasure that had come from wrecked boats. The man greedily eyed the stash but as soon as the mermaid began to sing to him he fell asleep. When he awoke he found himself chained up in the cave and eventually died. Whatever you do, do not mess with a mermaid!

In the village of Port Gordon, situated on the Moray Firth in Banffshire, there is a remarkable story that dates back to the 1800s. It concerns a group of fishermen who were frequently pestered by a warty, green-haired merman who they considered to be an omen of ill luck. Every time their boat set sail they would see him, and so troubled by his presence became the fishermen they headed back to the shore; always suspending their trawl for another time.

In 1900 a Scotsman named Alexander Gunn saw a mermaid at Sandwood, the local haunt of a ghostly seaman. He was walking his dog when he noticed his pet beginning to act oddly: she started to growl and it was then he saw was a beautiful woman with reddish hair. Upon being disturbed by Mr Gunn, the woman threw him an angry look and dived into the water.

In 1947 a fisherman saw a mermaid in the sea off the Island of Muck. The mermaid was perched on a herring box combing her hair and again, plunged into the depths when disturbed.

In Irish folklore it is claimed that the Cantillon family of Kerry would take their dead, in coffins, to the shores of Ballyheigue Strand. There they would be left until nightfall, when the sea beings came and took the casket to the bottom of the sea. These types of stories bring to mind the Finn Folk of the Northern Isles who, appearing as beautiful mermaids, would lure handsome young men to their watery abodes.

In Wales there is a fascinating yarn attached to Conway Bay, for it is here that a mermaid was found washed ashore by several fishermen. She asked them, kindly, to take her back to the water but they did not act in accordance with her wishes, and so before she died she placed an eternal curse on the area, which has been blamed for several fish famines.

In July 1826 a Welsh farmer from Llanllwchaiarn had taken a stroll to the coastline, which was only a few hundred yards from his house, when he noticed under the glow of the setting sun a woman who was washing herself in the sea. The farmer thought that it must be a local woman and so, out of politeness, turned his back on the woman. After a while the man, with curiosity getting the better of him, decided to creep down past the rocks to get a better look at the woman, whereupon he realised she was in fact a mermaid. So excited was the witness that he crawled back up the rocks to tell his family. They all then descended the path and watched, until the man's wife got too close and the mermaid, seeing her, dived into the water. The family saw her several times after this, but on most occasions she stayed out at sea, grooming herself near a rock before disappearing beneath the waves.

In the booklet *Myths & Legends of Wales*, Tony Roberts states that the most likely place to see mermaids is Pembrokeshire. Many years ago, a fisherman from St Dogmaels was fishing off Cemaes Head in his boat when his attention was drawn to a movement at the base of one of the cliffs. To his amazement, he saw a mermaid combing her hair and so decided to float his vessel softly alongside and then apprehend her. The fisherman dragged the mermaid aboard but, according to folklore, she begged the man to let her go in fluent Welsh. Of course the fisherman, now with the catch of his life, was reluctant but she granted him three wishes in an hour of need if he would release her, to which he finally agreed. One day when the fishing was

Is that a mermaid on a Welsh beach? No, it's a piece of driftwood. (Found and photographed by Simon Wyatt)

particularly bad the man was surprised to see the mermaid, who shouted to him to take up his nets. Moments later a terrible storm broke out, forcing him back to shore. Several other fishermen drowned that day because they were not privileged enough to hear the warning.

In 1791 a farmer, Henry Reynolds of Pennyholt, had a startling encounter with a Pembrokeshire merman. He spotted the creature at Linney Stack and noticed how it had pale skin and the tail like that of a conger eel. The figure was washing its hair and so Henry decided to go back and get his friends but by the time they returned, the merman had gone.

In 1934 there was a very eerie encounter at Holy Island, Northumberland. It involved two fishermen, Bob Armstrong and Jackie Stokes, who, whilst out fishing in their small boat, noticed several figures seemingly walking on the water. In the distance, under the eye of the moon, there appeared to be several men, women and children floating on the surface of the water. Were these figures ghosts, finally given up by the sea, or had the fishermen observed a family of merfolk?

Cornwall has quite a few mermaid legends. The most well known originates from Zennor, a village and civil parish in the county. The story goes that for a few years, albeit sporadically, a beautiful woman would visit Zennor church and each time she returned she had never seemed to age. A local man became enchanted by her, and vice versa, and he followed the mysterious woman out of the village and was never seen again. However, one afternoon a boat had cast its anchor off Pendower Cove when a beautiful mermaid rose out of the water to tell the captain that the anchor had in fact dropped on a secret door in the sea that gave her admittance to her abode where her children waited for her. The captain gladly raised the anchor but was quick to gather his men and move the vessel away from the spot, knowing full well that to see a mermaid was considered very bad luck. Ever since that encounter a carving has existed in Zennor church as a warning to the young men of the future.

Mermaid legends seem to have an element of repetition about them: in most yarns they are considered bad omens and in many cases the fishy females grant wishes, should the witnesses help them. Another of those types of tales comes from Cury in Cornwall, where it was once said that a man observed a creature sitting on a rock in a cove near Lizard Point. The mermaid asked the man if he could help her back to sea and, as he obliged, she granted him one wish. The man said that he wished he could help his neighbours and so, with that, the mermaid told him to return to the spot at another tide and she would give him her comb. All the man had to do was comb the waves and this would evoke the mermaid. So, when the man returned to the area he combed the waves and the mermaid appeared, and not only granted him his wish but gave him a gift for detecting stolen goods and an ability to 'charm disease'.

This, dear reader, is where I leave you. Thank you so much for accompanying me on this strange voyage, I hope you have enjoyed these nautical tales of terror. No doubt,

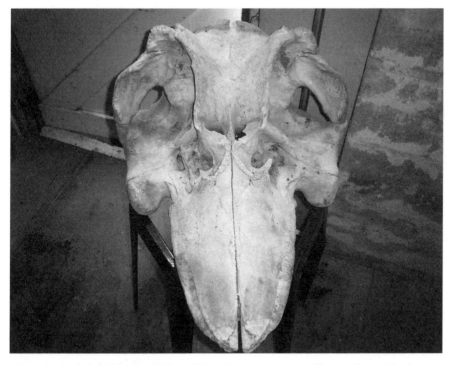

This 'serpent' skull, believed to be that of Cornish sea giant Morgawr, turned out to be from a whale. (Jonathan Downes)

like so many fishermen's yarns, they are exaggerations, but be careful not to dismiss all of these stories so hastily. By all means take them with a pinch of salt, but to scoff at such folktales may at once invoke the wrath of your local mermaid! The sea is very much a wondrous abode for folklore to dwell, but it is also a place of power, which instils great fear. It is because of this deep, inner dread of the roaring waves that we appreciate and crave the maritime mysteries of Britain so much.

The fishermen know that the sea is dangerous and the storm terrible, but they have never found these dangers sufficient reason for remaining ashore.

Vincent van Gogh

BIBLIOGRAPHY

Arnold, Neil, *Mystery Animals of the British Isles: Kent* (CFZ Press, 2009)

——, *Mystery Animals of the British Isles: London* (CFZ Press, 2012)

Baldwin, Gay and Anker, Ray, *Ghosts of the Isle of Wight* (IW County Press, 1992)

Bardens, Dennis, *Ghosts & Haunting* (Zeus Press, 1965)

Bord, Colin and Bord, Janet, *Modern Mysteries of Britain* (Grafton, 1988)

——, *Atlas of Magical Britain* (Sidgwick & Jackson, 1990)

Brooks, J.A., *Cornish Ghosts & Legends* (Jarrold, 1981)

——, *Ghosts & Legends of the Lake District* (Jarrold, 1988)

——, *Ghosts & Legends of Wales* (Jarrold, 1987)

——, *The Good Ghost Guide* (Jarrold, 1994)

Brown, Theo, *Devon Ghosts* (Jarrold, 1982)

Campbell, Grant, *Scottish Haunting* (Piccolo, 1982)

Chambers, Aidan, *Great British Ghosts* (Piccolo, 1974)

Codd, Daniel, *Mysterious Lincolnshire* (Breedon Books, 2007)

Cunningham, Gary and Coghlan, Ronan, *Mystery Animals of Ireland* (CFZ Press, 2010)

Curran, Bob, *Banshees, Beasts and Brides from the Sea* (Appletree, 1996)

Dixon, G.M., *Folktales & Legends of Kent* (Minimax, 1984)

Downes, Jonathan and Wright, Nigel, *The Rising of the Moon* (Domra, 1999)

Downes, Jonathan, *UFOs over Devon* (Bossiney, 2000)

Eisner, Will, *Spirit Casebook of True Haunted Houses and Ghosts* (Poor House Press, 1976)

Eldritch, Morven (ed.), *Ghosts* (Geddes & Grosset, 2004)

Fort, Charles, *Lo!* (Gollancz, 1931)

Garrett, Richard, *Great Sea Mysteries* (Piccolo, 1976)

——, *Voyage into Mystery* (Weidenfeld & Nicolson, 1987)

Green, Andrew, *Haunted Kent Today* (S.B. Publications, 1999)

——, *Our Haunted Kingdom* (Fontana, 1973)

Haining, Peter (ed.), *The Mammoth Book of True Hauntings* (Robinson, 2008)

Hallowell, Michael J., *Mystery Animals of the British Isles: Northumberland & Tyneside* (CFZ Press, 2008)

Hapgood, Sarah, *The World's Greatest Ghost & Poltergeist Stories* (Foulsham, 1994)

Harries, John, *The Ghost Hunter's Road Book* (Muller, 1968)

Hough, Peter and Randles, Jenny, *Mysteries of the Mersey Valley* (Sigma Leisure, 1993)

Hough, Peter, *Supernatural Lancashire* (Hale, 2003)

Howat, Polly, *Norfolk Ghosts & Legends* (Countryside Books, 1993)

Hoyle, Ronnie, *Strange Tales of the South West* (Bossiney, 1993)

Hurwood, Bernhardt J., *Ghosts, Ghouls & Other Horrors* (Target, 1971)

Johnson, W.H., *Kent Stories of the Supernatural* (Countryside, 2000)

Kirkman, Jo, *Ghosts of Rye* (Thomas Peacocke Community College, 2007)

Kristen, Clive, *Ghost Trails of Northumbria* (Casdec, 1992)

Lazarus, Richard, *Beyond the Impossible* (Warner Books, 1994)

MacGregor, Alasdair Alpin, *The Ghost Book* (Hale, 1955)

Macklin, John, *Beyond All Reason* (Ace Star, 1970)

——, *Dimensions beyond the Known* (Ace Books, 1968)

——, *The Strange and Uncanny* (Ace Star, 1967)

Mason, Phil, *Kent Chronicles of Catastrophe & Disaster* (Countryside Books, 2008)

Mawnan–Peller, A., *Morgawr the Monster of Falmouth Bay* (Morgawr Productions, 1976)

McAll, Kenneth, *Healing the Haunted* (Darley Anderson, 1989)

McAnally Jr, David Rice, *Irish Wonders* (Sterling/Main Street, 1993)

McEwan, Graham J., *Mystery Animals of Britain & Ireland* (Hale, 1986)

——, *Sea Serpents, Sailors & Sceptics* (Routledge & Kegan Paul, 1978)

McLaren, Calum, Livingston, Andrew, MacFarlane, Gail and Griffiths, Lorraine, *Strange Tales of Scotland* (Lang Syne, 1995)

Middleton, Judy, *Ghosts of Sussex* (Countryside Books, 1988)

Mills West, H., *Ghosts of East Anglia* (Countryside Books, 1984)

Newland, Robert J. and North, Mark, *Dark Dorset: Tales of Mystery, Wonder & Terror* (CFZ Press, 2007)

O'Donnell, Elliott, *Ghosts With a Purpose* (Digit, 1963)

——, *Dangerous Ghosts* (Consul, 1962)

——, *Haunted Britain* (Consul, 1963)

——, *Screaming Skulls & Other Ghost Stories, The* (Four Square, 1964)

Paget, Peter, *UFO-UK* (New English Library, 1980)

——, *Welsh Triangle, The* (Granada, 1979)

Piddock, Helen, *Tiswas Book of Ghastly Ghosts* (Carousel, 1981)

Robson, Alan, *Grisly Trails & Ghostly Tales* (Virgin, 1994)

——, *More Grisly Trails & Ghostly Tales* (Virgin, 1993)

Sampson, Chas, *Ghosts of the Broads* (Jarrold, 1976)

Sieveking, Paul (ed.), *Fortean Times: Yesterday's News Tomorrow* (John Brown, 1992)

Spencer, John and Anne, *The Encyclopaedia of Ghosts & Spirits* (Headline, 1988)

Thiselton Dyer, T.F., *Ghost World* (Ward & Downey, 1893)

Thompson, Francis, *Ghosts & Spectres of Scotland* (Lang Syne, 1984)

Underwood, Peter, *A Gazetteer of British Ghosts* (Pan, 1971)

——, *Ghostly Encounters* (Bossiney, 1992)

——, *Ghosts of Dorset* (Bossiney, 1989)

——, *Ghosts of North Devon* (Bossiney, 1999)

Various, *Dorset Mysteries* (Bossiney, 1989)

Wales, Tony, *Sussex Ghosts & Legends* (Countryside Books, 1992)

Weatherhill, Craig and Devereux, Paul, *Myths & Legends of Cornwall* (Sigma, 1994)

Wentworth-Day, James, *Ghosts & Witches* (Dorset Press, 1991)

Westwood, Jennifer, *Gothick Cornwall* (Shire, 1992)

——, *Gothick Norfolk* (Shire, 1989)

Whitaker, Terence, *Scotland's Ghosts & Apparitions* (Hale, 1991)

Williams, Michael, *Supernatural Investigation* (Bossiney, 1993)

——, *Supernatural in Cornwall* (Bossiney, 1974)

Wood, Charles Lindley, *Lord Halifax's Ghost Book* (Fontana, 1961)

www.bbc.co.uk

www.devlin-family.com/lordblaney

www.kenfig.org.uk

www.kentmonsters.blogspot.com

www.kent-online.co.uk

www.mevagissey.net/monster

www.orkneyjar.com

www.paranormaldatabase.com

www.somerset-online.co.uk

www.thisisbristol.co.uk

www.thisissomerset.co.uk

www.ufocenter.com

www.ufoinfo.com

www.waterufo.net